FROM BRUNEL TO BRITISH RAIL

THE RAILWAY HERITAGE OF THE CROSSRAIL ROUTE

Andy Shelley

with a contribution from Richard Brown

Published by Oxford Archaeology, Janus House, Oxford

A CIP catalogue record for this book is available from the British Library

Crossrail Archaeology Publication series designed and series-edited by Jay Carver, Marit Leenstra and Andrew Briffett

Production and design by Oxford Archaeology Graphics Office

Editing by Anne Dodd

Copy editing by Ian Scott

Front cover: archaeological recording at Paddington New Yard

Typeset by Production Line, Oxford

Printed in the United Kingdom by Henry Ling Limited, at the Dorset Press, Dorchester, DT1 1HD an ISO 14001 certified printer

CONTRIBUTORS

Principal author	**Andy Shelley**
Contributing author	Richard Brown
Picture research	Kirsty Smith
Maps and Geographic Information Systems	Gary Jones
Graphics	Magdalena Wachnik and Charles Rousseaux
Project manager (OA)	Richard Brown
Project manager (Ramboll)	Andy Shelley
Post-excavation manager	Anne Dodd

CONTENTS

FIGURES

ACKNOWLEDGEMENTS

Oxford Archaeology and Ramboll wish to thank Crossrail Ltd for commissioning this book, and Jay Carver, Crossrail's Lead Archaeologist, for assistance, commentary and guidance. We also wish to thank Jay's archaeological and built heritage colleagues David Keeley, Marit Leenstra, Suzanna Pembroke and Iain Williamson. Many other Crossrail employees have provided help during the fieldwork stages, and we acknowledge in particular the assistance of Paul Bayliss, Aaron Cowell, Ricky Harris, Steve Hunt, Scott Mackenzie, Simon Pledger and Abhi Purkayastha.

The authors have relied heavily on the reports of Crossrail's archaeological excavation and historic building recording programmes. These works were undertaken by Oxford Archaeology/Ramboll, Museum of London Archaeology (MOLA), Scott Wilson Ltd and Wessex Archaeology, and we acknowledge the contribution made by the many members of staff from these organisations. Most reports have an acknowledgement section; these may be accessed at www.archaeologydataservice.ac.uk

The excavations and historic building surveys were commissioned by Crossrail Ltd or Transport for London and facilitated by their contractors. These included Costain (Paddington New Yard), Costain Skanska (Royal Oak Portal), Taylor Woodrow (Old Oak Common), Morgan Sindall (Paddington New Yard), Vinci Construction (Connaught Tunnel) and Volker Fitzpatrick (Ilford). Once again, we acknowledge the contribution made by the many members of staff from these organisations.

We gratefully acknowledge the assistance of our colleagues at Oxford Archaeology, in particular Gary Evans, a mainstay of the project. Jon Boothroyd, Jon Gill and Vix Hughes all made important contributions during the fieldwork stages of the work. Other staff who have contributed to the project include Ben Attfield, John Grithin, Wayne Perkins, Peter Vellet and Leanne Waring of Oxford Archaeology and Pat Cavanagh, Fergal Donaghue, Matt Edmonds and Deborah Nedal of Pre-Construct Archaeology (PCA). Ramboll colleagues who have provided valuable help and assistance include Phil Emery, Jacek Gruszczynski, Simon Price and Hilary Quinn.

We also wish to acknowledge the help received from Gill Neal and Ally McConnell at the Wiltshire & Swindon History Centre, Nicola Herbert, Vicky Stretch, Tom Wilson and Andy Buckley at Network Rail, Nick Elsden at MOLA and Keith Priest and Vanessa Shrimpton from Fletcher

Priest Architects. Amongst those who have helped us source or granted permission to use images we acknowledge the help of Karen Thomas and Andy Chopping from MOLA, Charlotte Matthews from PCA, Elaine Arthurs from the STEAM museum Swindon, Mrs Riley and Rodney Lissenden on behalf of the late Mr RC Riley, Jovita Callueng from The British Library, Sophia Brothers from the Science and Society Picture Library, Julie Okpa from Rail Executive (Department For Transport), Stefan Popa, Gary and Linda Stratmann, Jenni Munro-Collins from Newham Archives and Local Studies Library, David Lennon, Peter Brumby, Ron Halestrap, 'Tulyarman', John Chalcraft from Rail Photoprints, Julie Cochrane from the National Maritime Museum London, Elizabeth Bowley from British Pathé Ltd, Tower Hamlets Local History Library and Archives, Groundsure and Javis Gurr from Historic England.

We are particularly grateful to Sir Neil Cossons and Tanya Jackson for reading drafts of this book and providing many helpful thoughts and suggestions.

Chapter 3 draws heavily on the work, gratefully acknowledged, of Guy Thompson, Malcolm Gould and Tomasz Mazurkiewicz of PCA, to whom, with the addition of Charlotte Matthews, we extend our thanks.

Of the many books, pamphlets and articles consulted during the preparation of this book two deserve singling out for particular acknowledgement. Joe Brown's London Railway Atlas has proved an indispensible aid; Chris Hawkins and George Reeve's magisterial Great Western Railway Engine Sheds has proved similarly invaluable.

FOREWORD

Those of us who worked on the railways in the 1970s and 1980s (I was then an adviser to the British Railways Board, appointed by Sir Peter Parker) rub our eyes in disbelief at how much the railway has been transformed in the last quarter of a century. Until the 1990s cost-cutting, contraction and decay were all too frequent a feature of life on Britain's railways; some 'experts' even questioned whether we needed a railway at all – wouldn't it be better and cheaper, they said, if we concreted over the tracks and created busways instead?

That madness is now behind us as demand for rail travel in Great Britain continues to grow at 5 per cent a year, regardless of national economic circumstances, and investment in our railways is running at unprecedented levels.

In all parts of Great Britain stations and lines have reopened, meeting the demands of a discerning travelling public for whom getting into a car and contributing to traffic jams on congested motorways now longer hold the attraction it did.

It is as part of that story that the Crossrail project comes into the picture – delivering a brand new high capacity railway linking lines of historic significance from Reading and the outer London suburbs to the west right through the centre of the city; and out to Essex and Abbey Wood via Canary Wharf. As with previous major rail investment schemes the Elizabeth line, as Crossrail will be known when it opens in 2018, will transform journey times and patterns, reinvigorate communities, and promote economic growth.

There is however one significant difference between Crossrail and other earlier railway projects, and that is the care that is being taken to map, chart and record every aspect of its construction that is of archaeological and railway heritage significance. Part of this process is the production of this excellent book, which describes in astonishing detail what today's engineers have found.

As President of the Heritage Railway Association I was delighted to read how heritage railways have been the beneficiaries of significant historical artefacts, whether it is Henley's footbridge from North Woolwich sent on its way to the Whitwell and Reepham Railway in Norfolk, or Old Oak Common's 70 ft turntable now performing sterling service on the Swanage Railway.

I was particularly pleased to see on page 43 a picture of the GWR cast iron column dating from 1903 that I came across at Old Oak in the autumn of 2014 during a visit kindly arranged by Crossrail. This was 'designated' by the trustees of the Science Museum in December that year, exercising their authority under the terms of the Railway Heritage Act to ensure the preservation of artefacts that play a significant part in the nation's railway history.

From what I have seen of the work undertaken by the Crossrail team, they have demonstrated a caring and sensitive approach to history and heritage unsurpassed by any other modern construction project. I commend this excellent book to all who care about these issues.

RICHARD FAULKNER, London June 2016

(Lord Faulkner of Worcester is deputy chairman of the Science Museum Group and chairs its Railway Heritage Designation Advisory Board. He is also President of the Heritage Railway Association).

ABBREVIATIONS

ac	alternating current
ARP	Air raid precautions
BG	Broad gauge
BR	British Rail or British Railways
BRB	British Railways Board
BRML	British Rail Maintenance Limited
BRT	BR Telecommunications Ltd
BT	Broad term
BTC	British Transport Commission
CL	Class name
CLR	Central London Railway
cwt	hundredweight
DLR	Docklands Light Railway
DDBA	Detailed desk-based assessment
DMU	Diesel Multiple Unit
ECR	Eastern Counties Railway
ECTJR	Eastern Counties & Thames Junction Railway
EH	English Heritage
ERO	Essex Record Office
ELR	East London Railway
EMU	Electric Maintenance Unit
ER	Eastern Region
EWS	English, Welsh & Scottish Railway
ft	foot
GER	Great Eastern Railway
GWR	Great Western Railway
GWT	Great Western Trust
HS2	High Speed 2
HST	High Speed Train
in	inch
kw	kilowatt
LAARC	London Archaeological Archive and Research Centre
lb	pound (weight)
LBLR	London and Blackwall Railway

LCDR	London, Chatham & Dover Railway
LMS	London, Midland & Scottish Railway
LNER	London & North Eastern Railway
LPTB	London Passenger Transport Board
LST	Liverpool Street Station
LSKD	London & St Katharine Docks Company
LTSR	London, Tilbury & Southend Railway
MDR	Metropolitan District Railway
MOLA	Museum of London Archaeology
MP	Member of Parliament
MPD	Motive Power Depot
MR	Metropolitan Railway
NG	Narrow gauge
NLBH	Non-listed built heritage
NLR	North London Railway
NMR	National Monuments Record
NRM	National Railway Museum
NT	Narrow term
OS	Ordnance Survey
PCA	Pre-Construct Archaeology
REC	Railway Executive Committee
RSJ	Rolled steel joist
SR	Southern Railway
SSWSI	Site-specific Written Scheme of Investigation
TfL	Transport for London
TMD	Train Maintenance Depot
TNA	The National Archives
TOPS	Total Operations Processing System
TWA	Transport and Works Act
WBR	Whitechapel & Bow Railway
WR	Western Region
WSHC	Wiltshire and Swindon Heritage Centre
WWII	World War II

GLOSSARY

Axlebox	A housing to attach the end of an axle to the frame of a vehicle
Broad gauge	Any rail gauge wider than standard, here referring to the GWR's 7ft 0¼in track gauge
Bull's-eye window	A small circular or oval window, usually resembling a wheel
Bullnose brick	A brick with at least one rounded edge
Burrowing junction	A formation in which a diverging line is carried beneath a main line
Condenser	A heat exchanger, often used to convert waste steam into water
Crow-step	An architectural term for step-like projections on a gable
Double-pitched roof	An architectural term for a roof with two flat slopes on either side of a ridge
Firedropper	A person who clears the remains of a fire from the firebox of a steam locomotive
Firelighter	A person who lights the fire beneath a steam locomotive boiler
Frog	An indentation or depression on the top face of a brick
Narrow gauge	Any rail gauge of less than standard width, here referring to gauges narrower than the GWR's 7ft 0¼in gauge
Purlin	A horizontal beam along the length of a roof
Raking strut	A structural component set at an angle and designed to resist longitudinal compression
Sand house	In slippery conditions dry sand was used to aid adhesion of a locomotive's wheels to the track. A sand house dried the sand so that it did not clog a locomotive's feeder pipes
Saw-tooth roof	A roof comprising a series of ridges with pitches of unequal length to resemble the teeth of a saw
Standard gauge	A gauge of 4ft 8½in, the most common width between the rails of a railway track
Tie-rod	A slender structural unit used to tie two or more components together
Traverser	A platform used to transfer rolling stock between parallel railway lines
Trussed roof	A roof supported by trusses (frames typically consisting of rafters, posts, and struts)
Turntable	A revolving table used to transfer rolling stock between railway lines

CHAPTER 1

INTRODUCTION

The building of Crossrail, London's new east-west railway, continues a tradition that has its origins in the short years of William IV's reign, but which became synonymous with the Victorian period. Crossrail is a major undertaking, perhaps the greatest civil engineering project in the capital since the construction of the Victoria Line in the 1960s or the Jubilee Line in the 1990s. Its aim is foster new opportunities, promote growth and revitalise neighbourhoods. For some it will be the source of new adventures; for all it will provide easier, quicker and more direct travel across the capital (Fig 1).

Trace a line across a map of London and one cannot fail to encounter an historic railway. Railways are more dynamic than people may suppose; over time stations are reconfigured, bridges replaced, tracks re-aligned. Sometimes, whole lines or tracts of land, particularly those associated with London's freight operations, fall into disuse. Crossrail's designers actively sought these out for use and adaptation. At many of these places historic buildings were adapted or removed to accommodate the new railway; elsewhere the construction work has unearthed the archaeological remains of some of London's earliest railways.

Historic buildings and archaeological sites, collectively known as heritage assets, have much to tell us about the lives and livelihoods of others. Crossrail ensured that their teams of archaeologists recorded any heritage

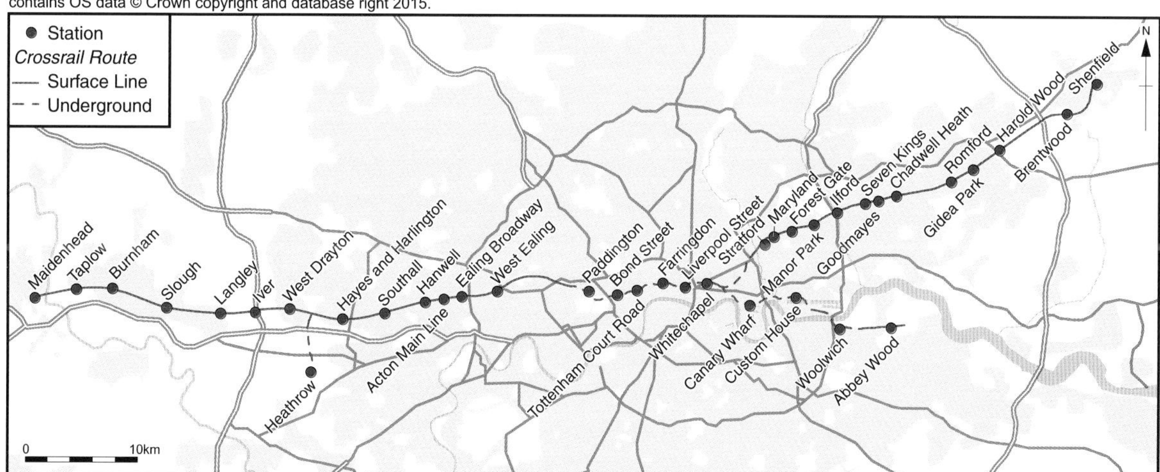

Fig 1 Crossrail's route and its stations. The dashed lines indicate tunnelled sections

contains OS data © Crown copyright and database right 2015.

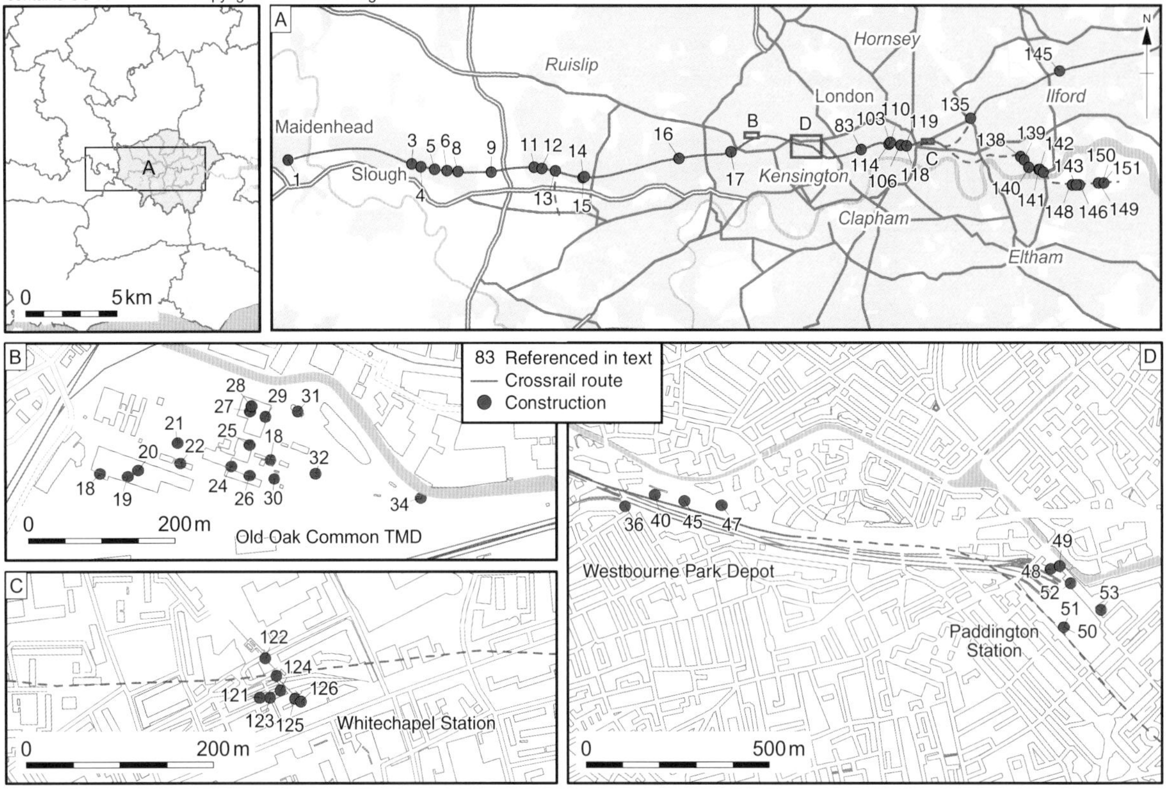

Fig 2 Location of heritage assets described in this book or the gazetteer

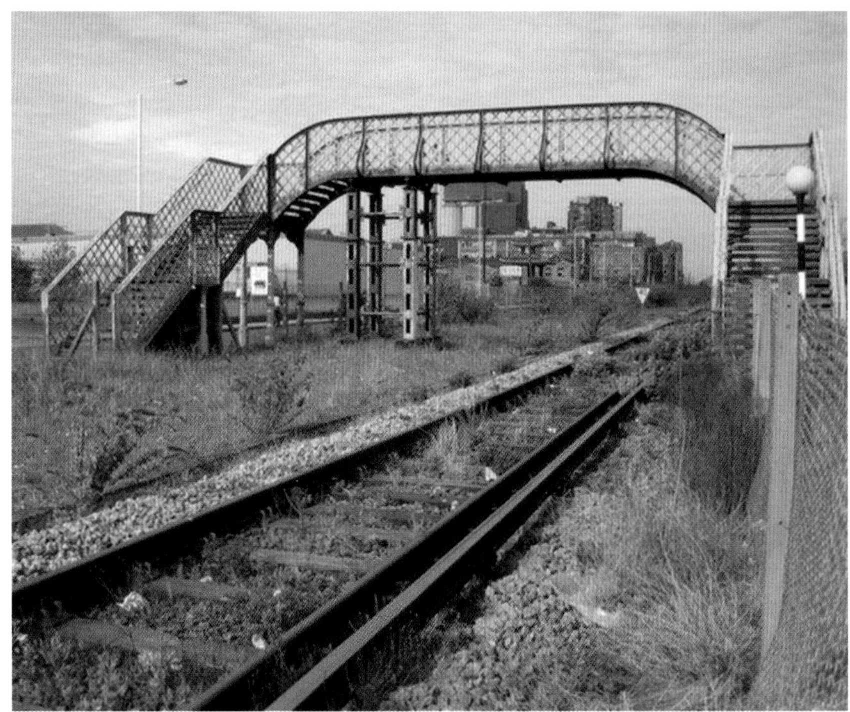

Fig 3 Henley's Footbridge (Gazetteer No. 142) was built in 1892 to allow workers at Henley's Electric Cable works to cross the North Woolwich Line in safety. Crossrail's archaeologists recorded it before it was carefully dismantled and relocated to the Whitwell and Reepham Heritage Railway in 2011

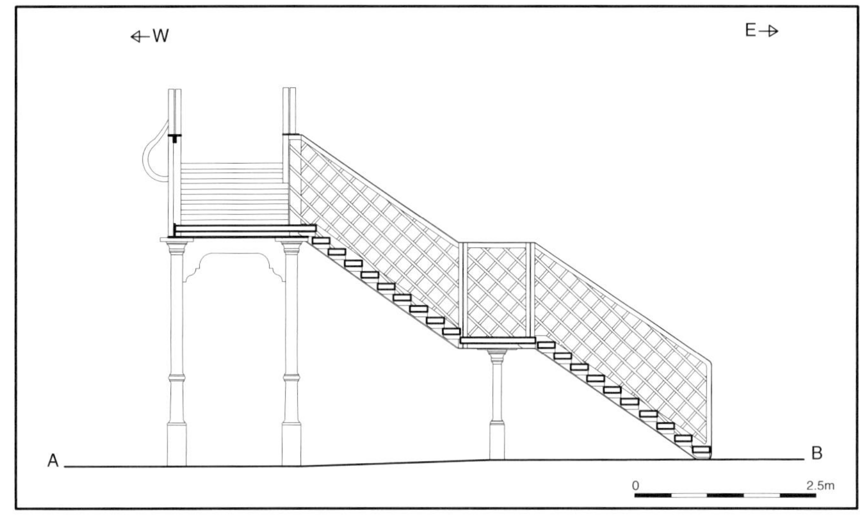

Fig 4 West-to-east elevation through the southern steps of Henley's Footbridge

asset affected by the works (see e.g. Henley's Footbridge Gazetteer 142, Figs 3 and 4, which was researched and recorded prior to relocation). Gathered together these records form an important and permanent corpus of information, but it is not one driven by a specific research agenda. Instead, the records embody a wealth of little details and observations from which broad themes and new insights might be teased. This book presents these themes and insights in the form of a collection of essays, largely based on the chronology of railway development in the capital. The intention has been to produce a synthesis of the new information gained; details of the buildings and structures recorded are reserved for the gazetteer and the reports of each building record, which are freely available through the Crossrail website.[1]

It is hoped the book is received as it is meant; as a celebration of buildings and structures, above and below-ground, each perhaps unremarkable but collectively an addition to the common wealth. It is also intended as a snapshot of the moment when Crossrail joins one of earliest and most extensive urban railway networks in the world.

NOTE

1 www.crossrail.co.uk

CHAPTER 2

EARLY RAILWAY DEVELOPMENTS ALONG THE CROSSRAIL ROUTE

The opening of the world's first public railway in north-east England in 1825 led to a rapid growth of rail companies and lines, and the entrepreneurs of this fledgling Victorian industry naturally set their sights on London. By 1901 there were fifteen major routes into the capital, each with its own terminus. But for various reasons, chief amongst them the conclusions of the 1846 Royal Commission on Railway Termini within or in the Immediate Vicinity of the Metropolis, there were for many years no main-line stations at all in the West End or the City of London. Like so many spokes of a wheel the lines remained divorced from one another until, by connecting Ludgate Hill to Farringdon in 1866, a direct north-to-south link was forged by the London, Chatham and Dover Railway (LCDR).[1] Early east-to-west routes of sorts were formed by the twin arms of the 'Inner Circle' (now the Circle Line), the first part of which, the Metropolitan Line, opened between Paddington and Farringdon in 1863. However, it took until 1900 and the opening of the Central London Railway (CLR, now the Central Line) for a direct route to be established.

Fig 5 Crossrail's 2018 route overlain on the London routes of the Great Western Railway, the Central London Railway (now the Central Line), the Eastern Counties Railway, the Metropolitan Railway, the North Woolwich line and the East London Railway.

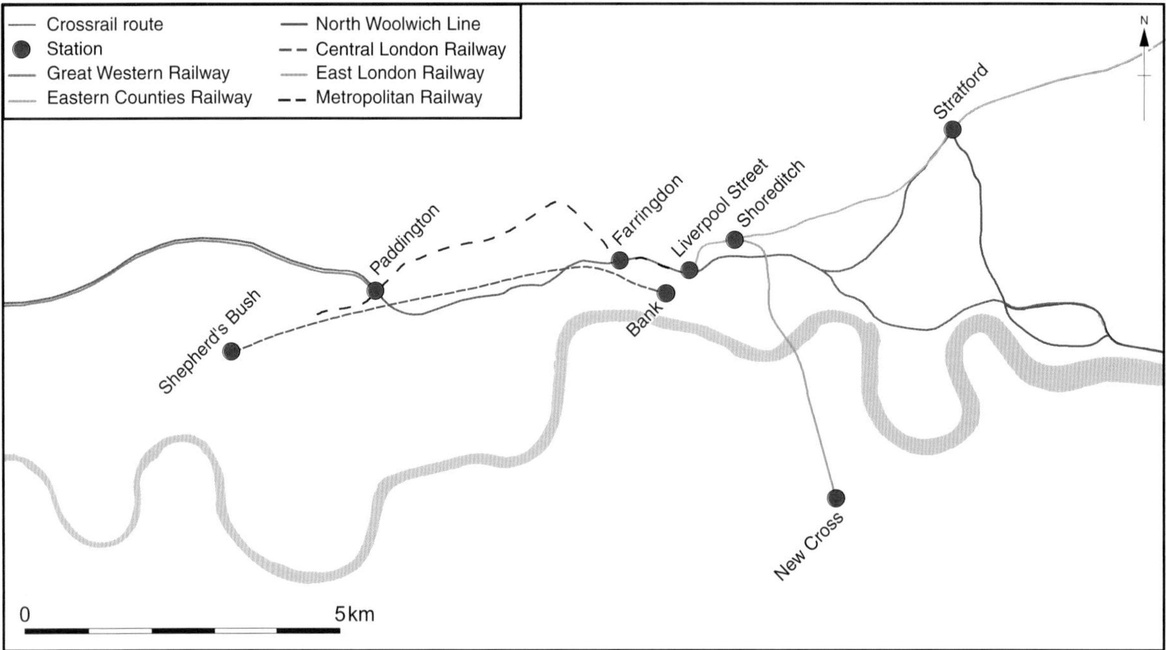

If the goods-only Post Office Railway of the interwar period is discounted, Crossrail will form only the second direct east-to-west route through central London, and will be the first to provide direct connections with the LCDR's route, now part of Thameslink, and the former South Eastern Railway's North Kent Line. In fact, Crossrail uses or connects many of the capital's earliest railways, from the Great Western Railway (GWR) in the west to the Eastern Counties Railway (ECR) in the east (Fig 5). This chapter details the new evidence that Crossrail's work has unearthed for the early development of these railways. It focuses primarily on the GWR, the ECR, the East London Railway (ELR) and the CLR.

Westbourne Park

The London and Greenwich Railway was the first such company to reach the capital, London Bridge station opening in 1836. The following summer the London & Birmingham Railway unveiled their terminus at Euston Square. They were soon joined by the GWR, whose line from Bristol was being constructed at breakneck speed by Isambard Kingdom Brunel. For a time the two companies believed they would share Euston station, but at the last minute the GWR board pulled out of the undertaking and instructed Brunel to pursue his idea of a station at Paddington. His site lay rather distant from the commercial centre, but it was convenient for the leafy crescents of Kensington, Marylebone and Mayfair from where wealthy passengers might be drawn. It also lay close to the Grand Junction Canal's Paddington Basin, already a significant transport interchange in its own right. The first station, like many of its contemporaries, was built in timber. It shared a cramped site with carriage sheds, workshops and an octagonal engine shed designed by Brunel's young Locomotive Superintendent, Daniel Gooch. The station opened in 1838, but was not anything like finished until 1845. By 1854 it was already being demolished.

Paddington had quickly neared capacity and in planning its replacement Brunel created space by switching the position of the station and its goods yard. This in turn displaced Paddington's engine and carriage sheds and workshops. A field in Westbourne Park, which had already been reduced in size by the construction of the Grand Junction Canal and Brunel's main-line railway, was chosen as the site for the new locomotive depot, with the carriage department moving to new buildings between Westbourne Bridge and Bishop's Road Bridge (Fig 6).

The move meant that the depot's workshops, stores and offices could for the first time be brought together into one building ('K', Fig 7). This structure (Gazetteer No. 44) is portrayed on a drawing from *c* 1853 (Fig 8). It consisted of a pair of two-storey wings, each with a double-height bay,

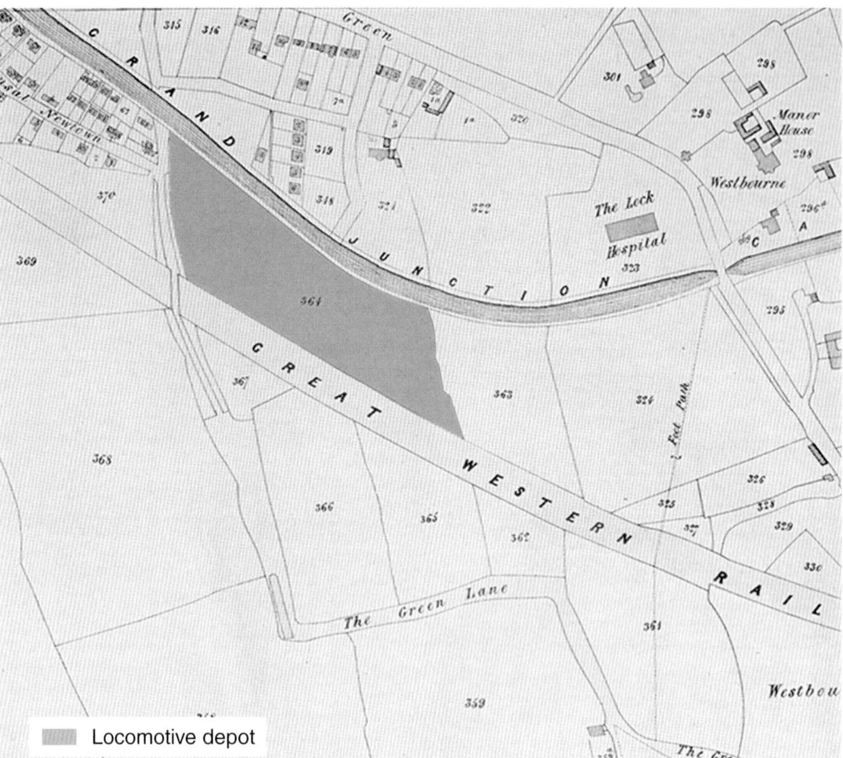

Fig 6 The trapezoidal parcel of land at Westbourne Park that Brunel and Gooch chose as the site of their new locomotive depot. From a George Oakley Lewis lithograph dated 1842 (British Library)

which book-ended workshops for carpenters, smiths and fitters. There were stores on the ground floor of the western wing (Block 1) and enginemen's sleeping and waiting quarters on the first floor. The eastern wing (Block 2) housed a general office, with an 'arch for men signing in', and individual offices for 'Mr Andrews', Gooch (who had opted to establish his head-quarters at Paddington rather than Swindon) and the necessary clerks.[2]

Fine though this building was, the undoubted centrepiece of Westbourne Park Depot when it opened was a four-road engine shed for Gooch's new generation of broad-gauge locomotives (Gazetteer No. 43, Fig 9).[3] The brick structure, later known as the 'BG' (Broad Gauge) Shed, was simply vast. It measured 663ft in length by 68ft in width. This was, as English Heritage's Steven Brindle has pointed out, a great deal longer than Winchester Cathedral, the longest medieval church in Europe.[4] The Camden firm of Locke and Nesham, at that time prolific builders of prisons, were awarded a contract of £14,130 to construct it.[5] The roof principals, each weighing 25.5cwt (1,300kg), were of wrought iron, there were smoke troughs above each road and a pit below that ran the length of the building (Fig 10).[6] Until about 1869 the roads were laid exclusively to Brunel's 7ft 0¼in broad gauge (2.14m), but the GWR's reluctant acceptance of Stephenson's 4ft 8½in standard gauge (1.44m)

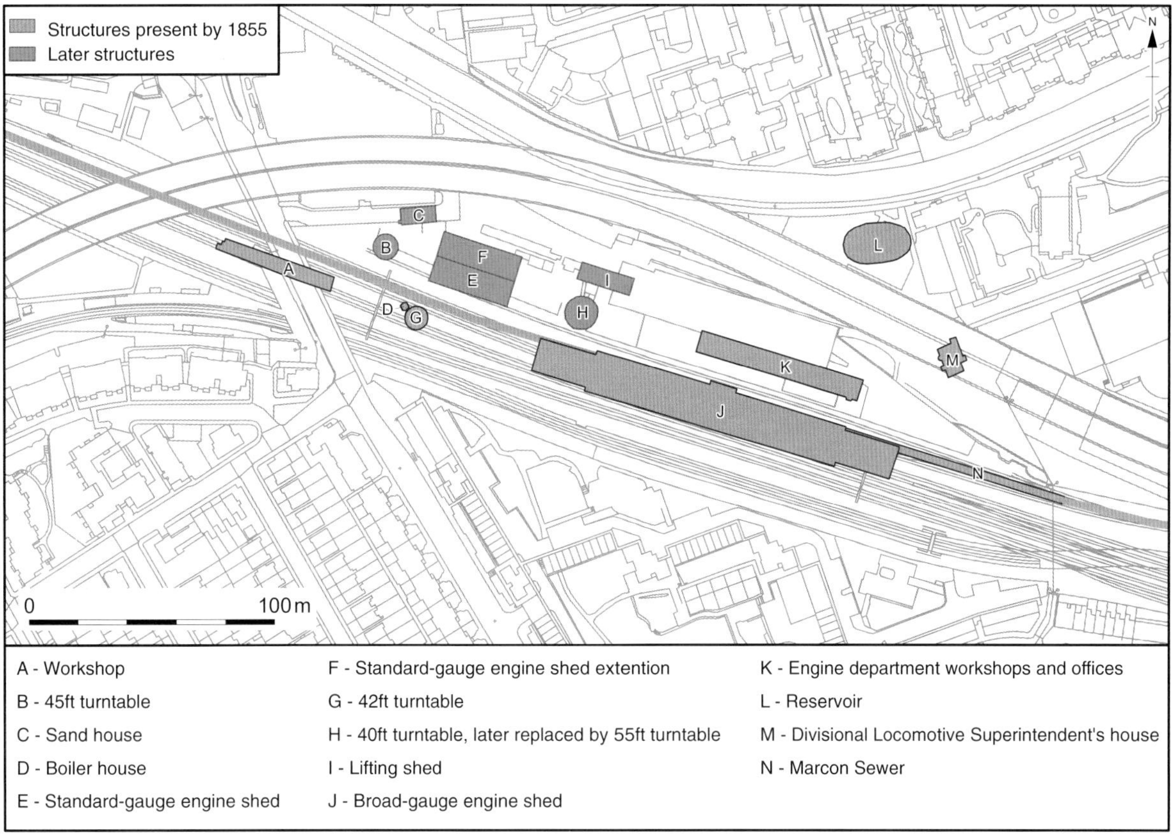

Structures present by 1855
Later structures
N
A
B
C
D
E
F
G
H
I
J
K
L
M
N
0
100 m
A - Workshop
B - 45ft turntable
C - Sand house
D - Boiler house
E - Standard-gauge engine shed
F - Standard-gauge engine shed extention
G - 42ft turntable
H - 40ft turntable, later replaced by 55ft turntable
I - Lifting shed
J - Broad-gauge engine shed
K - Engine department workshops and offices
L - Reservoir
M - Divisional Locomotive Superintendent's house
N - Marcon Sewer

Fig 7 The main structures at Westbourne Park Depot (see Fig 2 for location)

13314
TO BE RETURNED TO CHIEF ENGINEER'S PLAN OFFICE. G. W. R. PADDINGTON.
Plan of Upper Floor
Plan of Upper Floor
Ground Plan

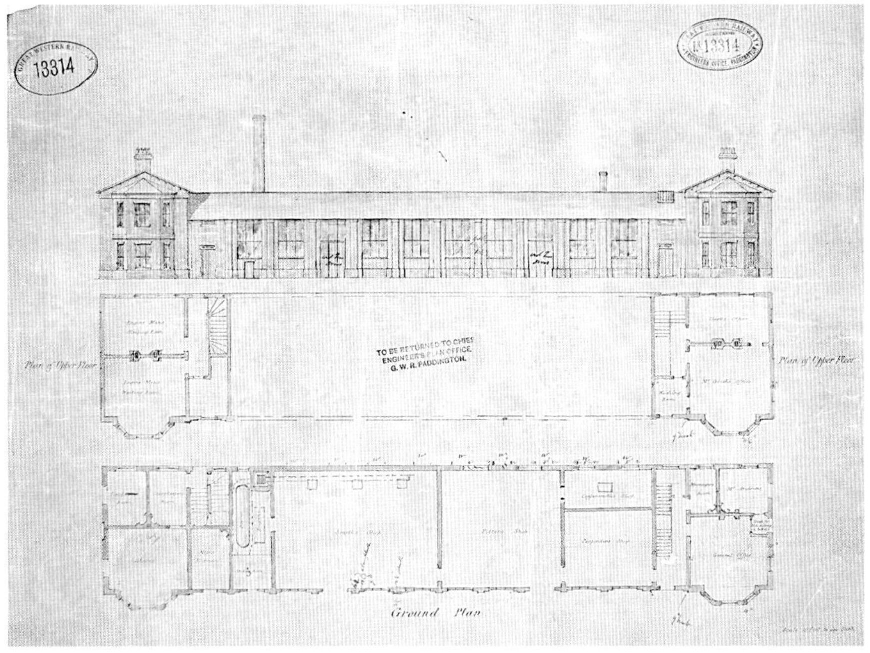

Fig 8 Westbourne Park's engine department workshops and offices *c* 1853 (Network Rail planroll 13314)

Fig 9 On 8 November 1862 the boiler of Perseus, a broad-gauge (BG) locomotive built in 1850, exploded at Westbourne Park, killing three. This is possibly the earliest photograph of the BG Shed (building J, Fig 7). (NRM/ Science and Society Picture Library)

meant that the roads had to be converted to mixed gauge. Crossrail's archaeological excavation in 2014 showed that this was achieved by bonding new walls to each side of the inspection pits, so that the standard gauge rails sat inside the broad gauge system (Fig 11). This arrangement of four rails differs from the one described as 'the addition of the third rail' in the *Great Western Magazine*'s description of the depot shortly after its closure in 1906.[7] The BG Shed was to be one of Locke and Nesham's last building projects; by August 1855 both partners had died and the firm was being wound up.

The depot layout was completed by a narrow workshop (A on Fig 7) beneath Green Lane Bridge, a small reservoir in the north-east corner of the former field (L on Fig 7) and an adjoining house for the Divisional

Fig 10 The pit beneath the northern road of the BG Shed was re-exposed in 2014. Looking east towards Paddington. The metal grille at the base of the pit covered a drain into the Marcon Sewer

Locomotive Superintendent (Alfred Villa, discussed in Chapter 4, M on Fig 7). However, Crossrail's excavations have demonstrated that the GWR also devoted much thought and expense in devising ways to drain the new depot. Their problem was that it lay within a cutting through the London clay, a notoriously impervious material. To remove the volumes of waste water that would be generated by servicing and maintaining the company's locomotives, not to mention the normal volumes of rainwater that might be expected, a brick culvert was built.

Fig 11 To allow the BG Shed to accommodate locomotives of mixed gauges the GWR reduced the width of the inspection pits by adding a brick skin to both sides of the pit. (Scale bar = 0.5m)

This was placed between the north wall of the engine shed and the northernmost inspection pit. At regular intervals catchpits in the base of the inspection pits were connected to the culvert by cast iron pipes. Inspection chambers were placed at intervals outside the north wall or inside the building itself (Figs 12-13). The culvert, now known as the Marcon Sewer after the name of a concrete supplier who based themselves on the site in the 1970s, flows to this day, in some places in its original oval-shaped brick form and in others in a Crossrail diversion.

Fig 12 (left) A Marcon Sewer inspection chamber that had once lain inside the BG Shed. The lighter-coloured brick chamber was a post-demolition addition

Fig 13 (right) One of the Marcon Sewer inspection chambers against the north-facing wall of the BG Shed

In 1861 the tracks into Paddington station were modified to accommodate standard-gauge trains, and the following year a standard-gauge shed known as the Narrow Gauge (NG) Shed (Gazetteer No. 35, Fig 14) was added to the depot.[8] There were probably further minor improvements to the site throughout the 1860s, and an early alteration would have been the enlargement of the reservoir (L on Fig 7). However, major changes started to become necessary during the 1870s as the volume of traffic increased. In 1871 two additional tracks were added to the main line between Westbourne Park and Paddington for the exclusive use of the Hammersmith and City Railway, and in 1878 the at-grade crossing of the main line by these tracks at Westbourne Park was replaced by a burrowing junction. In 1873 the NG shed was doubled in size to accommodate six roads, each furnished with pits and signs above the door which read NG1, NG2 etc. The use of the term 'narrow gauge' rather than the near-universally accepted 'standard gauge' shows just how prickly the GWR remained over the rejection of Brunel's beloved broad gauge system.

At around the same time that the NG Shed was being enlarged the workshops and offices were substantially altered (Fig 15). Block 2 and an adjoining section of the workshops were retained, but the rest of the building seems to have been heavily reconfigured. The smiths', fitters' and carpenters' shops now occupied the remaining length of the building (Figs 16-17), Block 1 having been removed and the building's internal partitions re-arranged. The revamped building was extended by 103ft to the west so that three roads of 89ft length, each with shallow concave pits, could be incorporated (Fig 18). Excavation suggests that the extension may have been a relatively lightweight structure. The southern elevation was formed from uprights supported on limestone blocks through which a cast iron downpipe passed, and the western gable was also carried by uprights, this time located by a pair of vertical steel bars embedded into brick bases.

Fig 14 The NG Shed's inspection pits were revealed during Crossrail works at Westbourne Park in 2014

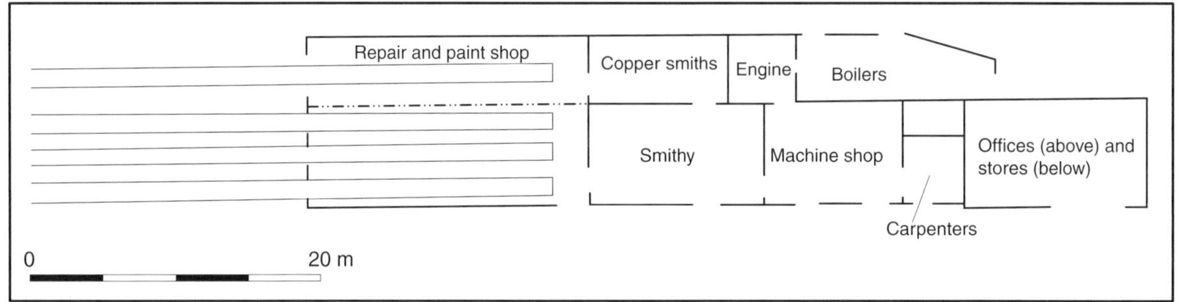

Fig 15 The locomotive workshops and offices in 1906. The least altered part of the 1853 structure was Block 2 (the offices and stores) (OA drawing after Hawkins and Reeve 1987, 67)

Fig 16 (left) In 2014 the remains of Westbourne Park's repair and fitting workshops were uncovered. The base of a forge in the smithy lies in the foreground, with two of the four pits beneath the roads of the repair and paint shop under excavation in the top of the picture

Fig 17 (right above) Westbourne Park's smithy contained a quenching trough built from large blocks of slate. The orange-coloured material at the base is waste from the process

Fig 18 (right, below) The eastern end of each pit in Westbourne Park's repair and paint shop was drained by a catchpit linked to the Marcon Sewer by a 6in pipe

Although the first depiction of a 42ft diameter steam-actuated turntable (Gazetteer No. 41) to the west of the BG Shed dates to 1872 it was presumably part of the original depot layout. A small, hexagonal building beside the turntable housed a boiler to power the chain which passed around the table in order to turn it.[9] A second turntable, of 40ft diameter and hand-operated by a pair of winches (Gazetteer No. 39; Fig 19), was

Fig 19 The concentric rings of the successive turntables which lay to the east of the NG Shed. The middle ring represented the outer wall of the earlier 40ft turntable (© Stefan Popa)

situated to the north of the BG Shed on the track that linked the NG Shed with the workshop.

In 1879 plans were issued for a lifting shop on the site (Gazetteer No. 42; Fig 20). This was to be erected to the north of the congested tracks between the NG Shed and the locomotive workshops. The building was referred to in a schedule drawn up in 1901 as the 'Shear Legs' Shed, presumably in reference to its cranes.[10] Of these there were two, one fixed, the other a hydraulic travelling unit. The roof was of saw-tooth construction rather than the double-pitched profile seen elsewhere on the site, and the roof principals were of timber rather than iron.

Proposals for development of the site continued to emerge from GWR's drawing office in Swindon. The following year plans for a sand house were issued (Gazetteer No. 38; Fig 21). (How dry sand had been supplied to the site before this date is not clear.) This elegant little brick building with its glazed roof vent and slated roof pitches survived until a ramp into the site was constructed in *c* 1975. At the same time as the sand house was being built, a new twin-track goods line between Paddington and Portobello Junction opened to relieve the main line approaches to the

Fig 20 In 1879 Swindon issued a drawing showing the proposed lifting shop at Westbourne Park (WSHC 2515/409/0056 ms 1879)

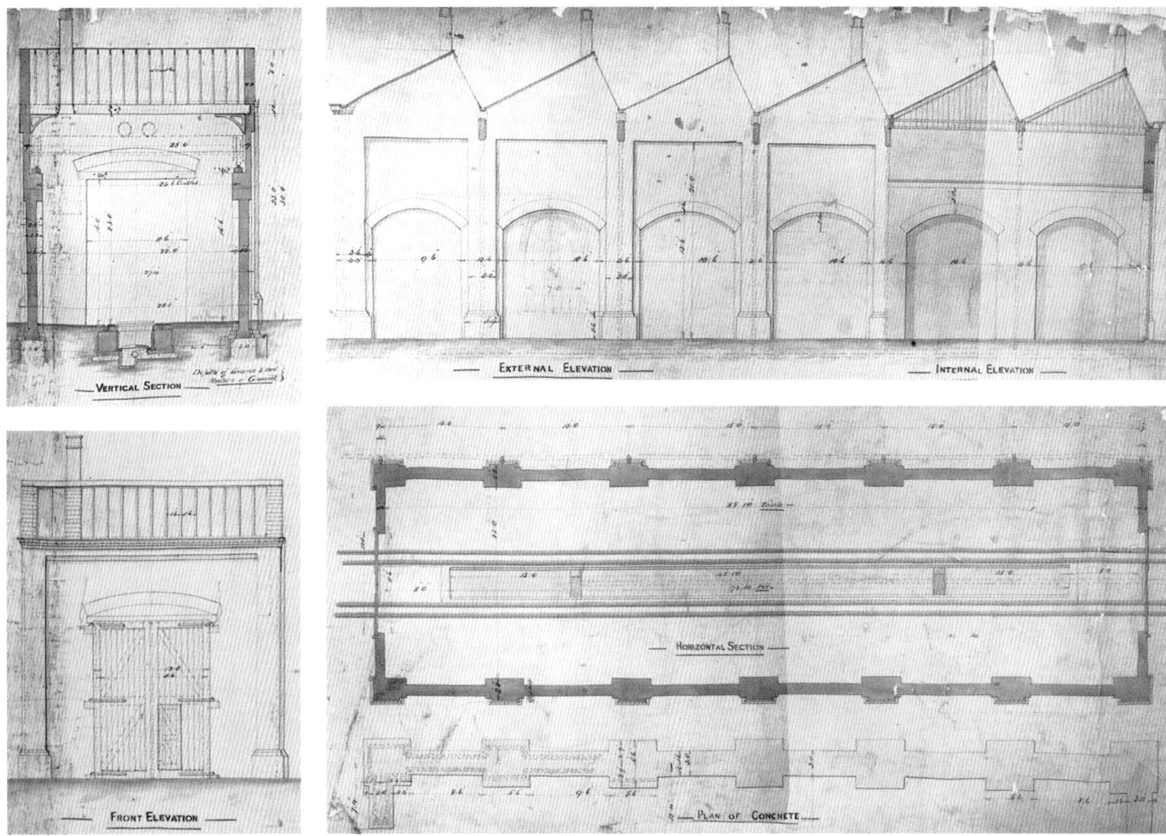

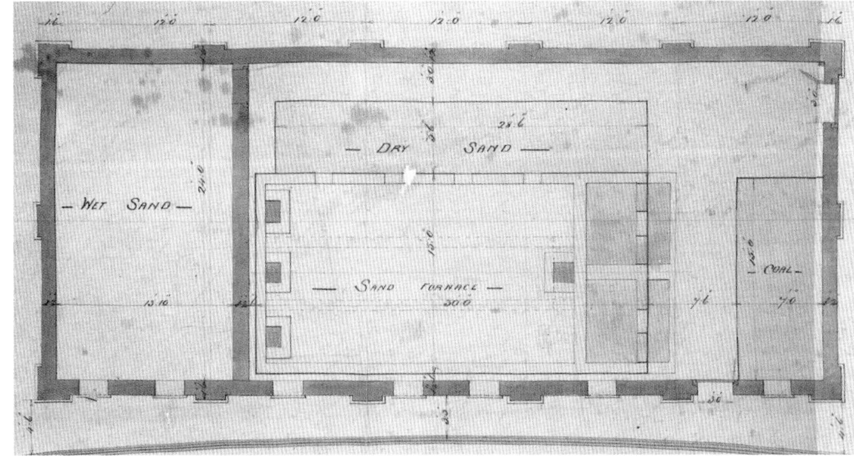

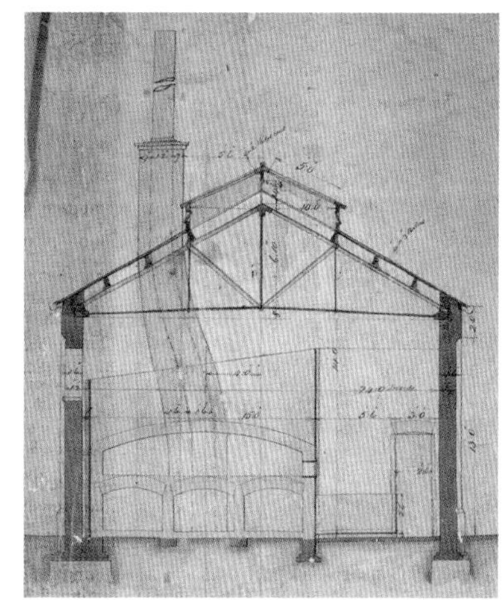

station. With no room between the BG Shed and the main-line this swept to the north of the depot before being carried under Great Western Road in a short stretch of tunnel later known variously as Cape Horn Tunnel or Mousehole Tunnel. In so doing it blocked the pedestrian route between Alfred Road and the site, and a footbridge was built to span the new tracks. This line remained operational until 1906 when it was replaced by another widening of the main-line corridor.

Fig 21 Plan and elevation for a sand house at Westbourne Park, issued by Swindon in 1880 (WSHC 2515/409/0051 ms)

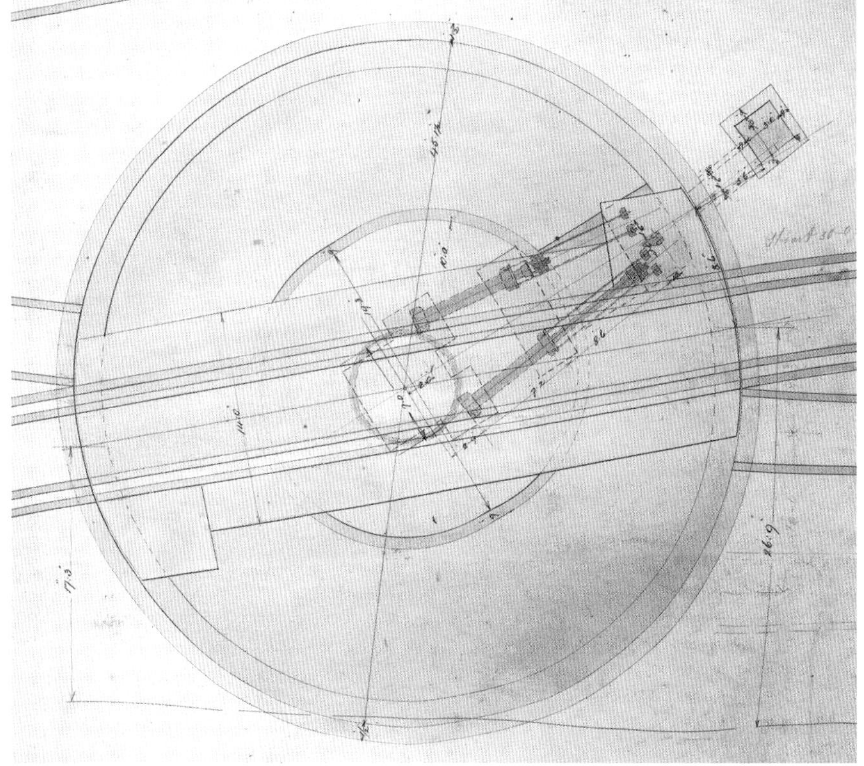

Fig 22 Plans for a new 45ft turntable were issued in 1881 (WSHC 2515/406/3201)

Fig 23 The 45ft turntable pit was briefly re-exposed in 2014. In this photograph the pit is bisected by a later service cable. Green Lane Bridge is in the background. (Scale bar = 1m)

In 1881 Swindon issued plans for a third turntable, this time to be situated to the west of the NG Shed and to measure 45ft in diameter (Gazetteer No. 37, Figs 22-23). Here, in the throat of the depot, space was limited, requiring the turntable deck to be equipped with a hydraulic slewing mechanism. The floor of the turntable pit was of brick, the full circle girders were of wrought iron and the deck, on which a small hut with windows sat, was of timber.[11] Once operational, the nearby 42ft turntable (G on Fig 7) was decommissioned and removed, presumably to eliminate it as an obstacle within the main line corridor.[12]

New tracks and buildings continued to be added to the site as traffic increased. In the later 1880s a double-pitched brick building was added to the northern elevation of the workshop, repair and office building. This allowed a fourth road to be added to the Repair and Paint Shop, and provided new accommodation for the coppersmiths and rooms for

Fig 24 This plan of the boiler and pump rooms at Westbourne Park has been dated to 1891 but may be earlier (WSHC 2515/409/0040)

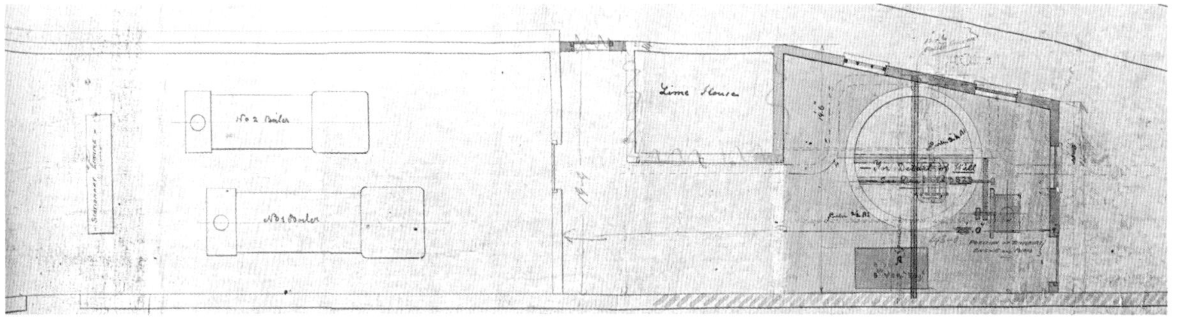

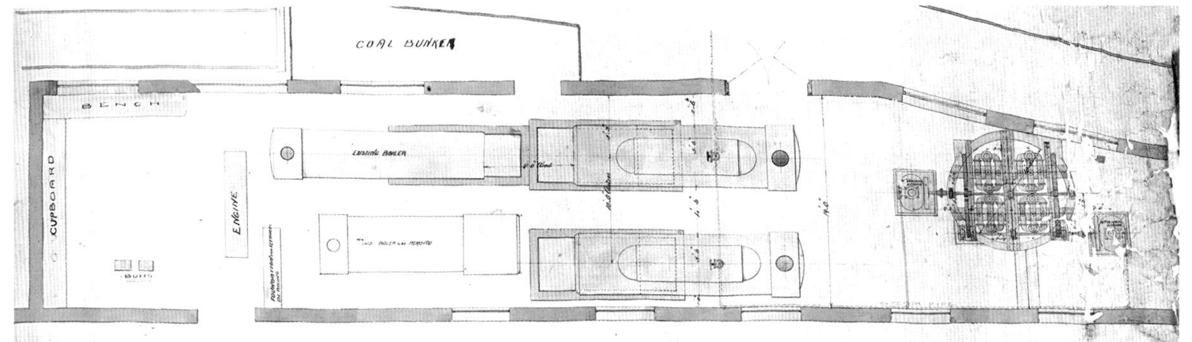

Fig 25 Westbourne Park's workshop engine, boiler and pump room, as proposed in 1886 (WSHC 2515/406/0852)

a stationary engine and a pair of boilers. These are shown on a drawing, which has been dated to 1891 but may be earlier (Fig 24). Also shown on this drawing are a limehouse, a vertical engine and a pump over a 10ft diameter well in a brick building roofed in corrugated iron. This was attached to the angle between the workshops and their extension.

In November 1886 Swindon detailed how one of the boilers was to be removed and two additional boilers installed (Fig 25). By demolishing the eastern wall of the boiler house it could be extended to accommodate the new boilers, which were to drive two vertical engines linked to a set of pumps seated over the well. An external coal bunker was accessed by a door in the northern wall of the boiler room.

What was the purpose of the well? Clues are provided by a drawing issued in 1898 (Fig 26), and also by the 2014 excavation (Fig 27). The archaeological work showed there to be no less than three shafts, of equal depth and interlinked at two levels, with culverts connecting them with the 'running shed', 'subway' and 'Paddington Electric Light'. 'Paddington Electric Light' was probably the power station built by the Telegraph Construction & Maintenance Company in a former carriage shed behind Gloucester Crescent in 1885.[13] Hot water returning from the latter's condenser was used 'to great advantage' by the depot to wash out boilers whilst they were still hot.[14]

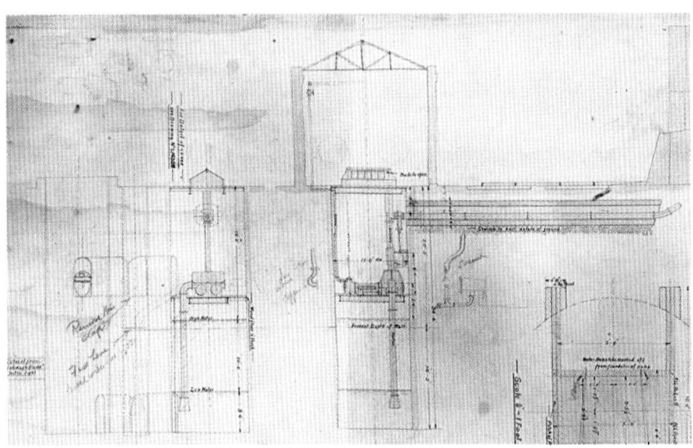

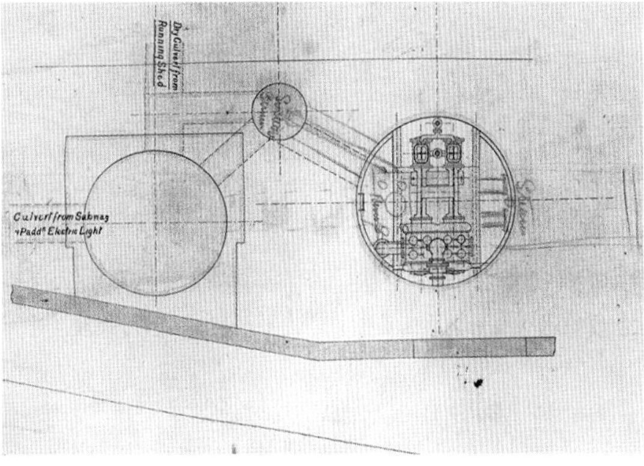

Fig 26 Two details from a 1898 GWR drawing showing the proposed arrangement of shafts and pumps at Westbourne Park (WSHC 2515/406/0881)

Fig 27 Westbourne Park's interconnected well shafts were exposed in 2014. Deep-level culverts linked the shafts to other nearby railway facilities

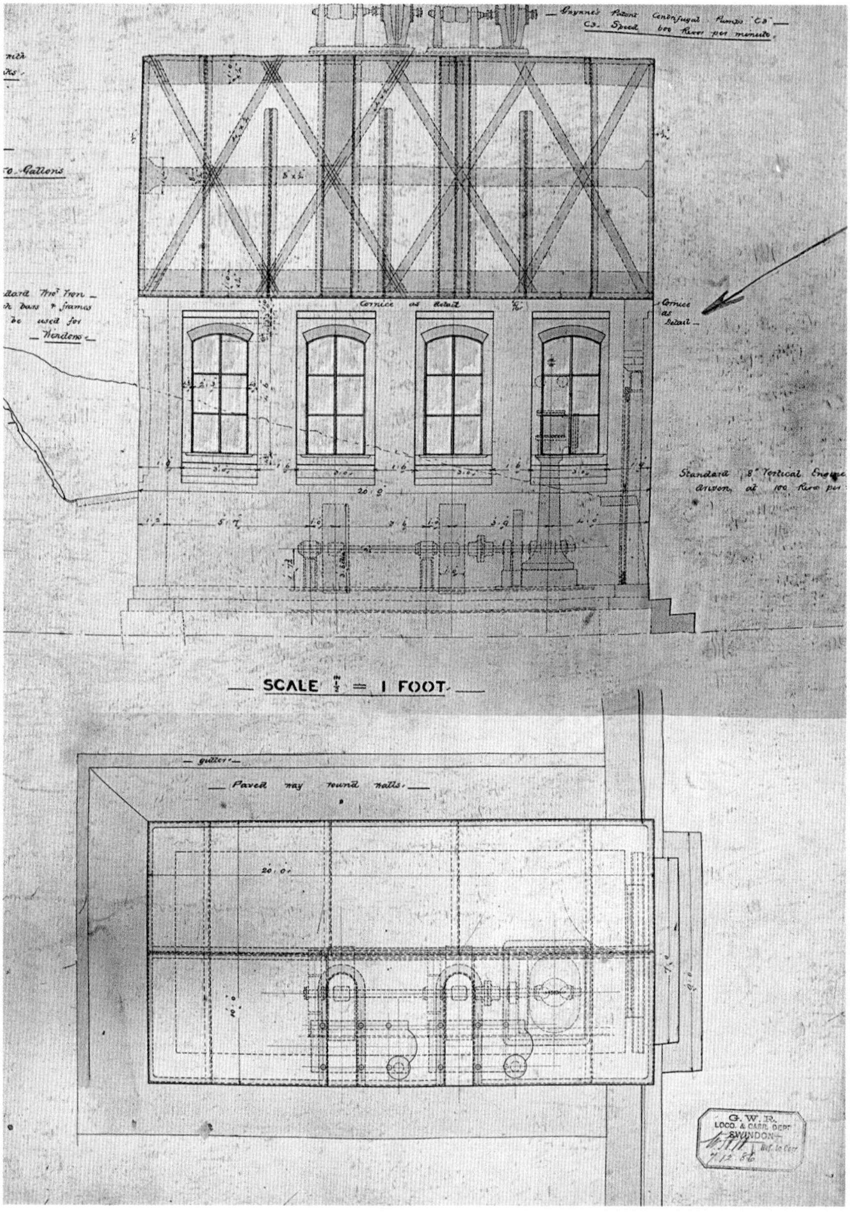

Fig 28 1886 design for a building to house centrifugal pumps and a tank at Westbourne Park (WSHC 2515/409/0119)

The 1898 drawing makes it clear that water was being pumped northwards under the goods lines to a pump house set in a cutting in the bank. Twin lifting pumps from 'Gwynne's Patent Centrifugal Pumps Co.', then lifted it into a tank surmounting the pump house (Fig 28).[15] Water may also have been transferred to the reservoir and tanks beside the canal, the intention in both cases being to add the water storage capacity the wells had brought to the site.

After 1898 the depot saw few new developments, works being confined instead to upgrades or replacements. Nearby a coffee tavern (Gazetteer No. 36) was constructed beside Cape Horn Tunnel in 1901, apparently as a direct replacement for one beside Green Lane Bridge.[16] Coffee taverns were one very obvious way that the company, through its Great Western Coffee Tavern Company Ltd, tried to encourage temperance amongst its workers. However, by 1912 such overt signs of paternalism were becoming antiquated and the Great Western Coffee Tavern Company was closed. A blueprint issued by Swindon in 1921 shows how the 1901 structure, which survives today as a furniture workshop and showroom (Fig 29), was to be converted into a Deeds Office.[17]

In one of the last major changes at Westbourne Park, the 40ft hand turntable was replaced in 1896 by a 'Swindon surface table' of 55ft 6in diameter, possibly with an eye on accommodating 4-6-0 locomotives.[18] By then the GWR had long since outgrown the site and the company were considering proposals that could relieve the chronic shortage of storage capacity bedevilling its Paddington operations. On 17 March 1906 a new depot opened at Old Oak Common and by June Westbourne Park's BG Shed, and probably also the NG Shed, had been demolished. A plan was drawn up in 1907 to show how Westbourne Park was to be converted

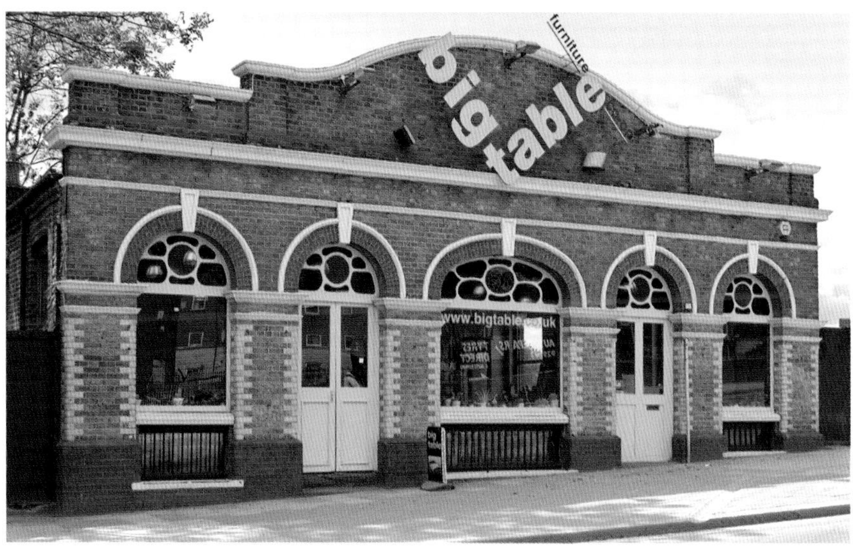

Fig 29 Now a furniture workshop and showroom, this building on Great Western Road in Westbourne Park originated as a GWR Coffee Tavern

into a goods depot, indicates that the east wing of the *c* 1853 workshop and office building had already been removed. The eastern gable of the foreshortened structure was now aligned approximately with the former east wall of the well house.[19] Two of the four roads in the repair and paint shop were extended through the building while the other two were removed. The former lifting shop, after its one through road had been removed, became a goods shed, but the 55ft turntable, scarcely 10 years old, was removed. Both sheds were eventually demolished in 1938 to make way for Alfred Road Warehouse (see Chapter 8), which was itself demolished in 2010 in advance of construction by Crossrail of the western approach to the tunnelled section of the new line.

Railways in East London

Railway companies were also pushing towards London from the east (Fig 30). The ECR (Eastern Counties Railway), whose prospectus was issued in August 1834, was formed with the remit of connecting Norwich

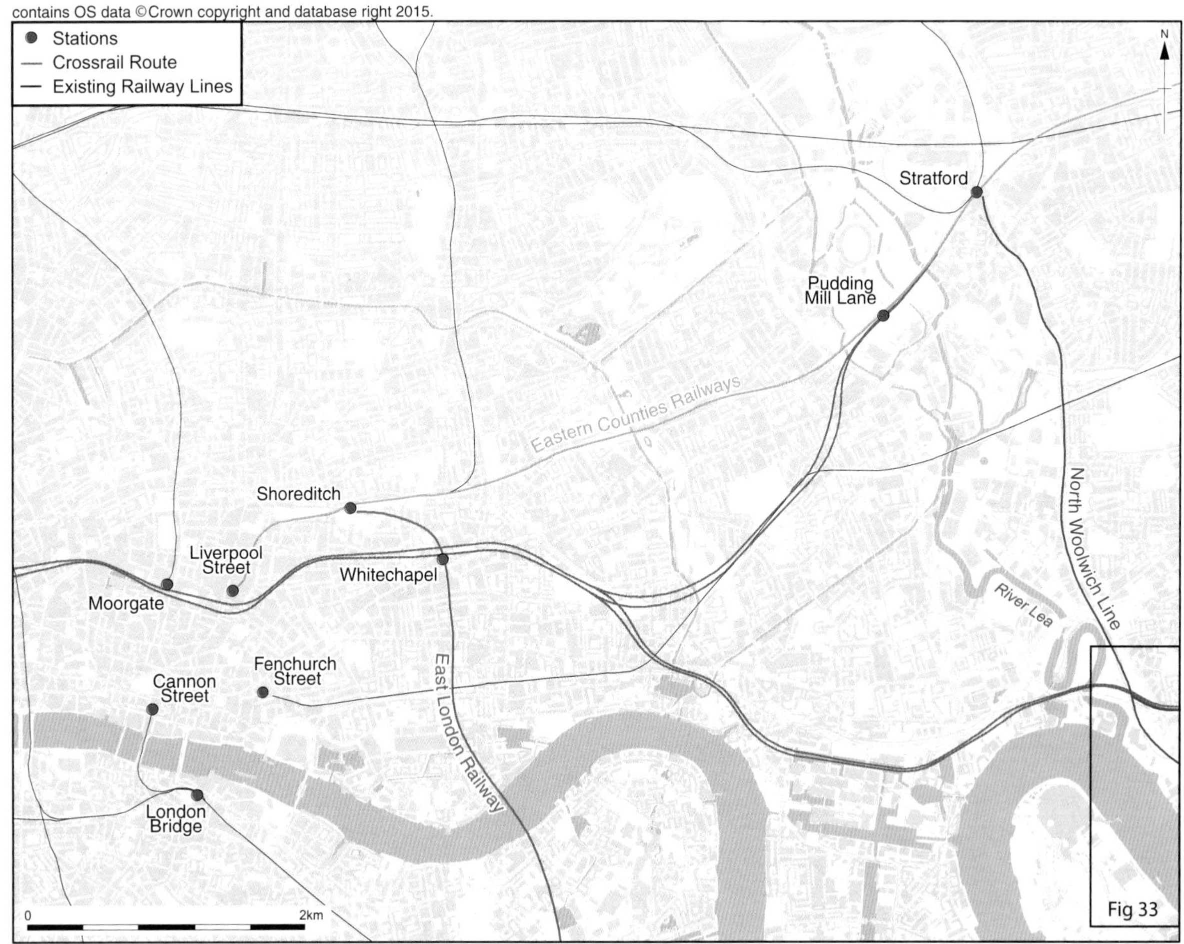

Fig 30 Railways in the Shoreditch, Whitechapel and Stratford areas

to London via a terminus in Shoreditch in the East End. Under the direction of its engineer, John Braithwaite, the Mile End to Romford stretch opened in June 1839. Initially, Braithwaite used a track gauge of 5ft but soon settled for the 4ft 8½in standard favoured by Stephenson. West of Stratford the ground was marshy, requiring a greater civil engineering effort, and much of the line had to be carried on raised viaducts, slowing progress.[20] Shoreditch station was completed in July 1840 and formed the line's London terminus until 1874, when Liverpool Street station opened.

Stratford was soon a busy hub, especially after the ECR's engine department relocated there from Romford. A number of railways joined the ECR's line at this point. The London and Blackwall Railway's (LBLR) link from Fenchurch Street crossed the tortuously named East & West India Docks & Birmingham Junction Railway's (later the North London Railway) line to Poplar only yards before it met the ECR line at its crossing of the River Lea. In the late 1980s the Poplar line, by then closed, was incorporated into the Docklands Light Railway (DLR) system. At its junction with the former LBLR it was re-engineered so that it could join the LBLR's lines into Stratford. There should have been a station between this junction and Stratford, but there were insufficient funds and it was not until 1996 that Pudding Mill Lane station opened (Gazetteer No. 135, Fig 31).[21] Few passengers were ever to be seen on its platforms (Fig 32). Once Crossrail had received approval this little station found itself directly in the way of the ramp down to its eastern tunnel entrance and in 2014 it closed, to be replaced by a much larger station a few metres to the south.

Another branch, the Eastern Counties & Thames Junction Railway (ECTJR), connected Stratford to Canning Town. The line opened in April 1846, and the following year it was extended across Plaistow Marshes to North Woolwich, from where a ferry provided a link with the munitions factories of the Royal Woolwich Arsenal (Figs 33-34). The North Woolwich line proved to be a popular service, but in 1849, by which time the ECTJR

Fig 31 (left) The first Pudding Mill Lane station opened in 1996 and closed in 2014 (Nigel Cox CC-SA-2.0)

Fig 32 (right) Pudding Mill Lane station was little more than a halt (Fletcher Priest Architects)

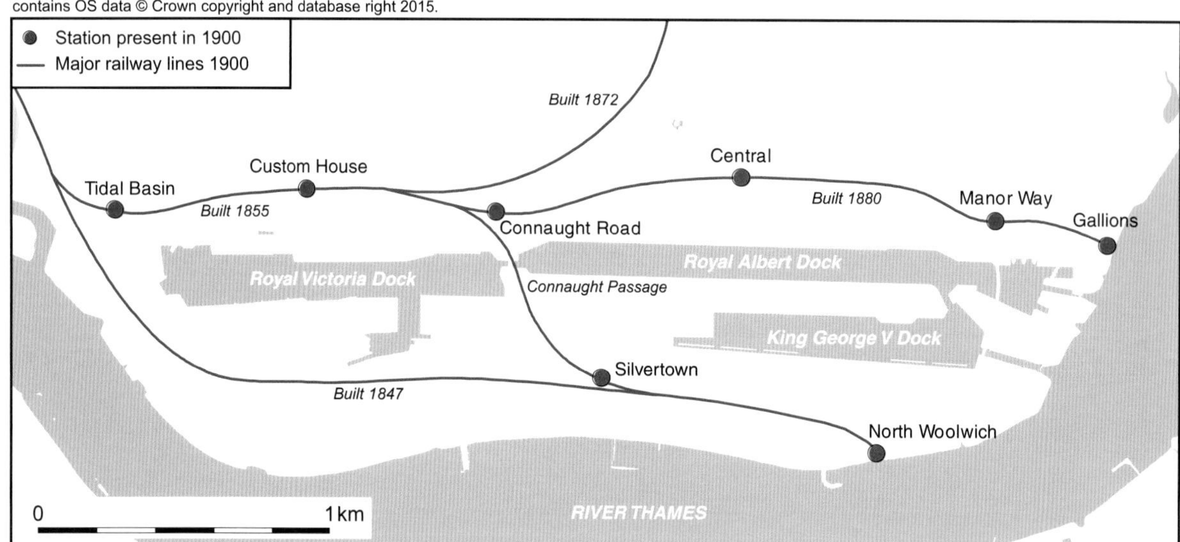

Fig 33 The North Woolwich line in the Royal Docks area of east London *c* 1900. The docks gained their 'Royal' prefix in 1921

had been absorbed into the ECR, the South Eastern Railway reached Woolwich along the south bank of the river and demand slumped. Fortunately, the ECTJR's chief proponent, the engineer George Parker Bidder, had also entered into a partnership with two leading railway contractors, Thomas Brassey and Samuel Peto, to construct a dock, called Victoria Dock, on a site close by the confluence of Bow Creek and the Thames.[22] In 1850 the scheme was granted permission. Its key advantage was its link to the ECR network. In order for the necessary channel to be dug between the new dock basin and the Thames, the North Woolwich line had first to be looped round the northern side of the dock. The revised route rejoined its original tracks near the south-eastern corner of the dock, and the abandoned section renamed the Silvertown Tramway after the settlement of Silvertown, itself named after the local cable manufacturing firm of S W Silver & Company, was adopted by the Victoria Dock Company.[23]

Victoria Dock very quickly became London's principal dock. Its many advantages lead to a meteoric increase in tonnage handled – 854,000 tons in 1860, already 70% more than the East and West India Docks combined.[24] Because the dock was connected by railway to Stratford, goods were able to travel directly from the quayside to most places in Britain. This encouraged the Midland Railway, the L&NWR, the GNT and the GWR to establish their own depots alongside the North Woolwich line.[25] The dock's exchange sidings were situated alongside Custom House station and were busy enough in their heyday to keep two dozen or more shunting locomotives active.

Victoria Dock's huge popularity encouraged its owners, by this time the London & St Katharine Docks Company (L&SKDC), to construct a second

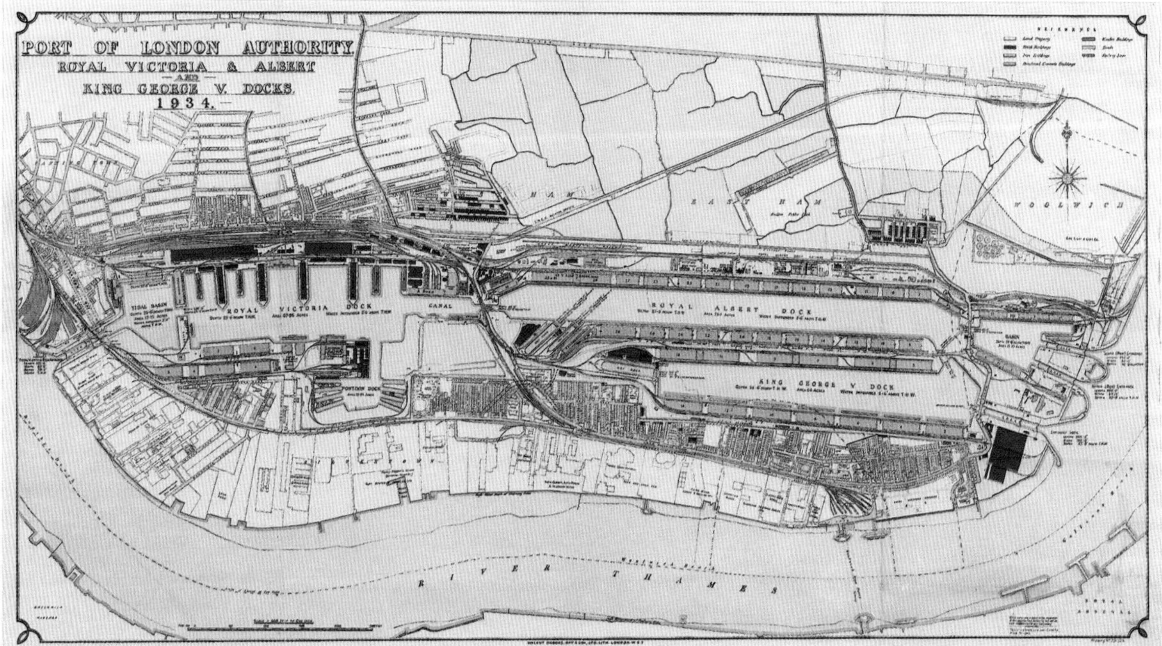

Fig 34 'Map of the Royal Victoria, Royal Albert and King George V Docks' 1934 (National Maritime Museum)

dock to the east. Once again the North Woolwich line lay in the way. Given that the proposal would link Victoria Dock with Gallions Reach it would not be possible to divert the railway any further eastward. Instead, the line was to be re-routed beneath the short canal between the two docks. Silvertown Tunnel, later known as Connaught Tunnel, opened in 1879 (Gazetteer No. 138, Figs 35-36).[26] As before, the high-level route was retained, the canal section being crossed via a swing bridge. The L&SKDC assumed ownership of both routes and the responsibility for maintenance of the tunnel and the flanking retaining walls of its approaches. The tunnel was constructed using the cut-and-cover method with approach gradients of 1 in 50. Since these were relatively steep, restrictions were placed on train weight. Because the tunnel was limited to trains of 25 wagons or less the surface crossing was popular.[27] Far from being a hindrance, it transpired that the number of level-crossings and swing-bridges around the docks hampered the development of road haulage more than the development of the railway.[28]

The walls of the cuttings were lined with Portland cement and braced with flying buttresses of brick and concrete (Fig 37). The tunnel section was enclosed below and to the sides by concrete, and above by clay. The stretch beneath Connaught Passage was divided into two by a brick central wall to add strength. Although the tunnel proved its worth the decline during the 1970s of the docks and the industries they had served signalled that the line would one day also close. With the opening of the DLR stations at Silvertown and North Woolwich the closure of the line came in

Fig 35 The point at which Silvertown Tunnel's single-bore divides beneath Connaught Passage. The base of the northern air vent is also shown. Looking south-east

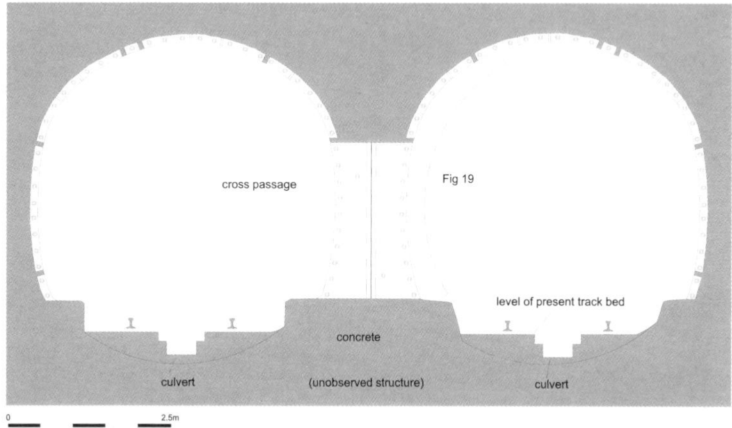

Fig 36 Between 1935 and 1936 the central section of Silvertown Tunnel was remodelled in order to increase the draft of Connaught Passage. The top of the bored tunnels was reduced significantly in thickness and cast-steel linings were introduced to maintain structural integrity

Fig 37 The buttresses of Silvertown Tunnel's southern approach

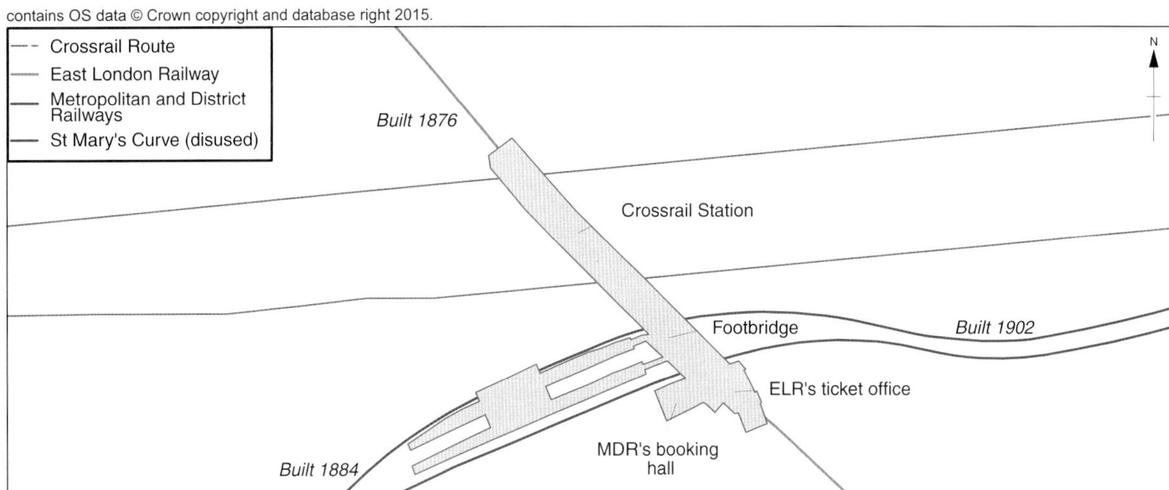

Fig 38 The layout of Whitechapel station showing its principal phases of historical development

December 2006. This was not, however, the end. In 2012 work started on deepening and strengthening what had become known as Connaught Tunnel in advance of the resurrection of the line as the eastern end of Crossrail's spur between Whitechapel and Woolwich.

In 2010 the North London Railway's (NLR) former spur from Dalston to Broad Street Station re-opened as the northern end of London Overground's East London line. This is chiefly a refashioning of the East London Railway's (ELR) link between New Cross and Shoreditch which had capitalised upon Marc and Isambard Kingdom Brunel's 1843 tunnel beneath the Thames. The ELR passed through Whitechapel, and there the company opened a station in April 1876 (Fig 38). In October 1884 the Metropolitan & District Railway (MDR) also reached Whitechapel and opened an adjacent station, which they named Whitechapel (Mile End) (Fig 39). From 2018, when Crossrail opens, a third line will use the station. In preparation, the station is being significantly modified and a new Crossrail station added.

Various elements of this complicated little station were recorded by Crossrail's archaeologists during 2012. These included a timber-clad footbridge (Gazetteer No. 124, Fig 40) that linked the MDR booking hall with its two island platforms, and for which plans had been issued in July 1901 when the station was being redesigned to service the MDR's extension to Bow. The islands were later linked to the ELR platforms by subways of 1936 vintage (Gazetteer No. 121). The subways were clad in London Transport's large ceramic tiles of the interwar period, where the main colour was oatmeal and edges and details were picked out in bands in blue, green and orange. The tiles were the product of Carter Stabler

Fig 39 The MDR Whitechapel Road station entrance in 1896, with part of the ELR station entrance to the right (Tower Hamlets Local History Library and Archives).

Adams's Poole Pottery which survives to this day. Above the staircases were two bronze-framed signs, which had been fabricated to a design from London Transport's 1938 Standard Signs Manual.

The MDR booking hall (Gazetteer No. 125) now acts as little more than a wide corridor between the current ticket hall and the footbridge, but it remains an impressive space (Fig 41). Its double-pitched roof is supported

Fig 40 Whitechapel station's footbridge dated to 1901. In the right-hand image the MDR booking hall can be identified by its white gable and bull's-eye window. To its left is the arched gable of the ELR ticket hall

Fig 41 The former MDR booking hall at Whitechapel station

on arched timber trusses, with a wide skylight providing natural light. More light is gained by a bull's-eye window in the northern gable. The hall was shortened considerably when its southern link to Whitechapel Road closed. The adjacent ELR ticket hall (Gazetteer No. 126, Fig 42) remains in use, and to reach Whitechapel Road from the platforms one must first walk through the MDR booking hall into the ELR ticket hall. The ELR hall is another tall and airy space with a double-pitched roof of glass supported by five cast iron trusses with floral spandrels. The top half of each side wall is panelled with wood. A tall arched opening in the northern gable formerly gave access to the ELR platforms via a cross-passage and stairs, but this now simply provides access to the MDR booking hall. An elliptical arch at the southern end of the hall probably helped carry the load of the buildings overhead, one of which provided accommodation for the ELR stationmaster (Fig 43).[29]

Fig 42 Whitechapel station's ELR booking hall

Fig 43 The ELR's Whitechapel station booking hall looking south to Whitechapel Road in 1957. The elliptical arch probably helped spread the load of the buildings overhead. (Collection of London Transport Museum, Image no: 440/199. © Transport for London)

Fig 44 The location of Broad Street Station ticket hall and Queen Victoria Tunnel in relation to London Liverpool Street station

contains OS data © Crown copyright and database right 2015.

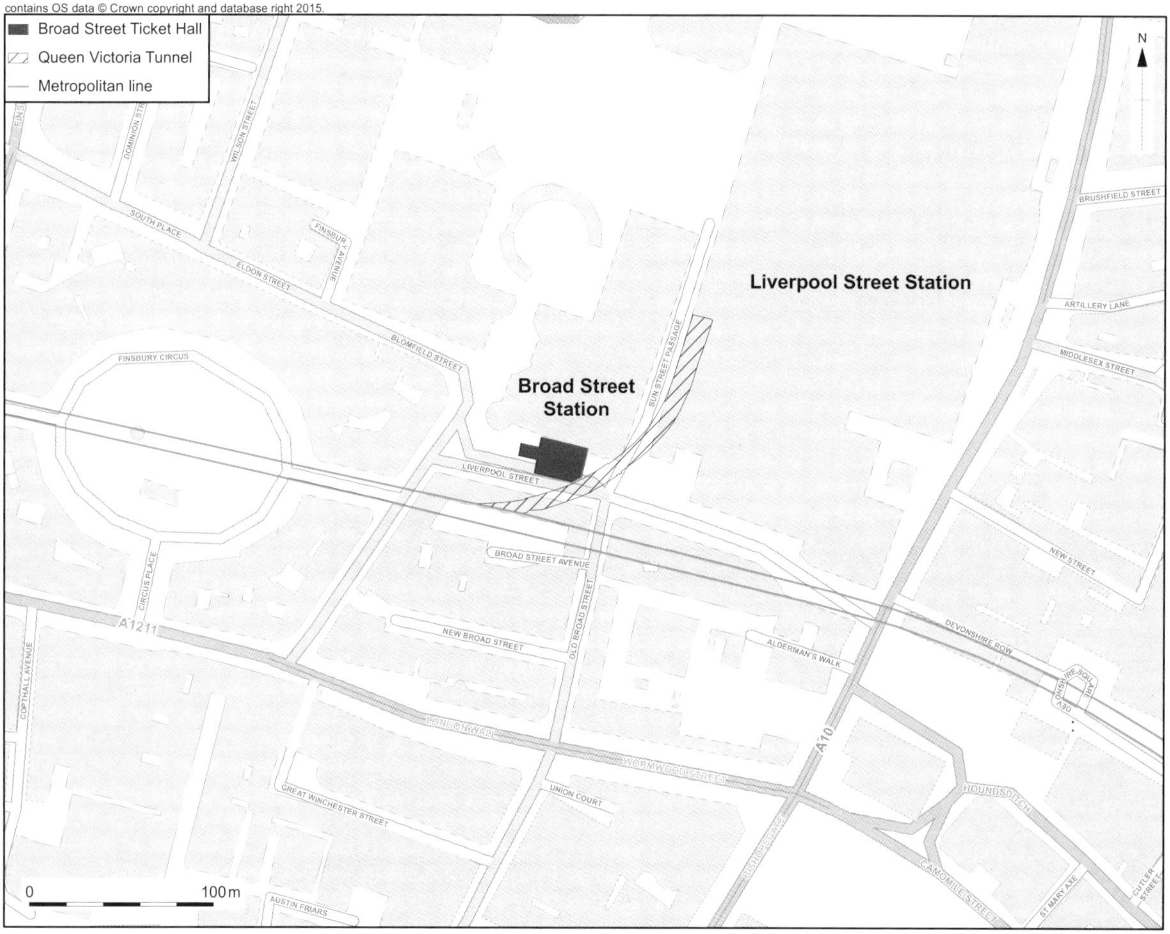

Broad Street Ticket Hall
Queen Victoria Tunnel
Metropolitan line

N

Liverpool Street Station
Broad Street Station
SUN STREET PASSAGE
LIVERPOOL STREET
BLOMFIELD STREET
FINSBURY CIRCUS
SOUTH PLACE
ELDON STREET
FINSBURY AVENUE
WILSON STREET
DOMINION STREET
BRUSHFIELD STREET
ARTILLERY LANE
MIDDLESEX STREET
NEW STREET
DEVONSHIRE ROW
DEVONSHIRE SQUARE
BROAD STREET AVENUE
OLD BROAD STREET
NEW BROAD STREET
ALDERMAN'S WALK
CIRCUS PLACE
A1211
COPTHALL AVENUE
LONDON WALL
WORMWOOD STREET
A10
UNION COURT
HOUNDSDITCH
GREAT WINCHESTER STREET
BISHOPSGATE
CAMOMILE STREET
ST MARY AXE
CUTLER STREET
AUSTIN FRIARS

0 100 m

Until 1865 the NLR, another of London's smaller railways, was content to use the LBLR's Fenchurch Street station as its City terminal. Eventually, however, the line's popularity persuaded the company to build its own station, and in November of that year it opened a spur from Dalston to Broad Street in the City. Broad Street station was once the third busiest in London but demand peaked as long ago as 1902. By the late 1960s only two platforms remained in regular use and in 1986 the station and its link to Dalston finally closed. All traces of the station above ground were swept away in the 1980s during the construction of Broadgate, an office and retail quarter which also wraps around Liverpool Street station (Fig 44). However, the Central London Railway's (CLR) underground ticket hall, which had been inserted beneath Broad Street station in 1912, survived this episode and became an electricity sub-station for London Underground. Parts of this will be re-used by Crossrail, and a survey in 2014 showed that historic fabric including glazed tiles, blocked-up archways, columns, stairs, handrails and advertising hoardings had survived in mothballed form (Gazetteer No. 119, Fig 45). A particular feature remains the 7.6m diameter lift shaft pit in the centre of the ticket hall. This accommodated two lifts, which rose 76ft to emerge in the concourse of Broad Street station.

Fig 45 Fragments of an advert for a football match at Wembley remain fossilised in an abandoned subway below Liverpool Street. This is likely to be advertising the match between England and Luxembourg, which took place on 15 December 1984

One corner of the ticket hall is chamfered to avoid Queen Victoria Tunnel (Gazetteer No. 118, Fig 46), a branch of the Metropolitan Line which lies beneath the carriageway of Liverpool Street and which was formerly known as the Great Eastern Railway Connection Tunnel. Constructed very much as an emergency measure to ensure connection between the Metropolitan Line and the Great Eastern Railway's (GER) main lines until

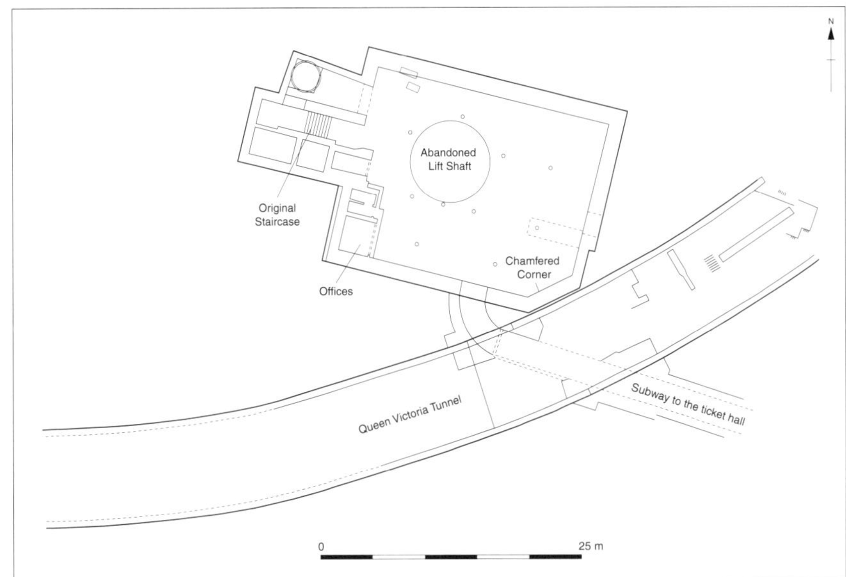

Fig 46 Broad Street ticket hall has a chamfered corner in order to avoid Queen Victoria Tunnel

Bishopsgate station could be completed, the tunnel opened for passenger traffic in February 1875 and closed little more than five months later. It was used only fitfully thereafter, and by the 20th century it had become a canteen for the GER.

The CLR had been established in 1889. Its proposition was simple; it would provide a link between the wealthy residential areas of west London, the fashionable shopping and entertainment districts of the West End, and the commercial 'Square Mile' gathered around Bank, and to do so it would use deep-level tunnelling and electric-powered trains. Both were relatively new technologies, and although costs soon rose as a result, the link opened in July 1900. As Jackson and Croome have noted, everything about the CLR was good and solid, and its stations, designed by Henry Bell Measures (1862-1940) were no exception.[30] Measures' Tottenham Court Road station at 9-15 Oxford Street (Fig 47) comprised a ticket hall, shop units and lifts down to lower-level platforms beneath Oxford Street (Gazetteer No. 83). The elevations fronting the street were of unglazed terracotta with Art Nouveau decorative elements. In common with his other nearby stations the upper storeys were designed by another architect, in this case Delissa Joseph (1859-1927) who designed the three upper storeys as an office development.

The ground floor entrance to the station contained two staircases leading to a ticket hall at basement level. That the public areas of the station once covered a larger portion of the ground floor was demonstrated by a number of architectural features which came to light during an inspection shortly

Fig 47 The Central London Railway's Tottenham Court Road station in 2009. The upper storeys have now been demolished to allow for re-development

before demolition in 2009. These comprised a large square skylight with a moulded surround, a tall moulded ceiling and an iron column with decorative neo-classical mouldings. To the east lay two smaller rooms, the northernmost of which was decorated with tiles similar to those used on Measures's station.

A new ticket hall was built in 1925, and in 1937 the first use of a continuous name frieze on a London Underground platform appeared.[31] The station was next refurbished, expensively, in the early 1980s. The artist Eduardo Paolozzi created mosaics of 'electrical colours' for some of the platforms, the rotunda and various lobbies. The mosaics highlighted the 'musical and hi-fi connections of Tottenham Court Road'.[32]

At the time of writing, Tottenham Court Road station is once again being comprehensively rebuilt. Its regular users will have noticed entrances being boarded-up, claddings being removed and, at street-frontage level, an airy new ticket hall taking shape. To a London rail commuter, changes like this are a familiar experience. As the early development of Paddington station shows, railway companies have always opened and closed lines, raised new buildings and demolished others. The experience of the DLR's little Pudding Mill Lane station was far from uncommon; on the contrary, its ephemeral existence is emblematic of a national railway system in constant evolution.

NOTES

1 An earlier north-to-south link had been formed by the opening in 1863 of the West London Extension Railway, but this was a circuitous route (Klapper 1976, 9)

2 Mr Andrews' role is not known, and he is not mentioned in Burdett Wilson's 1972 publication of Gooch's memoirs and diaries

3 The date Westbourne Park Depot opened is unclear. Brown gives a date of March 1852 (2013, 67), Lyons and Mountford March 1855 (1979, 203), and Brindle suggests some time between 1851 and 1855 (2004, 136)

4 White 1906, 85. Photographs from the turn of the century show that the entrances to each road were labelled as 'BG1', 'BG2', etc; Brindle 2013, 136

5 GWR Board Meetings 1852-1853, NA Rail 250/6, 71; www.littlehamptonfort.co.uk/wp-content/uploads/2014/04/Locke-and-Nesham-Research-Document accessed 1 Jul 2014

6 Hawkins and Reeve 1987, 64

7 The date of 1869 is given in White 1906, 86

8 White 1906, 85

9 White, 1906, 86

10 Hawkins and Reeve 1987, 66

11 Ibid, 65

12 White 1906, 61

13 Brindle 2013, 57

14 From a report by Westbourne Park's Assistant Divisional Superintendent William Stanier, given in February 1907, in Hawkins and Reeve 1987, 69. See page 45 for a description of the purpose and importance of boiler working

15 GWR drawing 'Tank and Engine House, Centrifugal Pumps, Westbourne Park', December 1886, WSHC 2515/409/0119. Gwynnes Limited was a London-based engineering company founded in 1849. The company was dissolved in 1927, but the pump-making business soldiered on as Gwynnes Pumps Limited until the 1960s.
16 This evidence comes from the 1894 1:1,056 Town Plan
17 GWR drawing 'GWR Coffee Tavern at Westbourne Park Station: Proposed Conversion into Deeds Office', 1921, WSHC 2515/403/0774
18 Hawkins and Reeve 1987, 65. A prototype 4-6-0 locomotive, No. 36, appeared in 1896 (Holcroft 1971, 73).
19 GWR drawing 'New Goods Depot at Westbourne Park', December 1907, WSHC 2515/410/1773
20 Brodribb 2009, 7
21 Designed by architects Fletcher Priest.
22 Greeves 1980, 9
23 Marden 2013, 101-103
24 Ball and Sunderland 2001, 222
25 Siviour 2006, 663
26 London & St Katharine Docks Company General Meetings Minutes (1874-90) recorded that it was stated on 29 July 1879 that *'the Railway Tunnel between the Custom House and Silvertown has been opened for public traffic'* (MLDSSC 5/15/219). It is only in recent times that it has come to be known as Connaught Tunnel
27 Marden 2013, 103
28 Siviour 2006, 663
29 Various items removed from the ECR's Whitechapel Station booking hall are being stored by London Transport Museum or have been donated to Epping Ongar Railway
30 Jackson and Croome 1962, 55
31 Day 2008, 126
32 Quotes from a London Transport advert shown on p.190 of Day 2008.

CHAPTER 3

MAINTAINING THE RAILWAYS: OLD OAK COMMON 1906-1939

By 1900 most railway companies with operations in London had workshops and running sheds in the capital, close to where their lines terminated. Some of these works, such as the ECR's at Stratford or the NLR's at Bow, were vast sites where all of the company's many requirements could be met. For the GWR, however, Swindon remained its principal base until the company's nationalisation in 1948. Away from its main works a company would establish district engine sheds, repair shops and yards in places convenient for the day-to-day needs of its trains. The GWR, with its London terminus at Paddington where there was little room for expansion, had yards, sheds and workshops scattered as far up the line as Kensal Green, with Westbourne Park established as its main locomotive depot by the early 1850s. The company had never satisfactorily resolved how to rationalise their operations in west London and, it has been said, were also held back by their dogged refusal to abandon broad gauge operations.[1] Daniel Gooch, Brunel's deputy for many years and the GWR's chairman from 1865, remained an advocate of the system until the last, but with his death in 1889 the GWR finally felt free to abandon Brunel's system. The last broad gauge train left Paddington in May 1892.

In November 1898 an ambitious scheme of works was put forward to solve the congestion affecting the approaches to Paddington station. A new engine shed, it was felt, could be sited at West London Junction, while general goods and a coal depot could be established at Old Oak Common in Acton.[2] The scheme was comprehensively revised the following October, when it was decided that Old Oak Common would be a better location for the engine sheds. Authorisation was duly granted for the purchase of a small strip of land in advance of the GWR board's anticipated approval of the plans.[3]

In December 1899 George Jackson Churchward, the Chief Assistant to William Dean, the GWR's Locomotive, Carriage and Wagon Superintendent, but effectively in charge because of Dean's failing health, reported that the new engine shed would cost approximately £70,000, exclusive of the cost of site preparation and excavation.[4] The minutes of the GWR board give little sense of any urgency to begin the project and by April 1900 the company had yet to acquire all of the land it would need between Paddington and Old Oak Common, despite the fact that the powers to purchase the land were due to expire the following August.[5]

However, the company pushed ahead with the related construction of their Acton to Northolt branch. In November 1899 it awarded this contract to Joseph Thomas Firbank of London Bridge for the sum of £155,846.[6] Firbank, the agreement specified, was also responsible 'for the removal of excavation from Old Oak Common within the line'. In May 1900 it was calculated that in order to prepare the site for the shed it would be necessary to remove approximately 240,000 cubic yards of material, at a cost of £20,000.[7]

Despite the general increase in activity it appears that by the end of 1902 the company had done little more than build a couple of carriage sidings and lay an oil gas main at Old Oak Common. The delay may have been due in part to William Dean's infirmities, which led him eventually to retire in June 1902. Churchward was promoted and revived the proposals the following year when he presented plans of the new depot, which he now estimated would cost £110,000 to realise (Fig 48).[8]

The centrepiece of the scheme was to be a vast engine shed (Gazetteer No. 23), a rectangular building that would provide more stabling in the

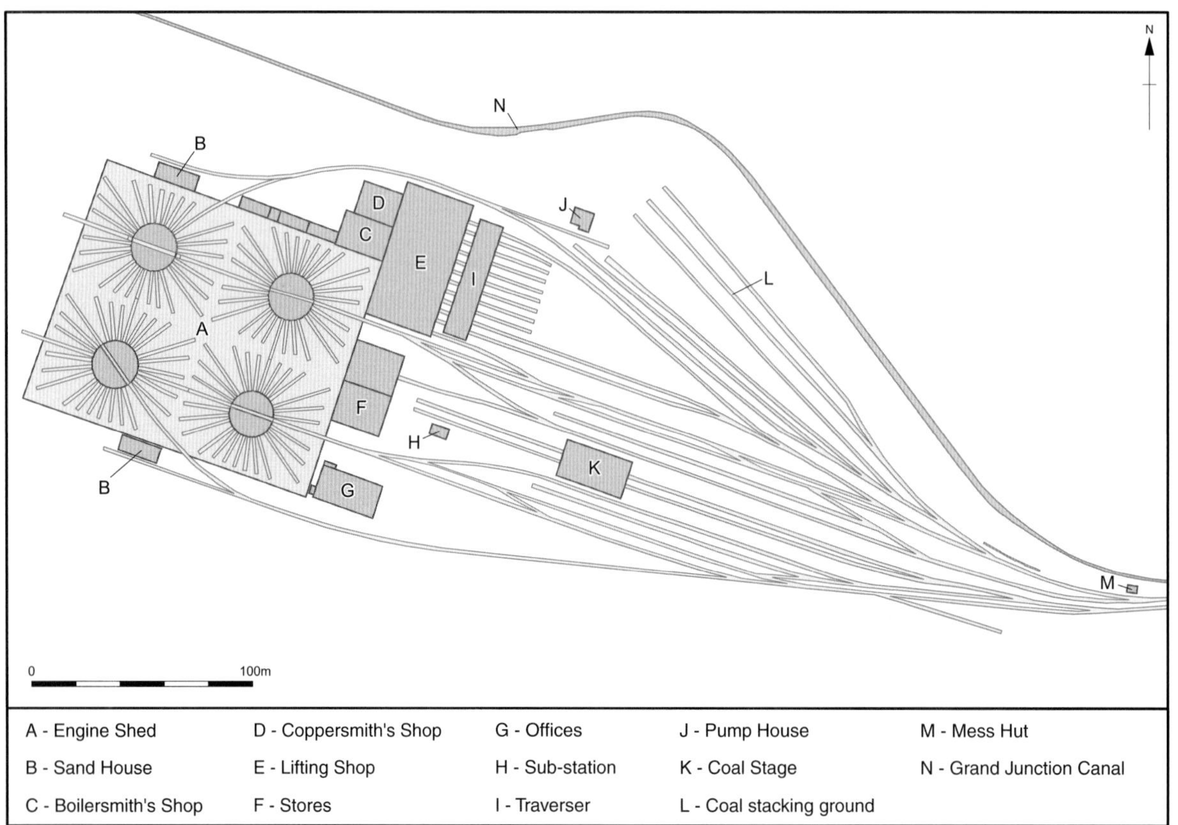

Fig 48 The layout of GWR's Old Oak Common Depot in 1906

corners than any previous GWR design. As Hawkins and Reeve have noted, Churchward knew that a cramped site 'was always a cramped site and there was to be no such problems with the new depots, whatever excavation or fill might be necessary. Vast acres were made available and the Churchward sheds set amidst them, with generous approaches, adequate sidings and enough open space about for whatever expansion might one day be conceived'.[9]

Holcroft, who worked in Swindon's drawing office during these years, noted that 'There was no going outside [Swindon] for assistance in any engineering matter, and planning and detail design of running sheds, shops, gas works, water supplies and plant of all kinds was undertaken in the Swindon office'.[10] The contract to construct Old Oak Common was awarded to Relford & Greaves, who offered to complete the works for £38,554. However, within a few weeks this decision had been revoked and the contract re-let to William Walkerdine of Bridge Street, Derby. Walkerdine had tendered to undertake the works for £40,313.[11] The instruction to proceed with construction of 'the offices, lifting shop, stores, carpenters', smiths' and coppersmiths' shops, sand furnaces, engine shed, WCs, messrooms, internal and external inspection pits, turntable foundations and a coal stage and elevated road thereto' was issued on 4 January 1904.[12] For its part the GWR agreed to supply and fix the timber baulks and rails, chairs, hydrants and standpipes, the sand furnace ironwork and bunkers, the coal stage tank and ladder, steel platforms, water pipes, valves, turntables, traversers and traverser foundations, and to lay tracks outside the shed.[13] The construction was to be undertaken under the supervision of the GWR's New Works Engineer, Walter Armstrong.

The architectural detailing chosen for the engine shed was to be repeated across the site. Walls were of red brick in Old English Bond over plinths of 'special-made' blue engineering bricks, a GWR vernacular also used, for example, in the recently completed stations at Truro and Westbury (Fig 49). Blue bricks recovered in 2015 from the fill of one of the turntables were stamped with the letters CBB, an abbreviation for Cakemore Blue Brick (produced in Rowley Regis, near Dudley). Elevations were formed from inset panels between plain brick pilasters, with double-chamfered plinths at the base of each panel. The tops of the panels were stepped so that the undersides of the frogs were sometimes visible and on the gables the panels were crow-stepped. Corners were generally formed from bullnose bricks with stop chamfers (Fig 50). Metal windows, often of four rows of six tall lights with an opening upper middle section, were set below segmental arches.

Walkerdine was instructed that all paved areas should have a 6in thick bed of dry ashes, 'well rammed on a layer of dry filling or ashes about 15in

Fig 49 (left) The eastern gable of Old Oak Common's stores building displayed many of the architectural details common to the depot's other Edwardian buildings

Fig 50 (right) Bullnose bricks detail the sub-station doorway

thick' while the floors of the offices of the shed foreman and clerk, the stores clerk and the messengers were to have a bed of cement concrete 6in thick, 'in which will be bedded dovetail joists to receive felt and boarding.' The floors of the lifting and carpenters' shops were to be similarly constructed, though they were to be laid with 5in creosoted wooden blocks.[14] In contrast, the engine shed, sand furnace houses, messrooms, enginemens' room, stores, coppersmiths' shop, WC and pits were to be paved with blue bricks laid flat, while the floor of the smith's shop was to consist of 3in of fine ashes on top of 6in of dry ash.

The walls of the shed's turntables and catch pits were to be of brindled brickwork in cement. Principal rafters were to be fashioned from sawn pitch pine and the majority of the roofs were to be clad with Bangor slates, although the raised roof over the lifting shop was to have glazed sashes, and the sides of the roof light were to be part-glazed and part louvred. Sliding doors, 4in thick and fitted with cast iron wheels, were hung at the engine shed, whilst folding doors were specified for the lifting shop. All of the iron and steelwork, including two box girders in the engine shed and six 30ft long plate girders for the lifting shop roof, was supplied by the GWR.

By October 1904 the works were sufficiently advanced for Churchward to begin ordering the fixtures, fittings and machinery. Orders were placed for an electrically-driven 30-ton crane from Vaughan & Son Ltd of Manchester, and for four under-girder turntables from Ransomes & Rapier.[15] Each turntable had a working load of 114 tons, was designed to revolve on hardened steel centres working in a dust-proof bath of oil, and with a 65ft diameter was clearly intended to carry Churchward's new Star class locomotive.[16] Churchward also recommended that the company accept a tender from Ransomes to supply an 80-ton electric traverser for a further £2,760 and in May 1905 Churchward proposed that the turntables also be electrically-driven.[17] Ransomes duly supplied two tractors for each turntable, placed diagonally at either end of the girders, which together turned the table at a speed of one revolution in 90 seconds.[18] The same month the GWR agreed to pay an additional £82 to Vaughan & Sons for the 30-ton electric crane, and a further £22 for Ransomes' electric traverser.[19] Other equipment purchased during the summer of 1905 included a £625 electric wheel lathe from Beyer Peacock, a pneumatic power hammer and a universal wood-working machine. Later a compressed air plant was supplied by the Consolidated Pneumatic Tool Co. Ltd.[20]

Towards the end of 1904 Walkerdine was awarded a £700 contract to ballast the approaches to the engine shed and a couple of months later the contract to lay the tracks leading up to and inside the new shed was awarded to Jackaman & Son of Slough for a further £940.[21] Contracts were also awarded during the summer of 1905 to Thomas Rowbotham of Birmingham and E C & J Keay for the construction of the adjoining carriage shed.[22]

The year 1906 was one of great expansion for the company, both in terms of increasing route mileage and the acceleration of their locomotive building programme.[23] Old Oak Common was a planned part of this expansion, and was described by the Railway Gazette shortly after it opened as the 'largest of its kind in Great Britain and possibly in the world'.[24] Despite opening on Saturday 17 March, work on completing it continued for the remainder of the year and all of the following year too. Utilities including the water supply and electrical lighting would continue to be fitted throughout the first half of 1906 and modifications started as soon as it opened for traffic.[25] In March the company issued instructions to modify the turning bars and stop levers of the turntables, alterations which may have been a consequence of the earlier decision to electrify them.[26] The construction and fitting out of the engine and carriage sheds had cost rather more than had originally been anticipated and it was not until the following year that the main contractors were fully recompensed.[27] It is likely that Walkerdine's contract was extended to include the construction of engine pits beneath certain roads leading to the engine shed. The pits were to measure between 88ft and 226ft 6in in length and were originally proposed during the autumn of 1906, while completion was scheduled for the following May.[28] In December 1907 it was proposed to construct two further pits beside the coal stage, one of 400ft length, the other of 500ft.[29] Westbourne Park Depot had been equipped with similar pits outside its sheds so it is not clear why those at Old Oak Common appear to have been an afterthought.

Minor cost and programme overruns on major capital expenditure projects are nothing new, and here should not detract from an appreciation of Old Oak Common. Churchward succeeded in creating an outstanding engine running and repair facility where before there had been only a 'ramshackle conglomeration of buildings, impossibly arranged'.[30] The depot, the largest

Fig 51 Old Oak Common's mighty four turntable engine shed nearing completion in 1906 (NRM/ Science and Society Picture Library)

on the system, served as the template for others that followed, and not only within the GWR empire. Critically, of course, it benefited from having to cater for only one gauge. The engine shed was exceptional in size, measuring 444ft by 360ft, with each of its four turntables servicing 28 roads, the bottom two being reserved for passenger engines (Fig 51). In all, 112 locomotives could be stabled and each had its own overhead trough through which smoke could be ducted through the trussed roof. The roof was supported with principals of 60ft span, secured with steel tie-rods and supported on steel girders carried on cast-iron columns. This was a monumental building, but size could not save it from obsolescence once double-cab diesel locomotives rendered the need to turn locomotives redundant. Demolition began in 1963, although fragments survived, fossilised within other buildings, until 2011 (Fig 52).

Fig 52 The north wall of one of the depot's two sand houses was formed from the south wall of the engine shed. It survived in fragmentary form until 2011

As well as being a locomotive stable the engine shed was where the inspections, regular maintenance, minor repair and daily preparation (cleaning, fire setting, lubricating *etc*) of locomotives took place. The leading fitter and boilersmith were guided in the distribution of work to their staff by the report sheets completed at the end of each journey by the engine driver.[31] When required, brick-arch repairmen re-mortared or replaced damaged firebricks in the firebox, and shed carpenters replaced broken floorboards and seats. Firebar setters re-set the fire grates, either from the cab or from inside the box. Boilersmiths regularly inspected the boilers and repaired leaking tubes.

Although many minor defects could be addressed in the engine shed by the fitters, problems like hot axleboxes or worn wheels required the locomotive to be booked into the lifting and repair shop (Gazetteer No. 29, Figs 53-55). This building, always referred to as the Factory was, *The Railway Gazette* noted approvingly on its opening, 'replete with every convenience'.[32] Overhead, Vaughan & Son's electric traversing crane had a span of 49ft and serviced the shop's twelve 52ft long pits. For the first time outside of a locomotive works, the crane allowed the partial raising of locomotive bodies to provide access to wheel bearings, and so relieved Swindon of some intermediate repairs. The Factory provided a heavy maintenance base for the largest of Churchward's new locomotives, and featured 'every potentially-required resource in one place'.[33] The east wall and central valley of the main shop and the runways for the crane were supported on compound steel stanchions set in pairs linked by batten plates, a practice which at the time could be regarded as very advanced. The central stanchions were spaced at double-width and were spanned by fish-belly plate girders, 'a distinctive and uncommon form in building structures'.[34] Altogether, the Factory represented a step-change in the facilities on offer to Churchward and his staff.

In the angle between the lifting and repair shop and the engine shed Walkerdine built a large smith's shop, and a smaller block for coppersmiths and carpenters. The smiths were provided with seven hearths, a fan and a power hammer, and the carpenters benefited from an electrically-driven

Fig 53 Old Oak Common's lifting shop is shown to good effect in a photograph probably taken not long after the depot opened in 1906. The locomotive is a Société Alsacienne de Constructions Mécaniques's four-cylinder compound which was unusual for having been bought by Churchward in 1903 specifically for evaluation purposes (NRM/ Science and Society Picture Library).

Fig 54 Old Oak Common's lifting shop (the Factory) in 1959 (Getty Image 90747063)

circular saw bench.[35] It was these trades that set Old Oak Common apart from some of its counterparts and allowed it to do the jobs that nearby depots such as Slough and Southall had to outsource.[36]

The depot's stores (Gazetteer No. 25) were attached to the centre of the eastern elevation of the engine shed, between the roads serving the eastern turntables. This rectangular building was formed by two identically-sized blocks and housed the stores, the chief running shed foreman's office and

Fig 55 Isometric laser-scan survey of Old Oak Common's lifting and repair shop and adjoining lifting bay, formerly the smith's shop

an adjoining room for his clerks, and the enginemens' rooms. By ingenious planning, the GWR's house magazine said, 'a gallery has been provided around the walls, thus appreciably increasing the accommodation' (Fig 56).[37] The job of storekeeper was an important one, and experienced staff would have been prized. Joby has noted that the mark of a good storekeeper would be to stock up with far more than was needed 'so as not to be caught short'.[38] Past experience taught that some items were produced in small batches between long intervals, or that some items were prone to failure in large numbers when the weather changed. As well as experience, vigilance would have been required. Henry Simpson, in a 1906 lecture, stressed 'Nothing whatsoever is given out from the Stores unless a requisition, duly signed by an authorised person, is handed in'.[39] Pilfering would inevitably have been a problem, and at Old Oak Common, bordered on two of its three sides by public footpaths, theft may also have been a risk. It can be no coincidence that a plan of alterations to the carriage shed messrooms and stores issued in 1911 stressed that 'Windows to be made burglar proof', for these were set directly beside Old Oak Common Lane.

Fig 56 (left) The stores at Old Oak Common remained operational until the site closed in 2010

Fig 57 (right) At first, John Armstrong and his staff worked from the offices at Old Oak Common, but they soon moved to Paddington. Behind their office block is the new amenity block, constructed in 1963. The cash transfer box is situated midway down the length of the building

The depot's offices were situated beside the south-eastern corner of the engine shed, and it was here that John Armstrong, the Divisional Locomotive Superintendent, and his deputy had their headquarters (Figs 57-58). On the first-floor there was a room 'for correspondence etc'.[40] According to Hawkins and Reeve office functions soon afterwards relocated to Paddington, freeing up the building to become the amenity block.[41] As constructed, the offices had been arranged in a series of four rooms on either side of a central corridor, accessed via doorways in each gable. This layout was substantially altered during the 1960s when the central corridor was partially blocked by a row of concrete columns to support the first floor, each with a heavy 'Y'-shaped head. The ground

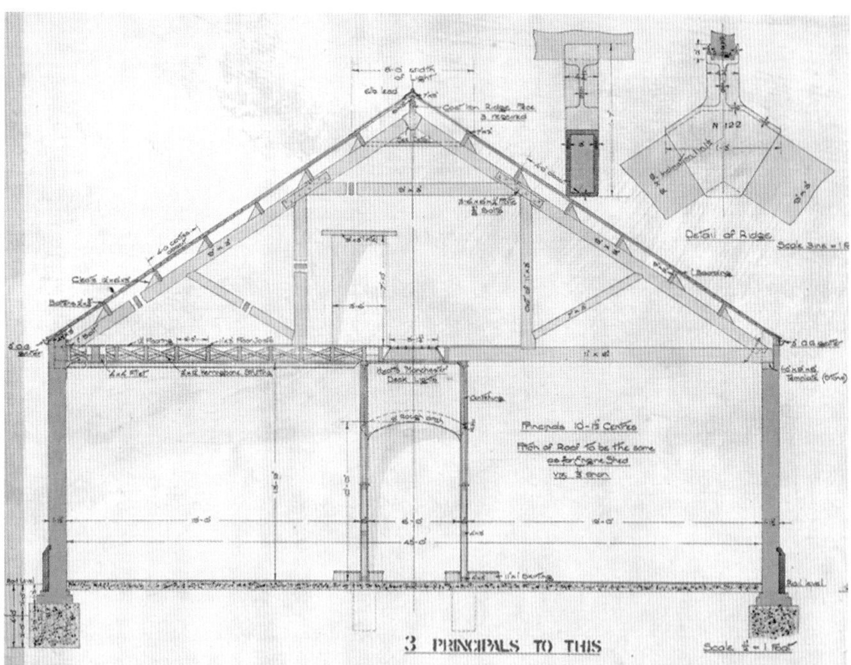

Fig 58 Detail of roof and partition to General Offices – Engine Shed, dated 1903
(WSHC 2515/406/1806)

floor was used to accommodate train crews; during Crossrail's historic building survey of the depot in 2010 it was noted that one office door retained a sign that read 'Virgin Trains booking on point', and in another there was a large clothes drying area.

The office block also retained another important function long after Armstrong and his staff had left. Men, noted Hawkins and Reeve, 'would queue at the shed office for an oval metal disc (later rectangular and in brass) which further entitled them to queue for their money, contained in a tiny tin box, which (after emptying) was tossed into a wooden collecting chest' (Fig 59).[42] This is a reminder that a worksite employing over 800 people when it opened had need of prodigious amounts of cash.[43] In earlier days, this had arrived at the yard in a cashbox on a light engine from the Treasurer's Office at Paddington.[44] However, in later years wages had clearly arrived by road because a rather well-disguised little brick box had been built against the foot of the building. This may have passed off for a gas meter housing had it not been for its heavy-duty brushed steel door and surround. Immediately behind this lay another steel door which opened into a narrow corridor between the external wall and a well-secured internal banking room. A further steel door in the wall of this room allowed cash to be quickly transferred from the corridor into a locked safe. From there, it could be dispensed via a banking counter on the opposite wall, beneath which a discreet panic button hinted at the quantities of cash being handled (Fig 60).

The last of the principal structures on the site was the coal stage (Gazetteer No. 32), built by Walkerdine to the standard GWR elevated platform design. The GWR did not use the mechanical coaling towers other railway companies favoured, perhaps because of the soft nature of Welsh coal or, as Holcroft has suggested, because the use of hand-filled 10cwt tubs allowed a more selective and consistent approach.[45] The iron tubs were filled by coalmen from adjacent wagons that had been pushed up a 1 in 50 incline onto an elevated waiting area beyond the stage, from where they could be gradually gravity-fed back throughout the course of the day. Coaling was classified as piecework and each man expected to shift between 20 and 25 tons a day. Once each tub was full it was wheeled to one of three openings in each side of the stage, at the base of which were hinged flaps. The tub was pushed against these until they lay flat, and was then wheeled out beyond the building so that its load could be emptied directly into the locomotive tenders that waited below. The ground floor of the building was reserved for accommodation and toilets, and the roof carried a 290,000 gallon water tank, divided into four parallel compartments. From here, water was distributed to five swinging jib water cranes, and to the hydrants and standpipes in the engine shed.[46] The coal stage lasted in operation until Old Oak Common closed to steam on 27 March 1965. By then it was antiquated; proposals to replace it with a 250 ton mechanical coaling plant had been considered in 1943 but were never enacted.[47]

Fig 59 Wages were collected in numbered tins that were exchanged for tokens (Steam Museum)

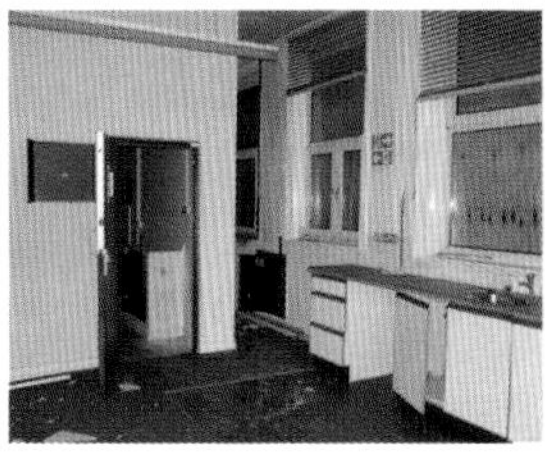

Fig 60 The staged arrangement of safes in Old Oak Common's office block enabled cash to be securely transferred into the banking room on the left of the picture

Minor buildings present on the site included an electricity sub-station, messrooms and toilets and, of course, the all-important signal box. There were also two sand furnace houses, one each against the north and south walls of the engine shed. Both were served by their own sidings. Sand was important to the efficient operation of the railways, aiding adhesion in slippery conditions. It needed to be dry and free from stones to prevent clogging the locomotive's feeder pipes, and Churchward's furnaces, which used a chamber between the furnace and the chimney, were estimated to dry five times the amount of sand that the company's older-type oven furnaces could process.[48]

In 1937 the southern sand furnace house (Gazetteer No. 22, Fig 61) was converted into messrooms for mechanics, cleaners and shed staff (Fig 62). While its northern counterpart disappeared in 1964 when the engine shed was demolished, the southern building became a detached structure and survived as stores until 2011. This survival allowed its simple and light-weight roof structure to be inspected in some detail (Fig 63). There were six trusses, each formed from full width tie-rods with 'T'-sectioned raking struts. Vertical tie-rods met the flattened ends of each strut, and their threaded ends passed through a flattened eye in the centre of the horizontal tie rod. The flattened ends and eye were bolted together by nuts on the

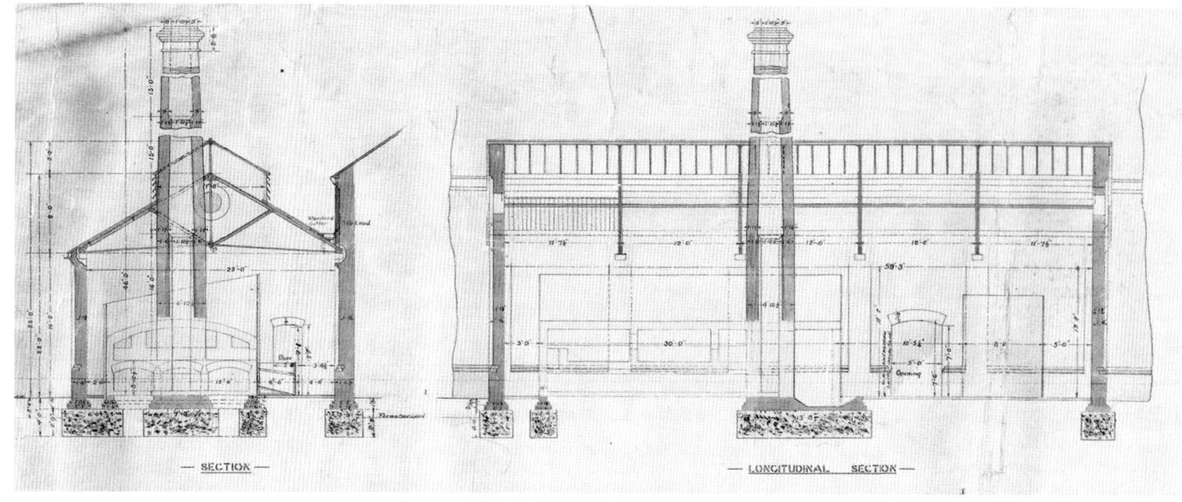

Fig 61 A GWR plan from 1903 illustrated Old Oak Common's southern sand furnace house (WSHC 2515-409-0869)

threaded end of the rod. 'T'-sectioned principal rafters were secured to the struts by riveted plates. The pitches each had two purlins formed from 'T'-sectioned steel carrying timber bearers. The bearer on the lower purlin of the north pitch was slightly offset, possibly because it supported a gutter.

For the depot's larger buildings heavy-duty roof trusses and details were specified. The valley between the stores' two symmetrical blocks was carried by a cylindrical central column of cast iron, which both supported the central roof joist and acted as a downpipe for the valley gutter (Fig 64). The column was stamped 'GWR W'hampton Dec 1903' and carried a

Fig 62 The southern sand furnace house was converted into messrooms in 1937 and in 1965 became a detached building when the remainder of the engine shed was demolished. The small structure in the foreground was an outside urinal, which first appeared on site layout drawings in the early 1960s

Fig 63 Simple and lightweight: the roof to the southern sand furnace house. Although both the sand house and engine shed were present when the depot opened in 1906 the sill on the engine shed window to the right of the photograph suggested that the sand house was an afterthought

Fig 64 A single cast iron column supported the valley trusses of the Stores building. This was salvaged during demolition and is to be incorporated into the site's new Crossrail depot

giant head that supported the bracing latticework that hung down from the main beams.

Like those in the stores the roof trusses of the Factory (and also the engine shed) were composite structures formed from timber, cast iron and steel. Each truss in the Factory comprised two timber rafters, joined at the apex by a cast iron ridge piece, which formed the head of the principal. The principal members were braced by two pairs of timber struts, formed from vertical pitch pine queen posts and angled outside braces. The structure was held together under tension by five steel tie bars. Two cast steel junction rings formed the points where the braces and the bars intersected (Fig 65). Each ring contained sockets for the feet of the timber struts, and holes for three steel tie bars. A paper presented by J H Baker to the Swindon Engineering Society in 1906 explained that the use of round bars, and the method by which they were attached to the junction ring, allowed for 'any slight discrepancy that may occur in the span', at the same time as obviating the costs that would be incurred through the use of flat bars, which would have required additional forging, machining and welding to ensure a satisfactory fit.[49] Each ring also had a hole at the bottom to accommodate a longitudinal steel tie bar which connected each truss to its neighbours. Set on top of the trusses in the Factory were twelve timber purlins, six each side, and a central ridge beam.

Fig 65 Cast steel junction rings in the stores building

Although by the turn of the 20th century the use of composite roof trusses had become relatively widespread, the elegant designs used by Churchward at Old Oak Common have been seen by industrial archaeologist Malcolm Tucker as representing 'a new level of sophistication' in the typology of composite trusses.[50] In particular, the decision to forge the junction rings from cast steel represents an early and innovative use of this material in this context. Tucker has described Churchward's lifting shop as a step-change in the level of facilities provided for the routine maintenance of locomotives on the GWR 'and probably nationally'.[51]

Churchward was alive to the need to improve the company's facilities and his genius, according to Hawkins and Reeve, was to 'take, adopt and improve what was best in existing practice'.[52] He paid particular attention to creating airy buildings that would remove some of the susceptibility to corrosion which had bedevilled the buildings of his predecessors. To do this he used a combination of tried and trusted methods, such as Brunel's system of timber roof structures trussed with iron rods, and the new and untested, such as the casting in steel of the roof's junction rings.

The GWR was an early convert to the use of electricity in its buildings (even if it was laggardly in electrifying its main-line traction), with experiments in electric lighting beginning at Paddington Station in 1880.[53] It was therefore natural that Churchward would seek to embed this new technology within Old Oak Common.[54] Electrical power (at 600V DC and 220V three-phase AC) was supplied by the GWR's new generating station at Park Royal which they had built specifically in connection with the Hammersmith & City Railway lines. It was distributed around the depot by a sub-station (Gazetteer No. 18) constructed by Pattinson & Sons. In October 1905 Churchward placed an order valued at £1,420 for a 400KW generator from Bruce Peebles & Co. Power would be distributed by cables provided by Siemens Bros, and high and low tension switchgear came from British Thomson Houston Co. Ltd and the Electrical Construction Company.[55] The *Great Western Magazine*, in a predictably glowing tribute to the new depot, described the provision of electricity at Old Oak Common as its 'outstanding feature'.[56]

The sub-station (or 'Electric Distributing Centre' as it was originally known) was situated between the stores and the coal stage (Fig 66). As elsewhere in the depot its architectural detailing drew on the company's

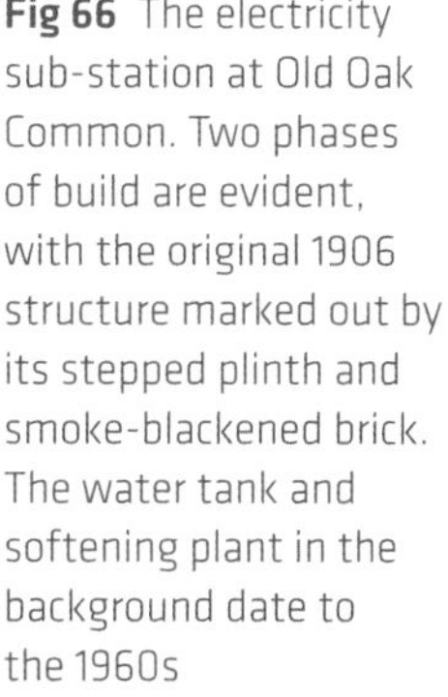
Fig 66 The electricity sub-station at Old Oak Common. Two phases of build are evident, with the original 1906 structure marked out by its stepped plinth and smoke-blackened brick. The water tank and softening plant in the background date to the 1960s

Fig 67 (left) Sign on Old Oak Common's electricity sub-station, photographed in 2010

Fig 68 (right) The ceiling of the electricity sub-station was barrel-vaulted

palette of red brick, blue engineering bricks, chamfered brick courses and bullnose bricks for corners. The building was recorded in 2010 prior to its demolition (Figs 67-68). The doorway contained a large steel four-panelled door with iron hinges, set into a steel frame. The heavy oval door handle was stamped internally with 'Ratner Safe Co Ltd' and Ratner's maker's plates were also attached to the upper exterior panels. This company was at the time a relative newcomer to the market for safe doors, having been incorporated in 1896. It is a question why Churchward felt the need to secure the sub-station so heavily.

From the day it opened, modifications, updates and repairs to the depot were required. Towards the end of 1910 it was decided to build a boiler washing plant. Boiler washing (which involved forcing hot water into the boiler by steam pressure) was a process undertaken weekly to remove scale.[57] Without hot water a boiler had to be left to cool before it could be washed out, for fear of damage under rapid contraction. At Westbourne Park, advantage had been taken (by means of conduits) of the hot water returning from the company's power station behind Gloucester Crescent at Paddington. This was so obviously a time-saver that it is a wonder Churchward delayed installing a similar provision at Old Oak Common until 1910. The Economical Boiler Washing Company's plant was one of a number supplied by the company to locomotive depots during this period, although the first of its type to be built on the GWR network.[58] The plant, inserted into the angle between the engine shed and the northern sand furnace house, consisted of a boiler washing plant house with a boiler house attached.[59] At the end of the 1920s plans were drawn up for a water-softening plant to be installed close by the boiler washing plant, with the aim of reducing the degree of scaling that occurred in the depot's boilers. In September 1931 the *Great Western Railway* magazine wrote of a water-softening plant to be installed by the Kennicott Water Softener Company of Wolverhampton.[60]

It would have been possible to build the water-softening plant alongside the boiler washing facilities had the company not recently acquired a refuse incinerator a short distance to the north of the latter.[61] This was supplied by the New Destructor Co. Ltd of Worcestershire, a company which at that time was riding a wave of municipal enthusiasm for industrial-sized refuse incinerators. In the 1960s it was to install another, much smaller incinerator in the new office and amenity building constructed alongside the original office building (see Chapter 7). The incinerator burned waste in specially designed furnaces which heated a boiler, the steam from which drove two new compound duplex pumps installed in the boiler house. In turn these pumps circulated hot water for the washing and filling of tanks in the boiler washing plant, replacing the existing boilers. The refuse was brought into the incinerator building by wagons using an existing siding, while smoke was expelled through a new brick chimney built at the south-west corner of the building.

The completion of the water-softening plant marked the beginning of a hiatus in the development of Old Oak Common, probably caused by the effects of the Great Depression of 1929-1932. GWR drawings and the minutes of board meetings show that various improvement schemes were put forward, mulled over, and laid to rest, only to be resurrected in later years. It is during this period (specifically, 1931/32) that, according to Whitehouse and Thomas, a whole group of shops including Old Oak Common ceased heavy repair.[62] There is no evidence that heavy repairs did cease at Old Oak Common and it may have been more a question of definition, for in 1947 H G Kerry, during a lecture entitled 'The Working of a Locomotive Shed', pointed out that what Swindon would have termed a light repair would for Old Oak Common have been a substantial repair.[63]

In conclusion, Old Oak Common can be seen as a significant moment for the GWR, and in particular for its new Locomotive, Carriage and Wagon Superintendent. The first ten years of the Churchward era were a period when the GWR went from being a rather antiquated railway to a decade or more ahead of its competitors.[64] As John Norris says, 1900 to 1910 was 'a decade of development [by the GWR] which was to see no equal on the railways of this country until the electrification of the west coast route from London to Scotland in the 1960s.' [65] Across the GWR empire new lines were inaugurated, new sources of traffic developed and former ideas on locomotive construction abandoned.[66] In particular, the locomotives Churchward developed were pioneers that set the standard for locomotive design for the new century. Production 4-6-0 locomotives (4-6-0 denoting the arrangement of wheels) appeared in 1905 as the two-cylinder Saint class, and were followed in 1906 by the four-cylinder Star class. An important aim in these years was the search for standardisation in locomotive design, particularly of parts. The same principle was extended to the facilities developed during the Churchward years. Fully understanding what would be required in an ideal depot enabled Churchward to preside over a design that was clear and confident; one is struck by the simplicity of Old Oak Common's layout. It became the template for all successive GWR turntable shed depots, at least until 1926, when the GWR's last roundhouse was built in Stourbridge, and by fate and circumstance outlived all of its successors.[67]

NOTES

1 Brindle 2013, 58
2 GWR Traffic Committee Minutes No. 6, 1897-99, TNA RAIL 250/339, 255-257
3 GWR Traffic Committee Minutes No. 7, 1899-1900, TNA RAIL 250/340, 146
4 GWR Locomotive, Carriage & Stores Committee Minutes No. 3, 1898-1902, TNA RAIL 250/270, 97
5 GWR Traffic Committee Minutes No. 7, 1899-1900, TNA RAIL 250/340, 253
6 GWR Acton & Wycombe Railway: Acton to Northolt Loop to Castle Hill, Mr J. Firbank Sureties to the GWR, 21/11/1899, TNA RAIL 252/1235
7 GWR Locomotive, Carriage & Stores Committee Minutes No. 3, 1898-1902, TNA RAIL 250/270, 132
8 GWR Locomotive, Carriage & Stores Committee Minutes No. 4, 1902-1904, TNA RAIL 250/271, 124
9 Hawkins and Reeve 1987, 2
10 Holcroft 1971, 96
11 GWR Minutes of the Board of Directors No. 44, 1903-05, TNA RAIL 250/47, 52, 86
12 'New Engine Shed & other works at Old Oak Common Acton', Specification, Schedule of Quantities & Contract, dated 04/01/1904, TNA RAIL 252/1340
13 General Conditions & Specification of Works, TNA RAIL 252/1340, 2
14 General Conditions & Specification of Works, TNA RAIL 252/1340, 18, 26
15 The crane cost £1,025 and the turntables £3,900 (TNA RAIL 250/271, 224). The crane was replaced with a 50-ton electrically-operated overhead example ordered in September 1928. It was supplied by Heywood & Co. of Reddish, Lancashire and remained in use until the Old Oak Common depot finally closed in 2010 (Arrangement of LT Gear for 50-Tons 4 Motor Crane, S.H. Heywood & Co. Ltd Reddish. Order no. 1872, date 26/09/1928, WSHC 2515/406/3394; Wiring diagram for 50 Tons 4 Motor E.O .T Crane, received 23/10/1929, WSHC 2515/406/3394; Arrangement of LT Gear for 50-Tons 4 Motor Crane, S.H. Heywood & Co. Ltd Reddish. Order no. 1872, date 26/09/1928, WSHC 2515/406/2621)
16 *The Railway Gazette*, June 1 1906, reproduced in Hawkins and Reeve 1987, 41
17 GWR Minutes of the Board of Directors No. 44, 1903-05, TNA RAIL 250/47, 405
18 *The Railway Gazette*, June 1 1906, reproduced in Hawkins and Reeve 1987, 41
19 GWR Locomotive, Carriage & Stores Committee Minutes No. 4, 1902-1904, TNA RAIL 250/271, 280-281
20 *The Railway Gazette*, June 1 1906, reproduced in Hawkins and Reeve 1987, 53
21 GWR Minutes of the Board of Directors No. 44, 1903-05, TNA RAIL 250/47, 310, 356
22 GWR Minutes of the Board of Directors No. 44, 1903-05, TNA RAIL 250/47, 461; 'New Carriage Shed & other works at Old Oak Common, Acton. Thomas Rowbotham & the GWR Award', 19/03/1907, TNA RAIL 252/1462; GWR drawing 'New Carriage Shed at Old Oak Common', n/d. *c.* 1905, WSHC 2515/409/338
23 Holcroft 1971, 102
24 *The Railway Gazette*, June 1 1906, reproduced in Hawkins and Reeve 1987, 41

25 GWR drawing 'Arrangement of Electric Lighting Carriage Shed Old Oak Common', April 1906, WSHC 2515/406/1551. It seems possible that the depot's water was supplied by a network of pipes originating in Westbourne Park Depot (GWR drawing 'New Goods Depot at Westbourne Park', 1907, WSHC 2515/410/1773)
26 GWR drawing 'Alteration to Turning Bar and Stop Lever, Ransomes & Rapier 65' Turntable Old Oak Common. Swindon', March 1906, WSHC 2515/403/0351
27 GWR Minutes of the Board of Directors No. 45, 1905-07, TNA RAIL 250/48, 291; 'New Carriage Shed & other works at Old Oak Common, Acton. Thomas Rowbotham & the GWR Award', 19/03/1907, TNA RAIL 252/1462
28 GWR drawing 'Old Oak Common Locomotive Yard Proposed Engine Pits', October 1906, WSHC 2525/410/0062; GWR drawing '88' Outside Pit (Chair Road) Engine Shed Old Oak Common', December 1906, WSHC 2515/409/1172; GWR drawing '226'6" Outside Pit (Chair Road) Engine Shed Old Oak Common', May 1907, WSHC 2515/409/1180
29 GWR drawing 'Old Oak Common 400' & 500' Outside Pits Coal Stage Old Oak Common', December 1907, WSHC 2515/409/0866
30 Hawkins and Reeve 1987, 39
31 Simpson 1906-1907, 'The Ideal Shed', *GWR Mechanics Institution Transactions for 1906 and 1907*, reproduced in Hawkins and Reeve 1987, 13
32 *The Railway Gazette*, June 1 1906, reproduced in Hawkins and Reeve 1987, 49
33 Tucker 2010, 2
34 Ibid, 3
35 *The Railway Gazette*, June 1 1906, reproduced in Hawkins and Reeve 1987, 53
36 Joby 1984, 131
37 'New Locomotive Depot at Old Oak Common' by A J L White, reproduced by Hawkins and Reeve 1987, 62
38 Joby 1984, 132
39 Hawkins and Reeve 1987, 25
40 'New Locomotive Depot at Old Oak Common' by A J L White, reproduced by Hawkins and Reeve 1987, 62
41 Hawkins and Reeve 1987, 61
42 Ibid, 97
43 Workforce total provided in *The Railway Gazette*, June 1 1906. The figure included 25 clerical staff.
44 Hawkins and Reeve 1987, 97
45 Selective in that the large lumps of first grade coal could be reserved for the principal express locomotives (Holcroft 1971, 136)
46 Information gathered from the text of a lecture given by H G Kerry on 30 January 1947 to the Great Western Railway (London) Lecture and Debating Society, and reproduced in Hawkins and Reeve 1987, 70. See also Leigh 1993, 2
47 GWR drawing 'Proposed New Engine Shed, Coaling Plant etc', December 1943, WSHC 2515/410/0720
48 Simpson 1906-7, 'The Ideal Shed', *GWR Mechanics Institution Transactions* for 1906 and 1907, reproduced in Hawkins and Reeve 1987, 11
49 Baker 1906, 161-2
50 Malcolm Tucker pers comm to Guy Thompson, August 2010
51 Tucker 2010, 1
52 Hawkins and Reeve 1987, 2
53 Brindle 2013, 56-7
54 A GWR drawing dated April 1906 shows the arrangement of electric lighting in the carriage shed. 8 amp double carbon open arc lamps were suspended from the ceiling over the walkways between roads. 6 amp versions were reserved for extremities of the building. WHSC 2515/406/1551

55 GWR Minutes of the Board of Directors No. 45, 1905-07, TNA RAIL 250/48, 22-23; see GWR drawing 'Old Oak Common Extension of Electricity Sub-Station', May 1939, WSHC 2515/403/0363
56 White 1906
57 Lyons 1972, 44
58 Ibid, 26
59 GWR drawing 'Boiler House Economical Boiler Washing Plant Old Oak Common', December 1910, WSHC 2515/409/0075; GWR drawing 'Arrangement of House Economical Boiler Washing Plant Old Oak Common', December 1910, WSHC 2515/409/0135
60 Reproduced in Hawkins and Reeve 1987, 80
61 GWR drawing 'Building for Refuse Destructor, Old Oak Common', May 1927, WSHC 2515/409/0772; GWR drawing 'Old Oak Common General Sections of Plant', July 1927, WSHC 2515/409/0774 (1); GWR drawing 'Old Oak Common Elevations of Furnace & Boiler', July 1927, WSHC 2515/409/0803; GWR drawing 'Old Oak Common Refuse Destructor Building', May 1927, WSHC 2515/409/0804; GWR drawing 'Old Oak Common General Plan of Plant, New Destructor Co. Ltd', June 1927, WSHC 2515/409/0862; GWR drawing 'Old Oak Common Boiler Setting & Flues, New Destructor Co. Ltd', July 1927, WSHC 2515/409/0863
62 Whitehouse and Thomas 1984, 85
63 Lecture reproduced in Hawkins and Reeve 1987, 21
64 Holcroft 1971, 136
65 Norris et al 1987, 1
66 Holcroft 1971, 86
67 As shown in Lyons (1972, 140). Birmingham's Tyseley Depot in particular was extraordinarily similar, right down to the relationships between the various buildings, differing in a major way only in the decision to build a two rather than four-turntable engine shed.

CHAPTER 4

WORKING THE RAILWAYS

In the beginning nobody had run a public railway, and so there were no railway workers. But once the first lines were open, staff numbers climbed rapidly. Some of the industry's first managers were former military officers, who naturally turned to ex-servicemen to fill the ranks. Other favoured pools of labour were the collieries and quarries of the Industrial Revolution, places where horse-drawn railways had been in use for many years. In rural areas a job on the railway paid handsomely above the agricultural wage, and recruitment was easy. In towns and cities workers were drawn to an industry that offered new opportunities for advancement and travel. Slowly, a body of expertise developed, and in time sons followed fathers into the industry.

Running a railway was a labour-intensive business. By 1847, as an era of speculative railway building drew to a close, there were already 47,000 people in the industry. A century later this number was to peak at a fraction under 650,000.[1] What did a body of people equivalent in size to the modern-day population of Sheffield do? The answer lies in the integrated services that railway companies sought to provide. Their employees did much more than simply build, service or roster trains. Rural staff kept a company's tracks and signals serviceable and its railway corridors free of obstructions. Level crossing keepers ensured the safety of road users, and signalmen and their telegraph operators kept trains apart from one another. Ranks of platform staff, from porters to stationmasters, were the public face of the railways. In what today is dubbed a multi-modal service, railway companies collected goods from the factory and the farm and delivered them to the customer's door. The wagons, lorries, carts and motorcycles that enabled them to provide this service required shunters, mechanics, draymen and drivers.[2] Wharfingers, ferry attendants

Fig 69 Stills from 'The Railway Today' (1960),' Computer for British Rail' (1957) and 'Princess Margaret Hovercraft' (1969) illustrate the many and varied roles undertaken by the staff of British Rail (British Pathé News)

and lock-keepers kept the companies' quays and waterways working. Bellboys, maids and maitre d's staffed the railway's hotels, and waitresses and crockery collectors helped keep hundreds of restaurants, bars and buffets open for business. Clerks, letter-sorters and superintendents administered the railway, and artists, writers and printers advertised it. In time, employees would come to develop computing systems, engineer fibre optic networks and captain hovercraft (Fig 69).[3]

Fig 70 The GER sewing machine shop in Stratford in *c* 1921 (NRM/ Science and Society Picture Library)

This was a vast army, but not one reflective of the population it served. In 1911 Britain's railway industry employed 460,055 people of which women accounted for little more than 0.5%.[4] There had been a few women on the railways from the beginning, typically in catering or clerical positions, and new technologies encouraged others to join. By 1900, for instance, the GWR's telephonists at Paddington were female.[5] Female employees were also favoured in the GWR's carriage workshops at Swindon, where they worked as upholsterers and seamstresses, as they also did at the GER's Stratford workshops (Fig 70).[6] The vast majority of jobs, however, were regarded as the preserve of men. Before WWI, for example, carriage cleaning was still regarded as men's work and in 1914 there were only 214 women carriage cleaners in the whole country.[7] It is probable then that the women employed in Old Oak Common's carriage shed in the early days of the depot were engaged in upholstery repairs. We know that women worked in this vast building because, in a drawing issued by Swindon in 1911, a proposal to alter and add to the stores and messrooms of the shed showed adjacent men's and women's messrooms (Fig 71).[8] While the men's room (at 72ft 2in) was nearly a third bigger than the women's, and the men had

Fig 71 A 1911 proposal for altering the mess-rooms and stores in the carriage shed at Old Oak Common shows how spaces were set aside for men and women (WSHC 2515-409-0138)

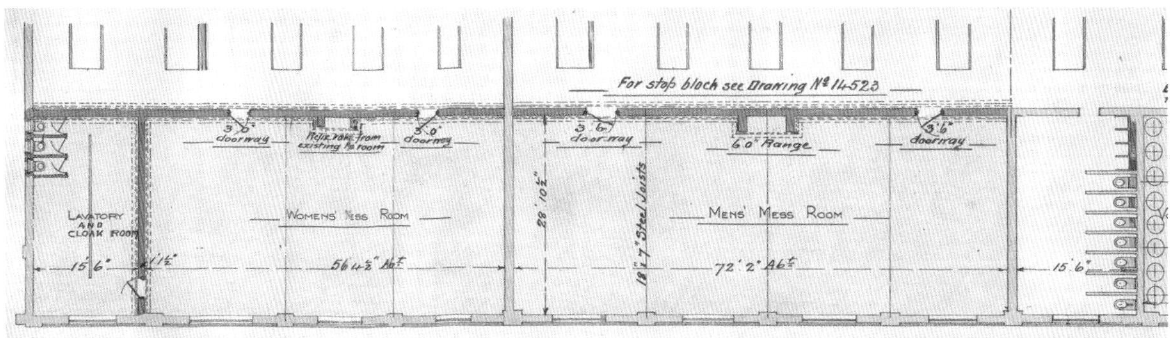

seven cubicles in their lavatory whilst the women made do with only three, there was nevertheless clearly a significant number of women in the shed. Although their wages would have been automatically lower than those the men received they did enjoy the luxury of cubicles furnished with doors (the men did without) and a lavatory with a cloakroom. The doors into the men's room were 3ft 6in wide while those to the women's were only 3ft wide. The reason for this disparity is unclear.

Numbers of female employees in the industry may have remained insignificant had it not been for the outbreak of war in 1914. This led quickly to shortages of labour and, for the first time, women were recruited in numbers to fill roles on the railways that previously had been seen as the sole preserve of men. Opinions of this change varied. Lady Doughty observed in the October 1916 edition of *The Great Central Railway Journal* that this change had taken place with 'none of the contretemps that might have been expected with such innovations upsetting the established order of things'. The *Railway Gazette* meanwhile was rather more circumspect in its view. 'Female labour' it stressed 'is limited to those grades in which experience is not of the essence … and the vocations must not entail contact with train movement'.[9] Returns to the Railway Executive Committee (REC) in 1916 show that the leading companies of the industry, finally galvanised into releasing men for the front, now employed over 33,000 women and girls.[10] Of the 22,000 or so where roles were specified, nearly two-thirds were clerks. While this was progress of sorts, there were no female engine drivers (and would not be until 1979) and only six wagon repairers. With the cessation of hostilities, the numbers of women employed on the railways collapsed. This was part of a phenomenon that saw three quarters of a million women made redundant in the UK during 1918.[11] Some women did remain with the railways, mainly in the clerical sector, but the numbers were small and remained so on the eve of WWII.

As war once again helped open the door to women, the GWR puzzled over how to engage them in work that was not 'of a repitition nature, but requires skilled craftsmen to see it through'.[12] At Swindon, as elsewhere, a Welfare Officer was appointed to liaise between the women and the management.[13] In time women were to be seen driving the walking cranes and traversers and, once trusted with this equipment, the larger overhead cranes. Other occupations into which women were eventually admitted included storekeeping, boilermaking, coppersmithing and tinsmithing. Although these trades were carried out at Old Oak Common it appears that there women were recruited solely to do the 'tube cleaning, ash removal, cleaning and canteen work'.[14]

Women stayed on after 1945, but not for long where they occupied traditionally male roles. Instead, companies like the GWR, having

Uniforms
British Rail Catering
Refreshment Room Staff

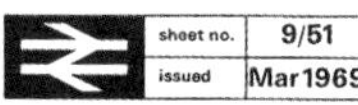

Attendants and Supervisors

This uniform, in a Rail Blue check, has been designed to present a fresh and attractive appearance whilst being practical in use and easy to wash. It is without a belt and purposely loose fitting to allow free circulation of air within the garment. A neck gilet is supplied for wear with the overall to hide other clothes which might appear above the neckline. A matching apron will be issued where necessary.

Supervisor

A title badge is supplied to Supervisors to be worn on the right lapel.

Uniforms
Ticket Office Clerk

Ticket Office Clerk

Ticket Office Clerks are issued with a lightweight jacket in pale grey 'Terylene' linen. The only embellishment is a gold symbol in the left lapel.

Fig 72 From British Rail's 1969 corporate style guide
(Secretary of State for Transport/ British Rail Corporate Identity Manual, Binder 4 Section 9 Uniforms, March 1969)

established a Training School for Girls at Paddington in 1947, steered new recruits into the office.[15] More commonly, women continued to find that opportunities were restricted to service industries like catering (Fig 72). Attitudes were slow to change. Dr Beeching's 1963 report on the future of Britain's railways mentions men nine times, women not at all. In 1975, the year the Sex Discrimination Act was passed, *Rail News* carried a piece on a visit to Old Oak Common by British Rail's prototype Advanced Passenger Train. The caption ran 'Pictured at Western Region's Old Oak Common depot, Derby research staff, including one woman – computer operator Thelma Taylor – who were aboard the APT-E controlling the test runs between Uffington and Goring.' There were 35 men in the photograph.[16] In 1981, the number of women employed in the industry was still less than 10% of the total.[17]

In industries where such imbalance was commonplace the word 'men' was used unthinkingly until recently to describe the workforce. It is therefore no surprise to see, in a 1937 drawing of a canteen for Old Oak Common, the provision of seating for 170 men.[18] The messrooms were to be created in a former sand furnace house (Gazetteer No. 22) attached to the depot's engine shed. What is striking to modern eyes is the institutional segregation of the workforce that the plan illustrates. In the shed mechanics and cleaners might have worked alongside one another, but when it came to breaks the GWR expected that there would be a physical separation as, it must be acknowledged, did their employees (Fig 73).

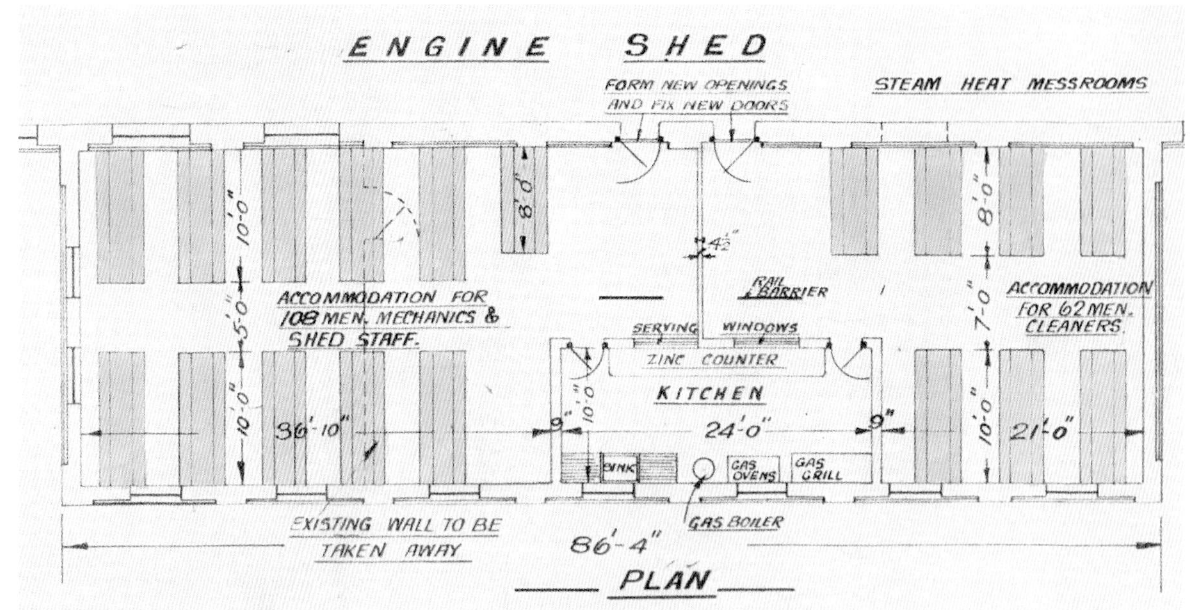

Fig 73 The 1937 conversion of Old Oak Common's southern sand furnace house into a canteen illustrates how segregation was designed into the site's fabric (WSHC 2515-406-1370)

Frank McKenna's 'minutiae of tasks, and the separateness they bred' was a powerful driver of division.[19] The workforce was rigidly demarcated according to the jobs they performed, and throughout the depot signs would have reminded them of their place. This system meant that even within the mixed workers grade at Old Oak Common there was a multiplicity of roles. As well as engine cleaning, for example, there were boiler washers, firelighters, firedroppers and ash pan cleaners. The cleaners, 'a wild bunch given to swimming in the canal and indeed the main coal stage tank', may have been of lowly status, but they were expected to rise through the ranks to the job of fireman and ultimately engine driver.[20] In consequence, they could lord it over the general labourers whose lot was a lifetime of moving the 'sheer volume of muck – oily, dusty, gritty, muddy or slushy' that was the constant byproduct of a railway.[21]

For much of its history the industry relied for efficiency on a mild totalitarianism. Although by 1940 when Albert Faultless started at Old Oak Common the toilet cubicles had gained doors, these came equipped with 'a large hole about 10" in line with the sitting position of the user, so that the Foreman could check that you were not wasting time by reading papers etc'.[22] Such behaviour was directly inherited from the depot's first superintendent, John Armstrong. A J Street has written that 'It was a serious crime to be caught smoking in the shed, the locomotive yard or on the footplate. Mr Armstrong was also very severe on anyone he saw entering or coming out of a public house, even if the men were off-duty'.[23]

As Hawkins and Reeve, and David Maidment (who worked at Old Oak Common in the late 1950s), have observed, the job of general mixed worker was for very many years the preserve of the Irish, and there were large Irish populations in the Acton and Willesden areas.[24] But in the aftermath of war a hitherto unknown problem emerged. Easier employment began to tempt workers, especially labourers, away from the railways. Old Oak Common lay between Acton and Park Royal, large industrial areas where national engineering and food production companies were offering cleaner, better paid work with regular hours. By 1957 Acton had 719 factories, workshops and other industrial premises and was said to have one of the two largest concentrations of industry south of Birmingham.[25] When in 1947 H G Kerry, the GWR's London Division Locomotive Carriage and Wagon Superintendent, was asked why strings of locomotives awaiting repair were to be seen outside locomotive depots rather than under cover, he could only reply that 'the Chief Mechanical Engineer is aiming at [getting] an engine straight from a running shed to the factory [but at the present time] this is not possible because of shortage of staff in running sheds and factories'.[26] What he did not consider worth mentioning was that these jobs might have been filled by the women so recently laid off in their thousands by the REC.

The lack of staff eventually became so acute that Old Oak Common began employing clerks to clean its engines during their weekends off.[27] Shortage of labour was a national problem, partially solved by the 1948 British Nationality Act which conferred on Commonwealth citizens the right to enter, work and settle in Great Britain. The newly formed British Railways was one of the earliest of the state-owned employers to tap this new pool of labour. In 1966 nearly a fifth of the inhabitants of the former Borough of Willesden, which bordered Old Oak Common, were still of Irish birth but by 1971 a new minority, those of Caribbean origin, had started to appear in numbers on the census (Fig 74). Nine tenths of these were manual workers, and at Old Oak Common Maidment remembers that the cleaners in the engine shed were exclusively drawn from the West Indian community (Fig 74).[28]

The shifting demographics of the railway industry coincided with a growing challenge to its rigid social hierarchies. Structural changes, as set out for instance in their 1955 Modernisation Plan, gave British Railways the opportunity to challenge long-standing workplace cultures, while an ascendant post-war liberalism hastened the decline of deference. British Railways's corporate identity programme was introduced in 1965, its purpose to promote a theme of unity. A new symbol, standard lettering, new liveries and new uniforms were the distinguishing features, and were supported by facelifts to the organisation's buildings. Often, the new

Fig 74 The demographics of Old Oak Common's workforce began to change in the 1960s (H G Forsythe/Gary Stratmann)

corporate identity was applied as a veneer, allowing fragments from former times to survive. The Victorian railway companies made extensive use of decoration to signal the differing levels of service on offer. This was important in public areas, where the social classes expected to be kept apart. Behind the scenes, the varied use of architectural detail to signal rank helped maintain discipline. Cornices and architraves in the Old Oak Common office of John Armstrong, for example, were moulded, whilst they were plain in the adjoining office of William Russell, his assistant. In another Old Oak Common example, the doors to the lifting shop's office were plainer than those in the general office (Fig 75).

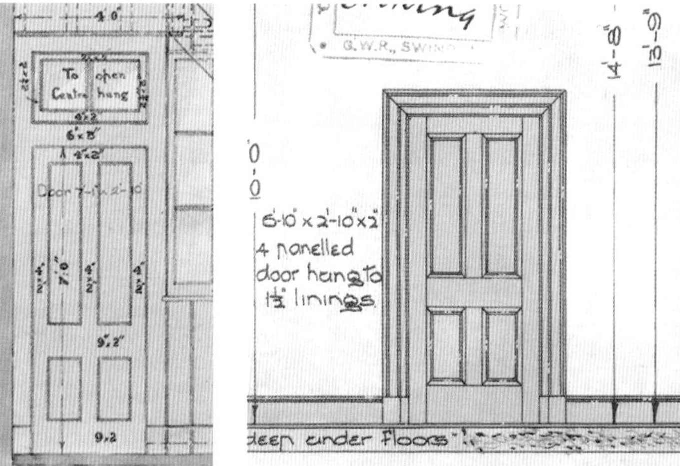

Fig 75 When Old Oak Common opened in 1906 its doors differed according to the status of the room's occupants. Lifting shop office (left), general office (right) (WSHC 2515/406/1806 and WSHC 2515/406/3348)

The size and quality of a company house was another very obvious way of rewarding rank. Until their nationalisation it had not been unusual for railway companies to provide housing; this policy ensured that staff were available night and day, promoted company loyalty and offered a useful means of control. Eastern Counties Railway, for example, built 300 houses for its workers in Stratford when it moved its engine works there in 1848.[29] The GWR was the main guarantor of the Great Western (London) Garden Village Society, a co-operative which built an estate of houses and shops between 1924 and 1931 on land close by West Acton station. There was another development at Hayes, and between the two there were eventually over 1,000 dwellings. The Acton houses were let to footplatemen 'who had to live near the running sheds at Old Oak Common'.[30] Other rail employees were also encouraged to live close to their place of employment, and thus tracts of agricultural land surrounding sheds and depots were gradually swallowed up by private housing.

When Westbourne Park, the GWR's locomotive depot outside Paddington station, opened in *c* 1853 it was furnished with a house, a drawing for which survives in Network Rail's archives (Fig 76).[31] Work by Crossrail in 2011 in advance of construction of the tunnel portal at Royal Oak uncovered the cellars of this building, the rest probably having been demolished in the early 1950s (Figs 77-78).[32] The building has been described by Steven Brindle as 'a house for the locomotive superintendent', but whether Daniel Gooch, who held this title at the time the house was built, ever lived there is questionable.[33] Gooch was a rising star who by 1847 had already moved into a substantial house in nearby Warwick Road.

Fig 76 GWR drawing of a company house at Westbourne Park Depot, later known as Alfred Villa (Network Rail)

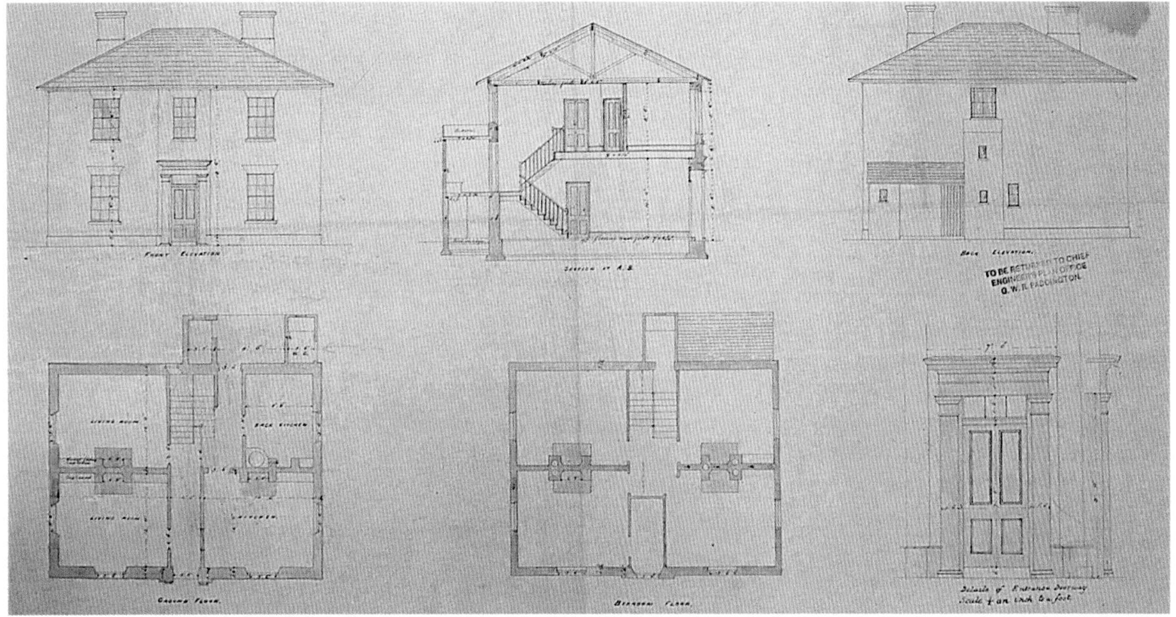

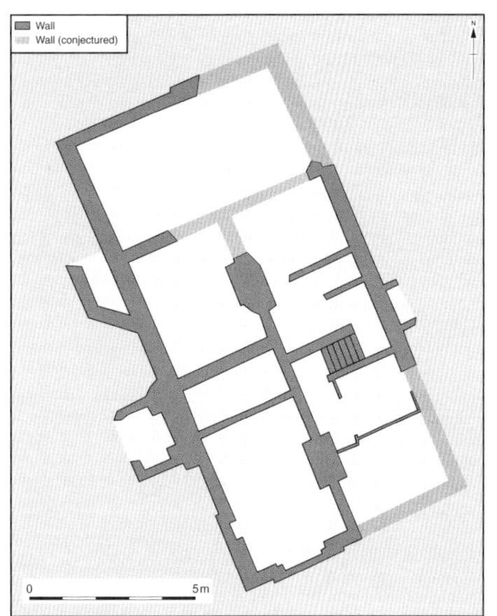

Fig 77 (left) Survey drawing of the excavated remains of Alfred Villa. The northern bay was added in the early 20th century

Fig 78 (right) Although Alfred Villa was demolished in the early 1950s its cellars survived and were briefly re-exposed in 2011

However, the Westbourne Park house was almost certainly later occupied by John Armstrong, who had been promoted in 1882 to Locomotive Superintendent of the Paddington Division, based at Westbourne Park. In 1896 John's son Ralph began an apprenticeship at the same depot and in 1916 followed his father to Old Oak Common as Assistant Divisional Locomotive Superintendent.[34]

By the 1960s what housing remained in railway hands was being sold off. The railways had been in retreat since the 1930s, dogged by a chronic lack of investment and harried by the rise of the private motorist and road haulier. After decades of contraction, arguably the industry's nadir was reached in the early 1980s.[35] Since then there has been some genuine progress, although commentators differ on how this has been achieved. Today, even though freight remains a shadow of its former self, passenger numbers are rising. Old lines and stations are being re-opened (and Crossrail is playing its part in this), and there are even a few new lines being planned. Employment levels have matched this change; by 2011, the number of UK employees in the industry was reported to have climbed to 138,100.[36] For these employees there is equal opportunity, although it remains the case that only 4% of the driving and maintenance workforce is female, and only 5% of the total engineering workforce is from an ethnic minority background.[37] Another statistic drawn from the Office for National Statistics' Labour Force Survey 2011 suggests that the workforce has an older profile than the economy as a whole. This data shows that there are clear challenges ahead for the rail industry. But it also highlights that, nearly two hundred years after the first timetabled passenger railway opened, many thousands of people continue to look to the railways for their career.

NOTES

1 British Railways Board 1963, 50

2 For a good introduction to working on Britain's railways in the days immediately before nationalisation see 'The Railwaymen: One of a Film Series About Jobs' produced for the Ministry of Transport by the Central Office of Information, B/C7228, June 1946. In 1948 the newly-formed British Railways inherited over 9,000 working horses and over 25,000 horse-drawn vehicles (British Transport Commission 1948, 6). Horses were still stabled at Paddington's Mint stables into the 1950s (Brindle 2004, 146). The last railway horse in Britain was retired in 1967. Rates of pay: drivers of motorcycles for delivery of parcels, GWR, Dec 1926–June 1927, RAIL 1172/1445

3 British Rail Business Systems grew out of British Railways' early experiments in applying computing to the business of railway organisation. British Rail Telecommunications (the successor of the telegraph operations founded by the earliest railways) controlled the country's second largest telecoms system after British Telecom (Gourvish 2002, 211). In the 1980s engineers from BRT worked with counterparts from Mercury Communications to exploit BRT's inter-city fibre optic network. Seaspeed, the trading name of British Rail Hovercraft Ltd, was formed in 1965. This was an extension of the interest British Rail held in maritime transport by virtue of the ferry services it inherited when the British Transport Commission was abolished.

4 *Employment in the Railway Industry: England and Wales, 1851-2001*, www.neighbourhood.statistics.gov.uk/HTMLDocs/dvc12/railway.html, accessed 7 March 2014

5 Brindle 2013, 88, Fig 5.19

6 Drummond 2010, 154

7 Wojtczak 2005, 11

8 GWR drawing 'Alterations & Additions to Stores & Messroom, Carriage Shed Old Oak Common. Swindon', June 1911, WSHC 2515/409/0138

9 *The Railway Gazette*, August 1915

10 Pratt 1921, 477

11 www.ww1hull.org.uk/index.php/ww1/women-in-the-first-world-war, accessed 27 March 2015

12 GWR 1942, 123

13 ibid, 124

14 Joby 1984, 101

15 Matheson 2007, 26

16 *Rail News*, September 1975, 3

17 Employment in the Railway Industry: England and Wales, 1851-2001, http://www.neighbourhood.statistics.gov.uk/HTMLDocs/dvc12/railway.html, accessed 6 March 2014

18 GWR drawing 'Proposed new Messrooms in Old Sand Furnace House and new Cloakrooms in old Messrooms, Engine Shed Old Oak Common', August 1937, WSHC 2515/406/1370. A larger canteen in the Engineman's Hostel by the main gate was in place by April 1949.

19 McKenna 1980, 93

20 Hawkins and Reeve 1987, 91

21 Joby 1984, 133

22 Faultless undated, 1

23 Street 1951, 23-24

24 Hawkins and Reeve, 1987, 94; Maidment 2014, 19

25 Acton Library, cutting from *Evening News*, 1957; *The Times*, 19 April 1956

26 Hawkins and Reeve 1987, 6

27 Joby 1984, 101

28 Bolton *et al.* 1982, 182-204; Maidment 2014, 19

29 McKenna 1980, 51

30 Jackson 1991, 349; McKenna 1980, 53; Hawkins and Reeve 1987, 91

31 GWR drawing, untitled, dated August 1853, Network Rail planroll 13314

32 It is possible that the house had been damaged beyond repair during the war, but the London County Council bomb damage maps do not attribute any damage to the structure (London Topographical Society 2005, Maps 59 and 60).

33 The drawing is reproduced in Brindle 2013, 48, fig 3.22, referenced as Network Rail Infrastructure Ltd (NMR AA031068); Burdett Wilson 1972, 64

34 Burdett Wilson 1972, 94; http://www.historywebsite.co.uk/Museum/Transport/Trains/Children.htm, accessed 8 March 2014

35 The low point in passenger miles, passenger numbers and revenue from passenger traffic is today seen as having coincided with the publication of the Serpell Report in 1982.

36 People1st, State of the Nation Report 2013: Passenger Transport and Travel, www.people1st.co.uk/getattachment/Research-policy/Research-reports/State-of-the-Nation-Passenger-Transport-Travel, accessed 27 March 2015, 29

37 Produced Sept 2010, using GoSkills AACS LMI report (Jun 2010) http://readingroom.skillsfundingagency.bis.gov.uk/sfa/nextstep/lmib/Next%20Step%20LMI%20Bitesize%20-%20Goskills%20-%20rail%20-%20Jun%202010.pdf

CHAPTER 5

DISTRIBUTION AND PROVISIONING

> *I wish that, in this age so enamoured of statistical information, ... that some M'Culloch or Caird would tabulate for me the amount of provisions, solid and liquid, consumed at the breakfasts of London every morning. I want to know how many thousand eggs are daily chipped, how many of those embryo chickens are poached, and how many fried; how many tons of quartern loaves are cut up to make bread-and-butter, thick and thin; how many porkers have been sacrificed to provide the bacon rashers, fat and streaky; what rivers have been drained, what fuel consumed, what mounds of salt employed, what volumes of smoke emitted, to catch and cure the finny haddocks and the Yarmouth bloaters, that grace our morning repast.*[1]

Supplying food to London was and is a monumental task. Journalist and statistician George Dodd, in his book *The Food of London* published in 1856, when the population of London was c 2.5 million rather than the current 8 million, observed that it is a task neither organised nor overseen nor assured by any government or authority.[2] Local government has had regulatory role in checking weights and measures, and more recently ensuring public health, and, but otherwise has not been involved in the supply and distribution of food. The Greater London Authority's remit in this area extends primarily to strategic aspirations for healthy and environmentally sustainable food.[3] Although specific produce has at one time or another been under government management, as for example with the Milk Marketing Board, the reality is that the supply of food to London is and always has been a commercial enterprise. And it happens every single day.

Since their construction the railways have played a pivotal role in this process. Although passenger services may be the more visible face of the railway, the impetus driving the expansion of the railway network and generating earnings was the movement of coal, raw materials, manufactured goods and food. The earliest horse-drawn railways and tramways were devised for the transport of coal, and passenger terminals were invariably accompanied by goods yards and depot facilities.

Until the mid-19th century London was able to source much fresh produce from the herds, cattle sheds, farms and market gardens within and at the margins of the City. George Dodd wrote that the 'fruits and vegetables which furnish a subordinate but valuable part of our food occupy a broad belt of market gardens around London ...'.[4] The Industrial Revolution bought expansion of the metropolis and its population, and it was necessary to look further afield for provisions. The new technology of the railways opened up fast and regular access to markets across the country'.[5]

Works during the construction of Crossrail at Paddington and Farringdon stations recorded elements of the historic railway infrastructure and particularly those employed in the transport of milk and meat to London.

The Great Western Railway's contribution

The Great Western Railway's (GWR) first London terminal at Paddington was a makeshift affair built to the west of Bishop's Bridge Road with passenger access through the arches of the bridge (Fig 79).[6] A temporary goods depot comprising a large timber-built shed was constructed on the site of the present day Paddington terminus. When the GWR began services in 1838 the Bishop's Bridge Road terminus was just under construction, but was certainly fully developed by 1845.

In 1850 the decision was taken to build a new terminus at Paddington and the temporary terminus was redeveloped as the Bishop's Road Goods Depot (Fig 80). The depot was linked via a rail coal depot to a coal wharf on the south side of the Grand Junction Canal. Following the opening of the Chepstow Railway Bridge over the River Wye in 1852-3, which allowed through trains to South Wales and its coalfields, a huge traffic in

Fig 79 Paddington station in *c* 1840. The passenger station is to the left of the painting, the goods depot to the right (NRM/ Science and Society Picture Library)

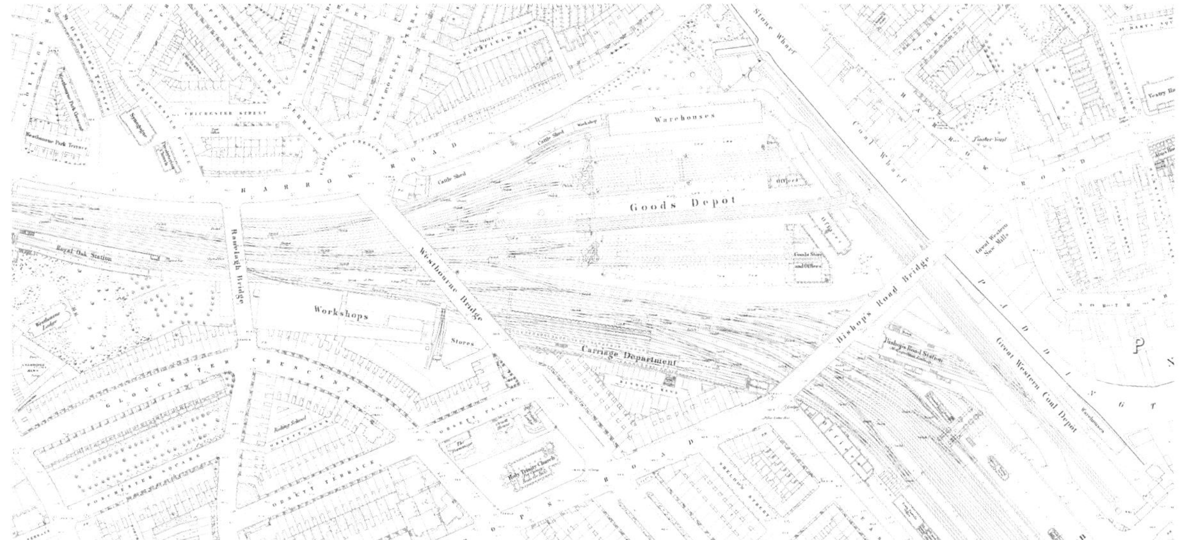

Fig 80 Bishops Road Depot with Paddington station to south on first edition OS map, dated 1872 (Groundsure)

coal developed. The 'high-level goods yard' was laid out alongside the canal basin especially for this trade.[7] By 1925 the Bishops Road Goods Depot had reached full capacity with 900 road vehicles a day and 900,000 tons of goods being handled each year. The depot was demolished during 1925-26 and a huge new goods depot building was erected in its place.

In the 1850s and 1860s the GWR also developed their own goods, parcels and milk delivery services, initially using hired carriers, stables and horses, but later purchasing its own horses and building its own stables at Paddington, Smithfield and Crutched Friars in the City of London (Gazetteer No. 53). The stables remained in use until after WWII.[8]

Goods didn't just come into the goods depot. Statistics from 1937 show that market traffic through Paddington station comprised the import of between 50 to 200 tons of flowers, fish, fruit, meat and vegetables each morning, as well as outward bound newspaper deliveries totally 203 tons every night and up to 394 tons on Saturdays.[9] The parcel and mail service was even larger. The parcels depot had its own platform, linked via a parcels subway to Platforms 1 to 8. In 1937 an average of 22,000 parcels a day moved through the parcels depot. The Royal Mail had a sorting office on London Street for traffic through Paddington, which amounted to 4,500 mailbags and 2,400 bags of parcel post a day. Outward-bound (Down) mail went along a conveyor from the Post Office into the station. Incoming (Up) mailbags were dropped down chutes onto another conveyor, which took the mail to the London Road office before it was sent on to Liverpool Street sorting office via the Post Office underground railway.[10]

Milk Trade

As already noted, London's immediate environs managed to provide most of the population's requirements for milk from urban and suburban cattle sheds until the mid-19th century.[11]

In 1865 the disease rinderpest or steppe murrain entered Britain through cattle imported directly from the Baltic, and it is estimated that 40% of the cattle in London perished.[12] Writing at the end of 1865 J C Morton estimated that there had been about 24,000 cattle kept in the metropolis before the outbreak, but that afterwards there were perhaps only 10,000 cattle left.[13] The rinderpest outbreak of 1865 is generally credited with bringing about a change in dairy farming practices in Britain, and it has sometimes be suggested that it was a material factor in the decline of metropolitan cattle sheds. However, although the 1865 cattle plague hit the London cattle sheds especially hard, the metropolitan herd did largely recover its numbers and metropolitan milk production again reached something approaching pre-plague levels.[14]

Furthermore, milk was being brought into London by rail well before the cattle plague outbreak. M M Milburn wrote in 1852 in his book *The Cow: Dairy Husbandry and Cattle Breeding* that 'the railway system has introduced a completely new mode of supplying our large towns with milk',[15] and George Dodd wrote in 1856 that:

> *in respect to dairy-produce, little is indeed furnished by any places near the metropolis. Our cheese comes from a dozen or more English counties, and from Holland and America; our butter from fully as many counties, from Ireland, and from America: even much of the milk we require is now brought from distances of twenty or thirty miles.*[16]

At first, the milk transported by train formed only a small proportion of the city's requirements. In 1861 only 4.4% of the milk supplied to London was brought in by rail, compared with the 71.7% from metropolitan sheds. Gradually, however, the proportion of the milk supplied to London by train increased. By 1884 76.2% of the milk supply was brought in by train, and only 21.5% came from local sheds. By 1891 83.1% of milk came in by train, and just 15% was from local sheds. The quantity brought in by train in 1861 was 1 million gallons, by 1891 the quantity coming in by train was 48.7 million gallons.[17] This change in the milk supply was caused by a number of factors, not least the growing rail network and advances in refrigeration. Thanks to fast delivery fresh milk from outlying farms could compete with urban suppliers. The costs of keeping cows in the metropolis seem to have risen to the point where it became increasingly difficult for metropolitan cow keepers to operate profitably, and as the city continued to expand in population the pressure

Fig 81 Milk churns awaiting dispatch at Paddington station in 1923 (NRM/ Science and Society Picture Library)

on the land available for development made it more and more difficult for to accommodate urban herds.[18]

The GWR transported just 8,954 gallons of milk in January 1865 but a year later it brought in 143,600 gallons during January. In May and June 1866 the quantities were 285,918 and 221,851 gallons respectively.[19] Up until the 1930s milk was transported in churns, and in 1878-82 a purpose-built milk platform was constructed on the north (arrivals) side of Paddington Station. The platform was covered in 1887. Empty churns were dispatched from Platform 1 on the departures side (Fig 81).

As part of extensive modifications to the station between 1909 to 1916 a series of new platforms were provided on the arrivals side of the station, all covered by a new roof which added a fourth span to the existing station roof. A new milk platform was amongst these changes.[20] The new lines were located beneath London Street, which had been raised on a steel frame and supported on a fire-proof jack arch structure. At platform level a sunken roadway was provided to facilitate the off-loading of milk churns from trains across the platform and onto waiting wagons without lifting. Access from the milk platform to street level was provided by a steel-framed 'milk ramp', which emerged on the north side of London Street at the junction with South Wharf Road (Fig 82). The ramp had a stone sett surface to provide footholds for horses and channel irons to guide the wagons.

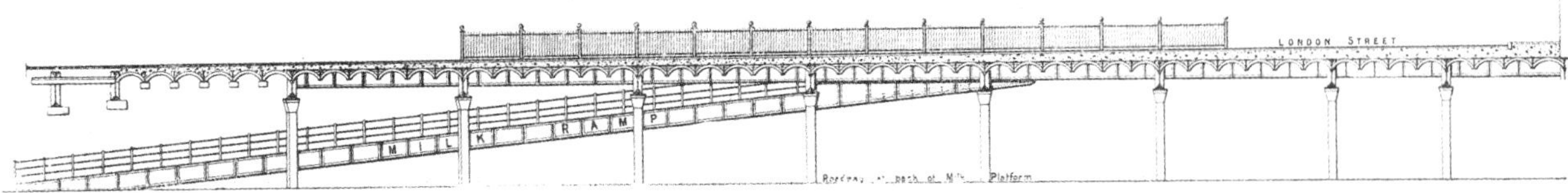

Fig. 4.—Longitudinal section of diverted goods approach and ramped approach to new milk platform.

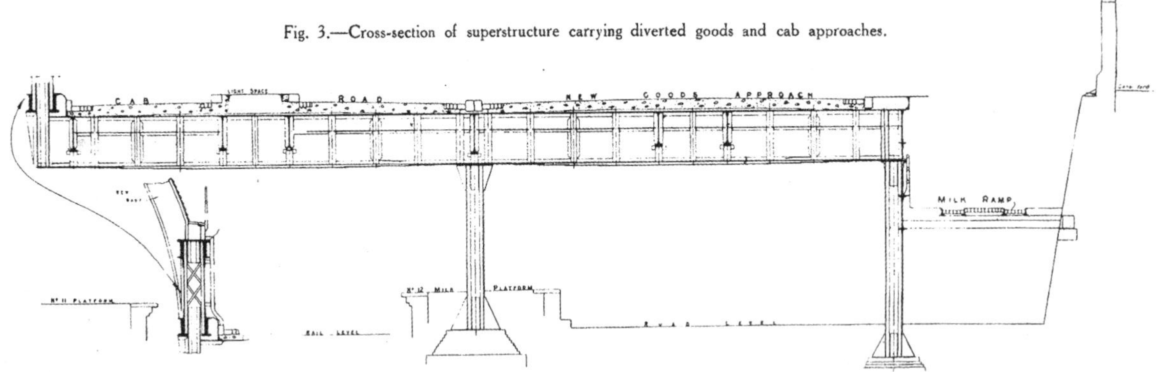

Fig 82 Section through the milk ramp showing sett surface dated 1917 (Steam Museum)

Most of GWR milk traffic for London came from Berkshire, Wiltshire, Oxfordshire, Somerset and Dorset and was carried in special express trains. In 1922 the GWR carried 75 million gallons (340,500,000 litres) of milk. There were typically 60 milk trains a day, and the milk depot handled about 7,500 churns daily. Most of the milk trains arrived at either midnight or midday. However, by the 1930s most railway milk traffic was carried in insulated tank wagons rather than churns, although some milk was still being transported in churns up until the mid 1970s (Fig 83). Milk deliveries by tank wagons were directed to a new milk depot at Wood Lane.[21]

Fig 83 Six-wheeled GWR milk wagon (David Merrett CC-BY-CA-2.0)

Modifications and extensions to Bishop's Road station between 1929 and 1934, together with the extension of the Metropolitan lines, provided better freight facilities at the new Bishop's Bridge goods depot and wrought further changes to the London Street deck. The most significant of these was the large Bowstring Girder that was erected at the west end of the station to carry London Street over the re-aligned and extended Bishop's Bridge tunnel. The milk platform was made redundant by this change and the milk ramp was closed and truncated, whilst the lines were converted to use by new suburban passenger services. The void left by the ramp was filled with concrete and a new road surface put down. The final remaining parts of the redundant and isolated milk ramp were recorded and removed during Crossrail construction work (Fig 84).

The boom years of milk supply by railway began to ebb in the 1960s with changing patterns of trade and the growth in road transport. Following the

Fig 84 The remains of the London Street milk ramp (with stone sett surface) prior to removal

Transport Act of 1962 the railways' statutory obligations to be a service provider for the public benefit were removed, allowing them to concentrate on the more profitable parts of their business. The import of coal fell dramatically following the Clean Air Acts and the transportation of milk and other foodstuffs moved onto the roads. The goods depot at Paddington was cleared in the 1970s in part to make way for the new Westway dual carriageway road, which opened in 1972.

Farringdon Station and Smithfield Market[22]

The GWR in the mid-19th century had probably the most extensive railway trade in foodstuffs.[23] This was further enhanced by the opening in 1863 of the Metropolitan Line, which ran from Paddington to Farringdon Street station. The world's first underground railway linked London's business district to the main GWR terminal at Paddington.[24] The Metropolitan Line was owned by the City Terminus Company but used by several other companies. It linked eastwards via Aldersgate Street (Barbican) as far as Moorgate Street station (Moorgate) in 1865 and southwards to the London Chatham and Dover Railway via its Ludgate Hill station in 1866. The GWR opened a new depot below Smithfield Market in partnership with Metropolitan Railway. This would be followed by depots at Poplar Dock (1878), The Royal Docks (1900), South Lambeth (1913) and Westbourne Park (1908).

The original Smithfield Market had been in existence since the 12th century and traded primarily as a market for live sheep and cattle. Before the advent of the railways fresh meat could only be transported on the hoof, which took time and was wasteful, as the animals lost weight en route, and caused chaos in the area surrounding the market as the herds moved through.[25] By the middle of the 19th century the city could no longer accommodate the herding and slaughter of the numbers of animals required to feed its growing population. There was also a growing concern for public health and sanitation, and concomitant concern with the impact of 'noxious trades'.[26]

Fig 85 Old Smithfield Market, from *London Pictorially Described*, by J F Porter (London, 1898)

The market on the original site at Smithfield was closed and replaced by a new Metropolitan Cattle Market which was opened at Copenhagen Fields in Islington by Prince Albert in 1855. This market proved short-lived and by 1860 a new wholesale meat market on the site at Smithfield was being planned (Fig 85).

The railways brought about a revolution in the movement of animals. Already by 1849 almost one million of the animals sold at Smithfield came to London by rail. Dionysius Lardner wrote in his *Railway Economy* of 1850 that railways not only reduced transport costs, but also travelling time, which meant fresher food, and in particular fresher meat and therefore better prices.[27] The speed of railway transport and its ability to carry large loads made it possible to transport fresh meat as carcasses rather than as live beasts into the heart of the city.

When plans for the new enclosed market were drawn up they included a basement area where meat could be unloaded from trains.[28]

Constructed in 1868 by the City Architect Horace Jones, who also designed and built Billingsgate Market, the meat market (which remains in use) is red brick with Portland stone dressings and corner towers. It is one storey high, measuring 36 bays in length and 6 bays across, and is roofed with Welsh slate and glass louvres with louvred dormers. The market was extended between 1873 and 1876 with the construction of the Poultry Market immediately to the west and further buildings – the General

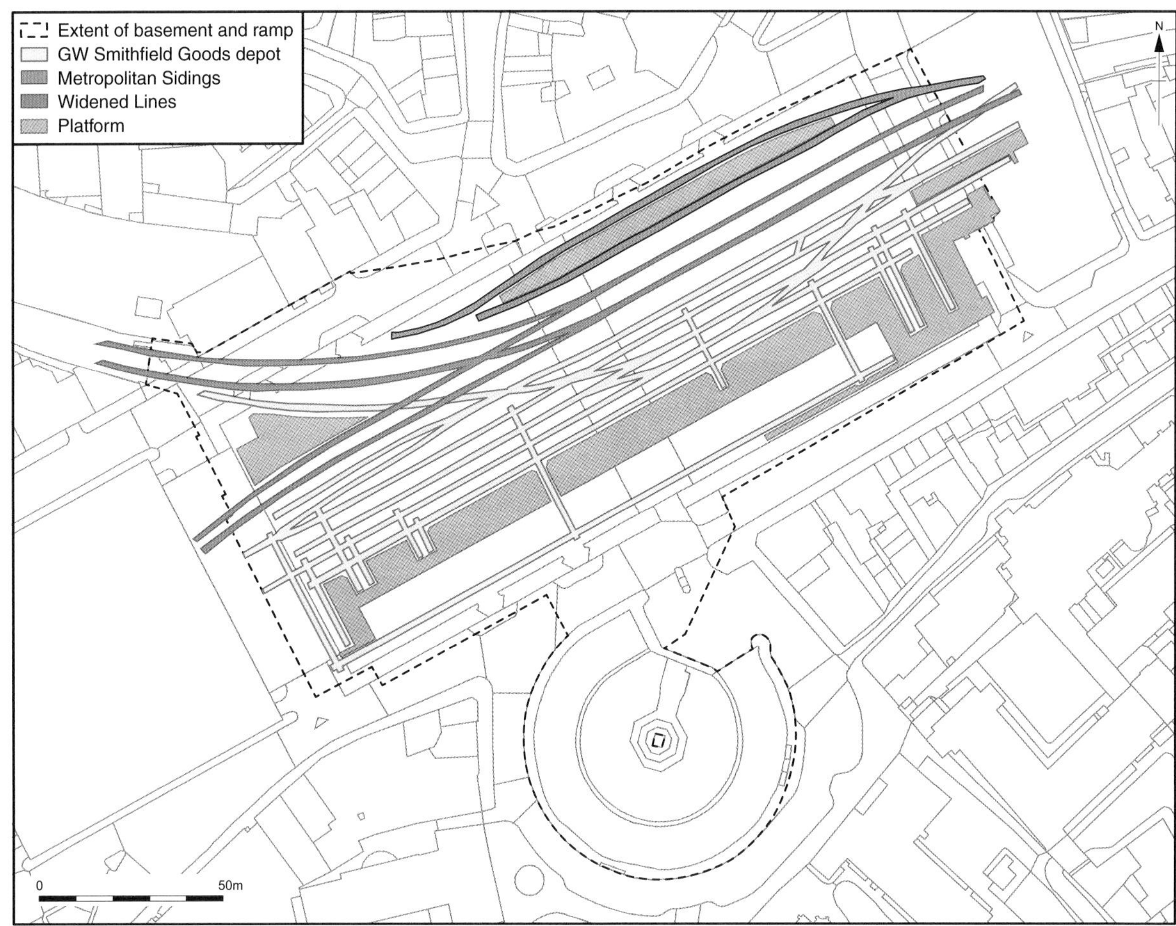

Fig 86 The railway system and associated platforms and ramp below Smithfield Market

Market (1879-1883) and the Fish Market (1888) – were added in later years.[29] From the early 1870s a trade in chilled meat imported from the USA had developed steadily, followed by imports from the Antipodes and South America.[30] These inspired the creation of cold stores in the UK. In 1884-7 the Poultry Market basements were converted to refrigerated storage using steam-powered engines. Access to these vaults was via a ramp to the south (Fig 86). Next to the Fish Market the 'The Red House' was built between 1898 and 1899 for the London Central Markets Cold Storage Co. Ltd. This was one of the first cold stores to be built outside the London docks and continued to serve Smithfield until the mid-1970s.

> *A visitor to the market, almost any hour after midnight and up to ten o'clock in the morning, will find salesmen, or salesmen's porters, busy at their laborious and not too pleasant work. There are a great number of Christian and Temperance men amongst the salesmen and porters; and at any time of the day when the market is open, visitors, whether they are buyers or mere sight-seers, may depend upon these persons giving respectful answers to reasonable inquiries,*

provided, of course, that they do not too far trespass upon their time. There are 162 shops in the market, each shop being about 36 feet by 15. Behind each shop there is a counting-house, and over every counting house and shop there are private apartments. The temperature of the market is generally about ten degrees cooler than the temperature in the open atmosphere, and in almost all weathers the comparative sweetness of the air is a surprise to visitors.[31]

The market still supplies inner city butchers, shops and restaurants with meat for the coming day, with the trading hours between 0400 to noon every weekday (Fig 87).

Fig 87 Workers inside the Central Market at Smithfield (Bettsy 1970 CC-BY-SA-2.0)

Some of the buildings on the north side of Charterhouse Street have access into the market's basement areas from their basements, and several commercial buildings to the east of Smithfield Market in the block defined by Lindsey Street, Long Lane, Charterhouse Street and Hayne Street were built over the railway depot and sidings that served Smithfield. The latter buildings were recorded by Crossrail's archaeologists prior to demolition to enable construction of Farringdon station's new eastern ticket hall.

'Smithfield House', Nos 54-64 Charterhouse Street (Gazetteer No. 104) was built on a steel lattice-work frame over the railway (Fig 88) and was linked to Nos 8-10 Hayne Street by a 10 ton travelling crane.[32]

No 3 Lindsey Street was tripe dresser's shop prior to closure and had a ceramic tiled frontage with the trader's name (Gazetteer No. 108). On a 1916 plan of the adjoining GWR offices, this little building was labelled as

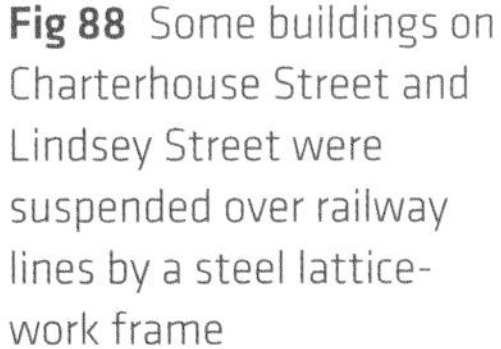

Fig 88 Some buildings on Charterhouse Street and Lindsey Street were suspended over railway lines by a steel lattice-work frame

Fig 89 The brick-built structure beneath No 3 Lindsey Street included a blocked-up archway which originally led to the railway sidings

Fig 90 The single pilaster which survived on the north corner of No 3 Lindsey Street had formed part of the adjoining GWR Correspondence Office

a 'Condemned Meat Store'.[33] The building was built on top of tunnels and structures belonging to the railway sidings beneath but had no direct access to the sidings (Fig 89). There was access from No 4 Lindsey Street to the north. This had been a GWR Correspondence Office, but the only trace of the structure remaining at the time of Crossrail's survey was a single pilaster surviving at the north corner of No 3 Lindsey Street (Fig 90).

Fig 91 The shopfront of Armour and Co. meat importers, who in 1938 were based at 23 Long Lane (Historic England)

Nos 8-9 Hayne Street (Gazetteer No. 109) was linked by a bridge over Hayne Street to a warehouse on the opposite side, and was served by a lift shaft that descended to the railway sidings below. In 1910 it was occupied by a printers and bookbinders. Nos 20-23 Long Lane and No 2 Lindsey Street were occupied in 1938 by businesses that included Armour and Co, meat importers, at No 23 Long Lane (Fig 91) and a cold storage company at No 20.

As with Paddington, the second half of the 20th century saw the emergence at Smithfield of a shift from rail to road supply. The railway tunnels below the market closed in the 1960s and were converted in the 1970s into car parks. They are now used for storage and parking. The distinctive cobbled access ramp still spirals downwards around a public park known as West Smithfield.

NOTES

1 Sala 1862, 78
2 Dodd 1856, 125-126, and 190.
3 *The Mayor's Food Strategy: Healthy and Sustainable Food for London. An Implementation Plan 2011-2013*
4 Dodd 1856, 103
5 See Lardner 1850, 6-11; Dodd 1856, Chapter 3 'Rapid Transit an Aid to Food-Supply'
6 Brindle 2013, 19-20, Fig 2.7
7 Ibid, 83
8 Ibid, 147-48, figs 8.25-8.26
9 Ibid, 87-88
10 Ibid, 88-89
11 Atkins 1977 argues that before the 1860s London's milk requirements were 'met entirely by urban and suburban producers located within easy reach of the consumer.'
12 Hall 1965, 799
13 Morton 1865, 74; but see Atkins 1977, table 1.
14 Atkins 1977, 388
15 Milburn 1852, 69
16 Dodd 1856, 102-03
17 Taylor 1971, 35, table 1.
18 Atkins 1977, 388-90, 392-95
19 Fussell 1988, 310
20 Brindle 2013, 59
21 Ibid, 88
22 See Brown et al 2016, 46-49 for further discussion of Smithfield Market and the meat trade.
23 Brindle 2013, 83
24 Ibid, 54-5, Fig 4.4-4.5
25 Metcalfe 2012, 90-92
26 The Public Health Act which was passed in 1848 provided a framework for the appointment of Inspectors of Nuisances but did not compel local authorities to act. http://www.parliament.uk/about/living-heritage/transformingsociety/towncountry/towns/tyne-and-wear-case-study/about-the-group/public-administration/the-1848-public-health-act/ Accessed 8 February 2016

27 Lardner 1850, 8-10

28 http://www.smithfieldmarket.com/content/market/history-of-the-market

29 The present Poultry Market building was built in 1961-3 by T P Bennett and Son to replace the original, which burned down in 1958. The shell dome conceived with Ove Arup and Partners was reportedly the largest of its kind in the world when constructed. It has a span of 225ft by 130ft and a height of 60ft, and cost £1,800,000. A complex system of more than one thousand pre-formed plywood shuttering sheets, each one a different shape, was used in the construction; For more detail of Crossrail work at Smithfield see Brown et al 2016

30 Western Buildings London Central Markets Smithfield. Report by the Historical Research & Conservation Support London Team. English Heritage 2003

31 Porter 1890

32 LMA, GLC/AR/BR/22/BA/043620

33 See Brown et al 2016 for more detail of No 3 Lindsey Street; Plan (LMA, GLC/AR/BR/22/BA/043620)

CHAPTER 6

LONDON'S RAILWAYS 1939-1945

Fig 92 *All Clear for the Guns* by Leslie Carr (NRM/Science and Society Picture Library)

Shortly before Britain and France declared war on Germany in September 1939 the British government once again took control of the railways. Its experience of running them between 1914 and 1921, under the aegis of the Railway Executive Committee (REC), had given it a valuable insight into the difficulties it might face. Most immediately, it had taught them to expect an exodus of staff to join the fighting forces as soon as the declaration was made public. This duly occurred, as did the corresponding rise in demand for troop transport trains. Almost overnight, the railways were transformed from a regular, timetabled service to a never-ending succession of 'special trains'. Within a few days of the outbreak of hostilities over 600,000 people had been evacuated from London, and by 1944 'special trains' were running at a rate of 500 per day above the ordinary, already heavily swollen, traffic.[1]

The footplate crews of these trains found that, amongst the many other problems they now faced, the quality of coal in their tenders declined.[2] This meant that it became harder to maintain good pressure in their locomotive's boilers, precisely at the time when best quality fuel was needed to help haul heavier trains. Worse were the hazards inherent in some of the cargoes they hauled. Explosions were mercifully rare, but they did occur. In one of the best-known incidents, James Nightall and Frank Bridges lost their lives when an LNER train loaded with aircraft bombs exploded at Soham station in 1944.

The availability of rolling stock became unpredictable. Locomotives, coaches and wagons were either displaced, in need of servicing, or damaged beyond repair. The mileage between major services was greatly increased, and engines would sometimes simply disappear, having been sequestered by another depot or exported overseas to help in the war effort there. The suspension of the GWR's locomotive, carriage and wagon construction programmes in the summer of 1940, and the increased workload borne by its existing stock, meant that the demand on the company's locomotive facilities at Old Oak Common was high. Repairs accounted for a substantial proportion of subsequent expenditure.[3] Eventually, to fill a widening gap, locomotives from the USA were ordered, and these started to appear at Old Oak Common during 1943.

Fig 93 *Railway Equipment is War Equipment* by Fred Taylor, 1943
(NRM/Science and Society Picture Library)

There was also a new danger. Railways, and sometimes even the trains using them, were specifically targeted by the Luftwaffe, especially from mid-1941 onwards.[5] Train crews were regularly displaced by the length of time journeys took, or because the lines they needed to return on had been damaged or destroyed. Special instructions were issued to staff about the methods of dealing with obstructions caused by drifting barrage balloons and crashing aircraft.[6] The blackout caused huge difficulties, especially in marshalling yards, where '*obstructions such as points levers, slippery rails, uneven sleepers and puddles of unknown depth*' presented many hazards.[7] Yards were even more confusing for the newly recruited. Isabella Anderson recalled that '*Going into strange yards, and listening to trains moving, and not seeing them, not knowing where the points are, and nobody to ask, is very alarming*'.[8]

To aid navigation, pillars, posts, the buffers of trains, the corners of buildings and countless other potential obstacles were painted white. Haphazardly painted pillars in Old Oak Common's engine shed were a remnant of this measure that remained in place until the shed's demolition in the 1960s. Conversely, the edges of carriage windows were painted black to prevent any light seeping beyond ill-fitting blinds. Paint was also used to obliterate the names of stations in order to confuse the enemy in the event of invasion. It was even deployed as a detection device. A fireman working out of Bristol during the war recalls that '*all locomotives had a portion of the cab eyeglasses painted with anti-gas paint which would change colour if ran into a contaminated area*'.[9]

A huge obstacle to an effective blackout was the glow from burning coal. The ash dropped into waiting pits at engine sheds remained red hot for many hours after its removal from a locomotive. In 1941 a contract was awarded to Smith Walker Ltd for the supply and erection of two asbestos-clad ash shelters at Old Oak Common (Gazetteer No. 33).[10] These straddled the ash roads on either side of the coal stage and were simple steel-framed structures with double-pitch trusses. The buildings proved too small for the job and were unpopular, and the sheets quickly became damaged. In 1952 Swindon issued a proposal to re-use Old Oak Common's structures to provide accommodation for their new gas turbine and diesel-electric locomotives, but in the end they were removed for re-use in Llanelli Docks.[11]

Old Oak Common lay in a heavily industrialised area, and it was inevitable it would be targeted during the Blitz. Its defence was provided by Army anti-aircraft batteries at nearby Wormwood Scrubs.[12] In 1940 Albert Faultless was a 16-year old avoiding the mines by working instead on the railways. In an unpublished memoir he described a typical night during the early years of war.

> *'There was an air raid on at the time. It was pitch black as we walked along the siding at Old Oak Common Carriage Sheds. The Wormwood Scrubs anti aircraft guns began to fire, with the drone of German aircraft above. My Driver said "Let's put on our tin hats as there will be a lot of shrapnel about". After about three steps, a piece of shrapnel two inches long, missed me by inches'.*[13]

As the number and duration of raids intensified, the footplate crews at the LNER's Devonshire Street yard took to sheltering overnight in the shunter's hut rather than risk the journey home.[14] Footplate crews at Old Oak Common could do the same. Their cabin was situated at the throat of the site, beside the foot of the embankment to the Grand Junction Canal, in a position where it might offer blast protection to staff working the

Fig 94 Old Oak Common's Shunters Cabin, formerly a WWII ARP shelter

remote eastern end of the yard. In place by September 1943 it survived until 2011 in modified form (Fig 94).[15] A thin, rectangular building, its walls were of red brick where they were visible to passing passengers, and of concrete block where they were hidden. The shallow double-pitched roof was of poured concrete, with internal shutter marks clearly visible. A thick, L-shaped blast wall of concrete blocks protected the original door in the eastern elevation.

The 1939 Civil Defence Act had compelled employers to implement measures to protect resources from aerial attack. Companies were expected to bear in full the cost of providing air raid shelters for their staff, and at Old Oak Common the Shunters' Cabin was joined by four other shelters built beside or into the site's boundary embankments (Fig 95). All were within easy reach of the engine shed and workshops. The LNER's Ilford Goods Depot also had four, this time buried beneath earth bunds.[16]

The SR's Plumstead Goods Depot had two subterranean shelters (Gazetteer No. 146). These provided protection for staff working in the carriage sidings between the main North Kent Line and the branch to the Royal Arsenal (Shelter 1, Fig 96) and at the eastern end of the goods yard (Shelter 2, Fig 97). Both shelters were recorded in detail by Crossrail during 2011.

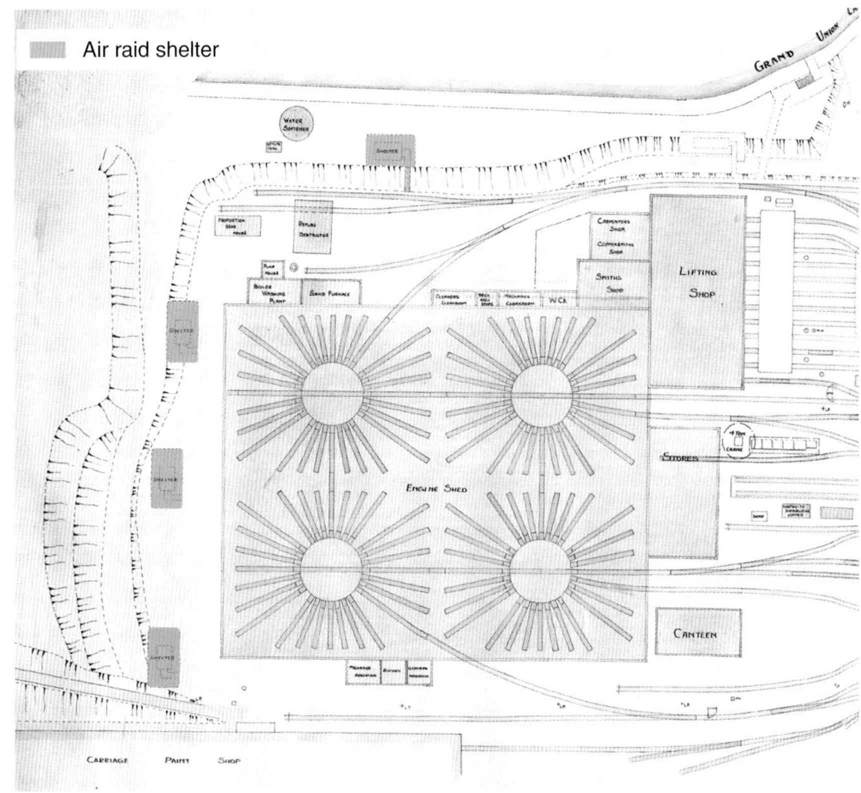

Fig 95 Four of Old Oak Common's air raid shelters are shown on this plan from September 1943 (WSHC 2515-410-0672)

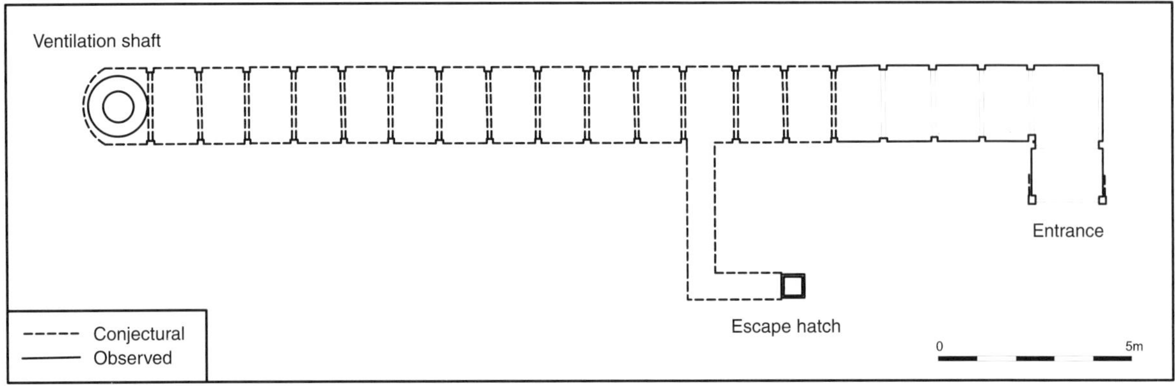

Fig 96 General arrangement of Plumstead Goods Depot's Shelter 1

Fig 97 An internal view of Shelter 2 at Plumstead Goods Depot, looking east

Although the shelters were not identical both had been constructed from grooved pre-cast concrete posts and trusses. Concrete slabs were slotted into the grooves to form the walls and double-pitched roofs. The risings from the trench formed a mound over the buried structures. The floor for Shelter 2 was formed from a concrete slab with a rebate at either edge to form a gully discontinued at each post. Both shelters had vents at the opposite end from the entrances, and hatches to provide a means of escape should the entrance became blocked.

Old Oak Common's carriage sheds were vast, and easily spotted from the air. On 24 September 1940 they were hit and a number of carriages were destroyed. Just over a month later the Luftwaffe struck again, this time in broad daylight. At least one 500lb bomb fell on the recently completed carriage paint shop, badly damaging a section of the roof and cracking brickwork in the south-east gable (Gazetteer No. 20). The offices of the

Fig 98 Old Oak Common's carriage paint shop after the air raid of 25 October 1940. The twisted pile of wreckage in the centre of the photograph is all that remained of TPO vehicle 836
(The National Archives)

yard master, passenger inspector and seat registrar were destroyed, as was Great Western Travelling Post Office vehicle 836 (Fig 98).[17] The nearby engine shed was also badly affected; bomb blast damaged the roof and the ties holding the smoke chutes in place.[18] In truth, however, the yard had escaped lightly; one bomb narrowly missed breaching the banks of the adjacent canal.[19] The following month the GWR board granted £1,275 for the repair of the damaged roads, and in April 1941 it authorised a further £2,519 to protect the glazed roofing of the carriage and locomotive workshops.[20]

It was obvious that the depot's existing air raid shelters could not guarantee the safety of carriage workers. Shortly after the second raid, plans were drawn up to convert the ground-floor office at the back of the carriage paint shop into a reinforced concrete dormitory and shelter (Figs 99–100).[21] Ninety-six bunks were to be provided. The drawings indicate that the existing 4½in brick walls were to be trebled in thickness, whilst concrete slab-roofed baffle walls of the same thickness were to be built to protect the two doorways. The structure was to be strengthened by the addition of an internal steel frame of re-used RSJs, whilst the roof of the (unreinforced) first-floor office was to be covered with sandbags. The conversion was undertaken by Terson & Co for £1,675.[22] Re-use was commonplace at a time when supplies were scarce and subject to stringent control, but even long after the war had ended the use of salvaged materials continued.

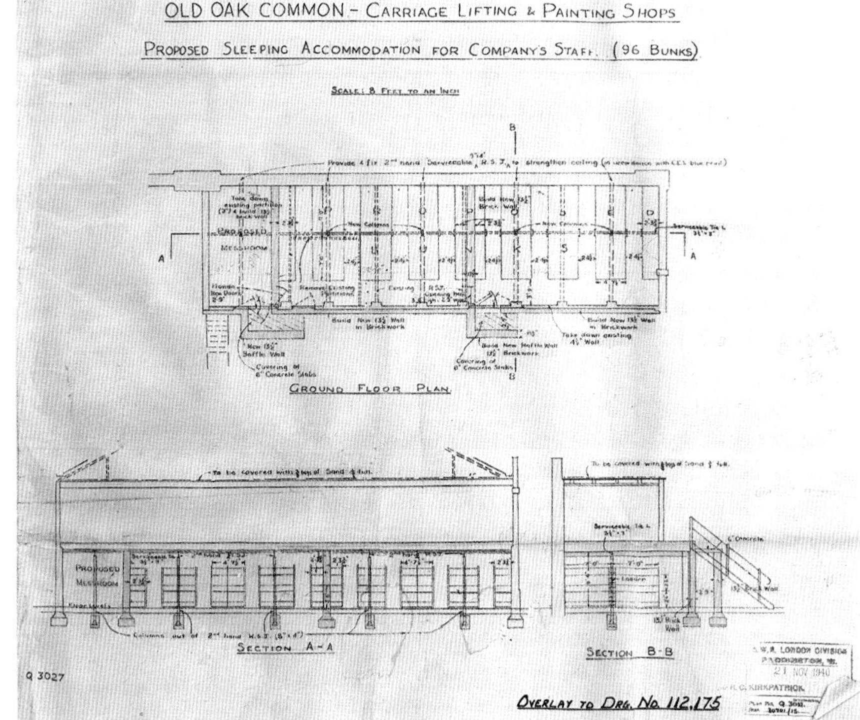

Fig 99 In November 1940 the GWR board approved a conversion of the carriage paint shop stores and offices into an emergency shelter and dormitory (WSHC 2515/403/0361(A))

Fig 100 The internal shelter and dormitory in Old Oak Common's carriage paint shop survived in adapted form until the depot closed

An example came to light during the partial demolition of the paint shop's offices in 2010. A partition was found to have been made from the planks of an ex-LMS or LNER standard goods wagon, the base of one over-written with the script '… ON' above a black painted panel on which had been written '12T'.[23]

On the other side of London the LNER's Ilford Goods Depot was also suffering. A high-explosive bomb destroyed the engine shed, and the main line railway and stabling sidings also suffered direct hits. But by far the worst affected area was London's docklands, which were peppered with over 25,000 bombs (Fig 101). Little escaped damage. The eastern side of the northern single tunnel section of Silvertown Tunnel (Gazetteer No. 138), which carried the North Woolwich line beneath the passage between

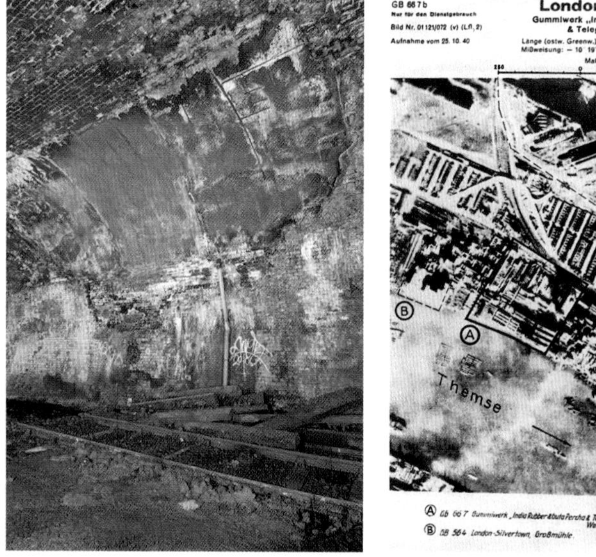

Fig 102 (left) Silvertown Tunnel required patch repair after it was punctured by a bomb

Fig 101 (right) 1941 Luftwaffe photograph of the North Woolwich line as it threaded through Silvertown
(H1763, Newham Archives and Local Studies Library Collection)

Royal Victoria and Royal Albert docks, was penetrated by a bomb and hastily repaired with shuttered concrete reinforced with steel mesh (Fig 102).[24] Custom House station was damaged on the first night of the Blitz on 7 September 1940, and worse befell North Woolwich station during the same raid.

Oddly, given that Paddington station was as much a target as Old Oak Common, the clerical staff at the depot were transferred to new office accommodation at the station during 1942.[25] The depot's offices were then converted into a canteen. During the opening ceremony the GWR made much of its munificence, and the chairman of the canteen committee, driver Henry Holsgrove, spoke 'of the hardships which the men had experienced under rationing conditions without the facilities they had now been granted'.[26] Although railway work was a reserved occupation, which already entitled footplate staff to extra cheese, tea, condensed milk and soap, the provision of the canteen would undoubtedly have been very well received. In an era where provisions were scarce, food was a constant source of conversation. Across the land, railway staff had joined the Dig for Victory campaign and all manner of out-of-the-way patches of railway ground were cultivated. The sports field and flower plantations at the GWR's Hayes Estate were turned over to allotments for the duration of the war, and it may be that the allotments sandwiched between the coal stacks and sidings of Ilford Goods Depot, first mapped on the Railway Executive's detailed site plan of 1953, originated in the same way.[27] Even the edges of canals were used – a GWR plan of Old Oak Common from 1946 shows allotments balanced precariously between the towpath of the canal and the yard's coal stacking grounds.[28]

Towards the end of March 1944, as the war entered its final phase, the Ministry of War Transport instructed the GWR on its behalf to build accommodation at Old Oak Common for US Army troops.[29] It is not known where this accommodation was, but the £2,920 allocated was an insignificant sum, which suggests it was strictly of a temporary nature. Indeed, it may have been little more than an upgrading of the carriages which a gang of Direct Labour men, excavating space for three extra stock lines beside the carriage sheds, had 'retrieved from various scrap yards' and converted into living quarters.[30] These were still being lived in by railwaymen in February 1947 when they were mentioned in an exchange in the House of Commons.[31] Walters, in his book *London: the Great Western Railway Lines,* refers to Italian prisoners-of-war (POWs) being billeted in Old Oak Common's carriage paint shop.[32] This is certainly possible, for of course it boasted a secure dormitory, and there were many hundreds of thousands of Italian POWs in the country between 1941 and 1946. Indeed one of them, John Salvatore Zuncheddu, remembers being held briefly at a camp in Acton during July 1941.[33] However, supporting evidence for such billets is hard to come by and it is equally likely that the POWs were simply brought in every day to clean carriages, as happened at Bristol Bath Road during 1943.[34] In fact, by 1944 Italian prisoners had much freedom, and a number were found to be living in government requisitioned houses in Acton.[35]

War in Europe ended in May 1945. Six years of hostilities had left Britain's railways in a parlous state. Nearly 400 railway staff had lost their lives whilst on duty, and over 2,400 had been injured.[36] The Big Four railway companies had collectively lost many hundreds of locomotives, coaches and wagons. Investment had stalled, as had practically all idea of modernisation. Some lines, like the LNER's branch from Custom House to Gallions, never reopened to passenger traffic after they were bombed.[37] To mark the end of the war the REC published several celebratory posters (Fig 103). At the bottom, the names of the Big Four were prominently displayed. Within three years these names had passed into history. On 1 January 1948 'British Railways', the new name for the country's nationalised railway, was born.

IN WAR AND PEACE
WE SERVE
GWR · LMS · LNER · SR

Fig 103 *In War and Peace We Serve* by Reginald Mayes, 1945 (NRM/Science and Society Picture Library)

NOTES

1 Bell 1946, 69; Drummond 2010, 53

2 The supply of coal to power the industry was a perennial problem. In August 1941, for instance, it was noted that the railways were down to their last three weeks supply (Hansard HC Deb 05 August 1941 vol 373) and severe weather in December 1944 and January 1945 meant that by February 1945 stacks contained only the equivalent of two week's consumption (Bell 1946, 114).

3 GWR Minutes of the Board of Directors No. 55, 1938-1941, TNA RAIL 250: 58, 120, 225; GWR Minutes of the Board of Directors No. 57, 1943-1945, RAIL 250/60

4 The first 43 locomotives were transferred to the LNER works at Doncaster for completion. Eventually, each of the four British railway companies was deploying the locomotives to replace lost stock and increase the capacity of the British railway system. The first American locomotive was handed to the GWR at Paddington on December 11 1942 (Bell 1946, 112).

5 Bell 1946, 5

6 Ibid, 56

7 Joby 1984, 110

8 Wojtczak 2005, 147

9 Marc Nusbaumer, *A Bristolian Train Driver Recalls WW II*, www.britain-at-war.org.uk/WW2/Bristolian_Train_Driver, accessed 14 March 2014. Mustard in colour, gas detection paint turned red on contact with gas.

10 GWR Minutes of the Board of Directors No. 55, 1938-1941, TNA RAIL 250/58, 418; Hawkins and Reeve 1987, 97

11 BR WR drawing 'Old Oak Common MPD Proposed Accommodation for Gas Turbine & Diesel Electric Locomotives', August 1952, WSHC 2515/403/2194; Hawkins and Reeve 1987, 97. They raise the possibility that their removal to Wales did not occur.

12 These consisted of 3.7in Heavy Anti-Aircraft guns, augmented in 1943 by a complement of 5.25in guns and a nearby 'Z' battery of 64 static rocket launchers (Dobinson 2001, 249, 573)
13 Faultless undated, 6
14 Joby 1984, 112
15 GWR drawing 'Old Oak Common Loco Yard Survey, September 1943', WSHC 2525/410/0672
16 ERO D-Z 346-3003-53
17 Old Oak Common Division, Damage Caused by Enemy Action, 1940, TNA RAIL 253/309; Hosegood 1991, 22
18 Hawkins and Reeve 1987, 104
19 Wilson 2006, 242
20 GWR Minutes of the Board of Directors No. 55, 1938-1941, 305, TNA RAIL 250/58; the roof protection contract was awarded to James Clark & Eaton Ltd (GWR Minutes of the Board of Directors No. 55, 1938-1941, TNA RAIL 250/58, 396)
21 21 November 1940, drawing number Q.3027, an overlay to Swindon drawing 112175, dated 26 Sept 1938, WSHC 2515/403/0361(A)
22 GWR Minutes of the Board of Directors No. 56, 1941-1943, TNA RAIL 250/59, 474
23 I am grateful to Tanya Jackson for this identification.
24 Silvertown Tunnel was later known as Connaught Tunnel.
25 GWR Minutes of the Board of Directors No. 56, 1941-1943, TNA RAIL 250/59, 90
26 Hawkins and Reeve 1987, 96
27 McKenna 1980, 54: Railway Executive Eastern Region drawing 'Ilford Carr Depot', dated 1953, ERO D-Z 346-3003-53
28 GWR drawing 'Old Oak Common Locomotive Yard Proposed Locomotive Oil Fuelling Plant', received 08/10/1946, WSHC 2525/410/1187
29 GWR Minutes of the Board of Directors No. 57, 1943-1945, TNA RAIL 250/60, 154
30 Hawkins and Reeve 1987, 95
31 Hansard HC Deb 17 February 1947 vol 433
32 Walters 1993
33 http://www.bbc.co.uk/history/ww2peopleswar/stories/02/a3936602.shtml, accessed 26 Mar 2014
34 Marc Nusbaumer, *A Bristolian Train Driver Recalls WW II*, www.britain-at-war.org.uk/WW2/Bristolian_Train_Driver, accessed 14 March 2014
35 Hansard HC Deb 04 October 1944 vol 403
36 Wojtczak 2005, 148
37 Marden 2013, 95

CHAPTER 7

FROM NATIONALISATION TO MODERNISATION: LONDON'S RAILWAYS 1945–1965

Almost from their inception there have been calls for Britain's railways to be nationalised, and tracts like Emil Davies' 1908 'The Nationalisation of Railways' circulated widely.[1] It is not surprising, therefore, that in the years following the end of war there was a groundswell of opinion in favour of the railways, like the coal mines, being taken into state ownership. As early as October 1940 a paper advocating the creation of a national transport monopoly was circulating within Government, and the post-war debate was not of whether to nationalise, but of how far public ownership would extend into the nation's hitherto privately-owned transport network.[2] In November 1946 the Government finally published its Transport Bill. This far-reaching proposal set out to establish 'a publicly-owned system of inland transport (other than by air) and of port facilities'.[3] The Transport Act followed in 1947, and on January 1 1948 the four main-line railways and nearly all the smaller railway undertakings in Britain were vested in the newly formed British Transport Commission (BTC). The BTC in turn delegated the management, operation and maintenance of the railways to the Railway Executive, which became the employer of all railway staff.

Until nationalisation the railways remained marshalled as they had been during the war. The Railway Executive Committee continued to meet, and did so throughout 1946. The 'Big Four', to a greater or lesser extent, busied themselves in a defence against impending nationalisation, and found time to plan for a rebuilding and modernisation of their networks. Much effort was also spent in addressing the practical difficulties of operating a railway in the aftermath of a war, in a time of shortages, industrial disputes and the bitter winter of 1947.

One immediate difficulty was securing a reliable supply of fuel. A national shortage of coal developed during 1946 and led the railway companies to actively pursue conversion of their coal-fired steam locomotives to oil. In March 1946 the GWR decided to convert ten freight locomotives, and four months later sanctioned the conversion of thirty-four express passenger locomotives.[4]

Fig 104 The fuel delivery siding at Old Oak Common in 2011. Almost everything in this picture was installed in 1946

At the same time they ordered that oil storage tanks be installed at Plymouth, Bristol, Newton Abbot, Cardiff, Swindon and Old Oak Common in Acton.[5] Plans for a fuelling point (Gazetteer No. 31) on the former coal stacking ground along the northern perimeter of Old Oak Common were issued at the end of September, and a contract with Simmons & Hawkes was signed in March of the following year.[6]

The plans show two heavy fuel oil tanks, each with a capacity of 176,000 gallons and each of 34ft 6in diameter and 30ft 2in height (one of these later being referred to as a temporary tank). A boiler house surmounted by a 400 gallon water tank drove steam pumps accommodated in the adjoining pump house, and there were three fuelling stations and ten unloading points beside a new, dedicated siding (Fig 104; building N, Fig 115).

By July 1946 the Minister of Fuel and Power was telling the House of Commons:

> *'I realised some time ago that it would be necessary to effect a measure of conversion from coal burning to fuel oil, if we were to survive next winter. We entered into negotiations with industrial concerns, and, in particular, with the railway companies, and I am very glad to say that, so far as one company is concerned—the Great Western Railway—they have already effected the conversion of 10 locomotives, and are in process of converting, I think, round about another 40.'*[7]

The Government decided to sponsor a large-scale programme of conversion, and in October 1946 they estimated that when the scheme was fully operational the national saving in coal would be 20,000 tons a week and the consumption of heavy fuel oil 16,000 tons.[8] The whole experiment floundered once it became obvious that the country had insufficient foreign exchange to pay for the oil, which of course had to be imported.[9] Few mourned its passing. The fuel had by all accounts been thoroughly unpleasant to handle, so viscous that it had to be passed through a heater before it could be pumped into a locomotive's tender, and then steam-heated again before it could be injected into the fire box.[10] The project did, however, have at least one benefit. The refuelling points were easily converted and allowed the newly formed British Railways (Western Region) to begin experiments with gas turbine and, later, diesel locomotives.

At a time when Britain was in thrall to the power of technological advancement, the use of gas turbines to power locomotives (and, indeed, road vehicles) was enthusiastically received. In the summer of 1946 the GWR's board placed an order for a prototype gas turbine-electric locomotive from the Swiss manufacturer Brown, Boveri.[11] The new locomotive, delivered in 1949 and entering service in 1950, was designed to run on heavy fuel oil (Fig 105). A second, British-built locomotive was supplied by Metropolitan-Vickers and arrived in 1951. The latter used aviation fuel and proved to be more expensive to run than its Swiss counterpart.[12]

By March 1949 drawings had been issued to illustrate how Old Oak Common's heavy fuel oil facility could be converted to fuel gas turbine and diesel locomotives.[13] Both heavy oil tanks, now labelled as having a

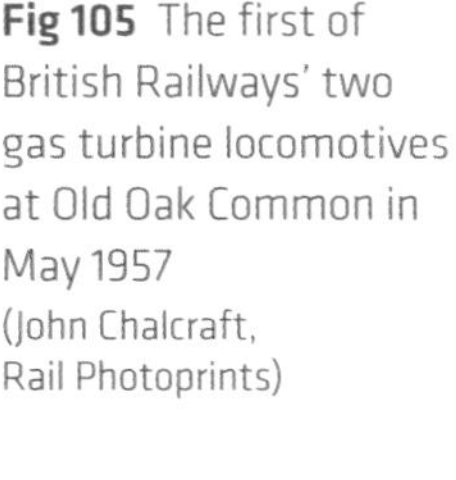

Fig 105 The first of British Railways' two gas turbine locomotives at Old Oak Common in May 1957
(John Chalcraft, Rail Photoprints)

capacity of 170,000 gallons, were to be removed and the hexagonal brick base of one was instead to carry a pair of 30ft x 9ft horizontal heavy oil tanks 'from Didcot'. In addition, a 6,000 gallon diesel oil tank was shown to the east of the pump house (this is sketched in pencil onto the 1946 plan). One existing steam-driven pump was to be used for the heavy oil, the other was 'to come away'. Steam would now also be piped from the shed. The scheme appears to have been modified during 1952; a plan issued in February of that year shows that one of the large-capacity heavy oil tanks was now to be retained, and one of the 12,000 gallon diesel oil tanks from Didcot would instead replace the 6,000 gallon diesel tank.[14] Inside the pump house there was a Lee-Howl double-acting piston pump driven by a 2 bhp motor to pump the diesel oil, and a J P Hall horizontal duplex steam-driven pump for the heavy fuel oil (Fig 106). With little money for new investment British Railways opted to install second-hand boilers from two Victorian 2301 Class locomotives to generate the steam.[15] Presumably, the planned increase in diesel oil storage capacity shown on the 1952 plan reflected the impending arrival at Old Oak Common of D3000 diesel shunters.[16]

The new gas turbine locomotives were 'the apple of Swindon's eye and cossetted accordingly'.[17] In August 1952 the company issued a drawing for a shed to house both them and diesel-electric locomotives.[18] This rectangular building was to sit to the east of the refuelling facilities and be formed by the 'recovered structure from the ash shelters'. It would span two roads, one through and one stopping inside the building over a 100ft pit. A small oil and materials store and an inspector's office were to be attached to one of the gables. This plan, never enacted, is interesting for its suggestion that at the time the Western Region were readying themselves

Fig 106 Detail from a 1952 drawing showing the proposed fuelling arrangements for diesel and gas turbine locomotives at Old Oak Common (WSHC 2515/406/1388)

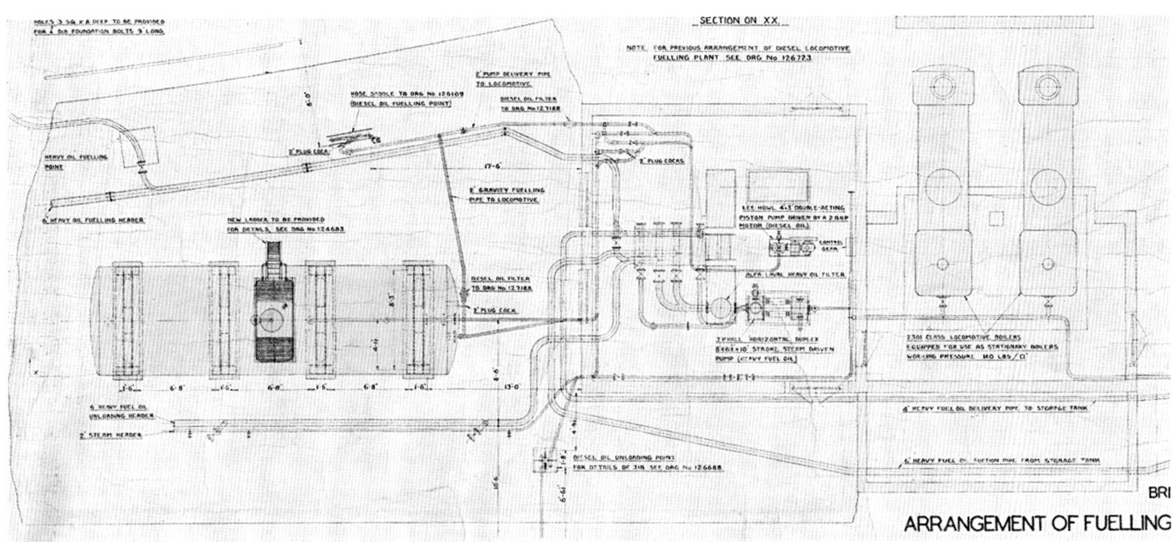

to operate diesel-electric locomotives, whereas it transpired that the BTC chose them as the test bed for diesel-hydraulic traction.

Despite wishing otherwise, Swindon soon found that their gas-turbine locomotives could not be run frequently enough at optimum speeds to deliver good fuel economy. They were also complicated to service and proved less reliable than had been hoped. Locomotive 18000 was eventually withdrawn from service in 1960, two years after its sister had been returned to Metropolitan-Vickers for conversion into a bespoke electric test locomotive.

While the GWR experimented with gas turbine propulsion, the LNER resumed their electrification of the London Liverpool Street to Shenfield line.[19] Engineering work had begun in the late 1930s but had been deferred on the outbreak of war. Finally finished in 1949 this major project required that Ilford Goods Depot, hitherto primarily a coal yard and stabling area for suburban services, be converted into an Electric Maintenance Unit (EMU, Fig 107). By July 1948 the site, now known as Ilford Car Sheds, was dominated by new buildings to house inspections, running repairs and carriage cleaning.[20] A detailed plan drawn up by British Railways (Eastern Region) in 1953 provides the detail necessary to understand how the depot worked.[21] A vast running shed (Workshop A, Figs 108, 110 and 111) housed a repair area serviced by three roads; in a smaller conjoining building to the south trains were inspected on a four-day cycle. Smaller buildings attached to the northern elevation provided accommodation for a large machine shop, stores, offices and lavatories (Fig 109).

A large cleaning shed and its ancillary stores and welfare buildings lay to the east (Workshop B). These buildings, like Workshop A, survive, albeit in altered form. The coal depot and its sidings to the north-west of the yard were retained, as were the cattle dock, milk wharf and general goods sidings to the south of the running lines.

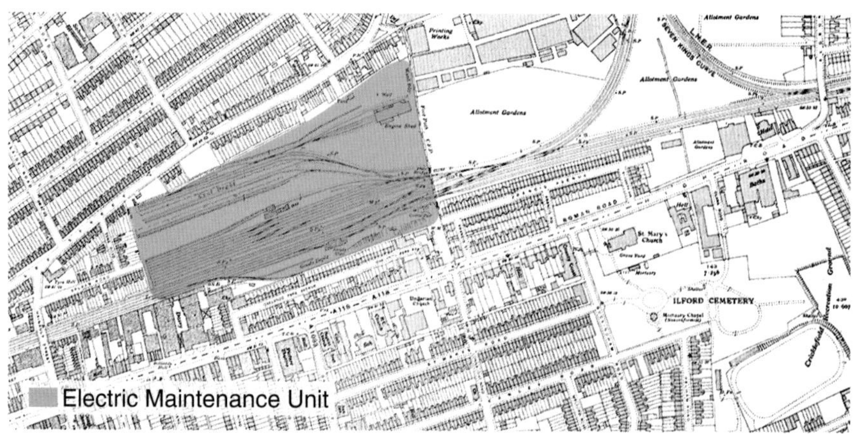

Fig 107 Ilford Goods Depot in 1938. The following year works to electrify the main line reached Ilford (detail from the 1938 Ordnance Survey New Series 25in Sheets 78-15 and 78-16) (Groundsure)

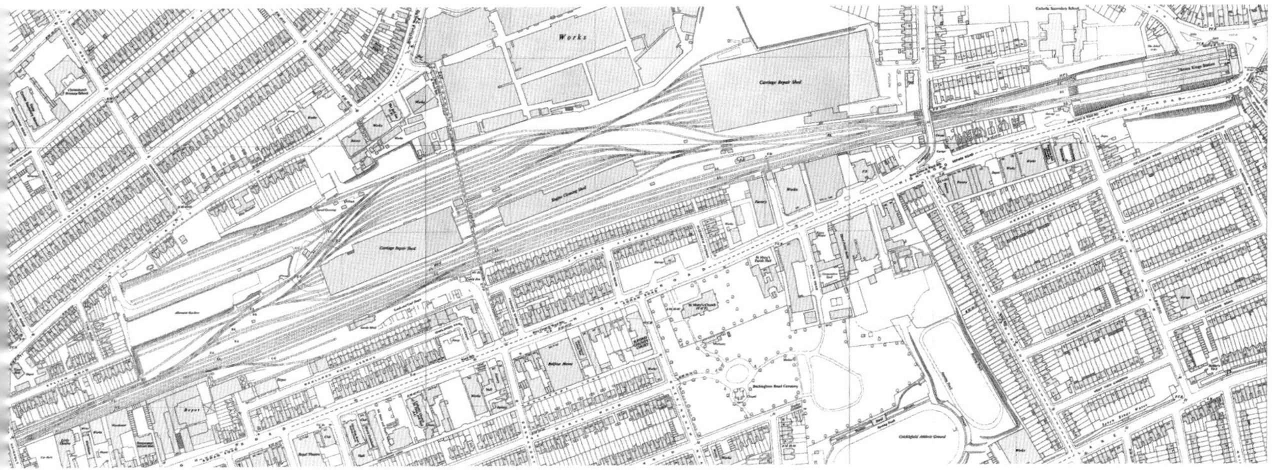

To the east of the goods depot the Fairlop Loop, a branch line to Woodford which had opened in 1903, formed a triangular junction with the main line. To accommodate the EMU it was necessary to remove the western arm of this triangle, and in 1955, with a 16-road carriage shed being proposed for the site, the removal of the remaining arm of the junction was decided upon. Passenger connections through the loop duly ceased on 19 March 1956.[22] A detailed plan drawn up in January of that year shows the new carriage shed, labelled as the 'New Inspection Shed', to be so vast (656ft 6in by 257ft 6in) that it required the demolition of some of Plessey's adjoining buildings, described on the plan as being 'on BTC land'.[23] The shed remains operational. At the same time there were new proposals for Workshop A. The inspection area was to have two of its three

Fig 108 An Ordnance Survey map of 1962 shows how the former goods depot at Ilford had evolved into a fully functional maintenance depot

Fig 109 The workshops and offices attached to Ilford EMU's Workshop A, pictured in 2013

Fig 110 (left) A 1930s design (although not delivered until the late 1940s), the LNER's Shenfield AM6 rolling stock survived in service until the 1980s. Pictured here being overhauled in Ilford Depot's Workshop A in 1969 (NRM/ Science and Society Picture Library NRM 1995-7233_LIVST_RC_251)

Fig 111 (right) Ilford Depot's Workshop A is now used by Bombardier to service Abellio Greater Anglia rolling stock. Photo taken in 2013

roads removed and its pits infilled. The stores were then to be relocated to the western half of this newly created space. In addition, a second washing plant was confirmed for the site. In a sign of the times, all of these post-war drawings show that a small car-park was now deemed necessary.

Several other significant railway schemes for the capital had their gestation in the years immediately following the war. In January 1946 and again in March 1948 the Railway (London Plan) Committee reported on the results of their studies into railway planning, the need for which Patrick Abercrombie had identified in the County of London Plan of 1943 and Greater London Plan of 1944.[24] The various recommendations included proposals for cross-London railway tunnels, several of sufficient size to take main-line stock. The proposals were taken forward by the London Plan Working Party, and approved by the BTC.[25] In the event, only Route C was ever built – as the Victoria Line – and the proposals for east-west links were not to resurface again until 1974.[26]

The Modernisation Plan 1955

If by 1953 the Railway Executive could point to a number of successes, including the restoration of Britain's main-line tracks to their pre-war condition, their continued existence was in doubt.[27] There was a sense amongst some politicians that the body formed an unnecessary layer of bureaucracy, and with the impending demise of the Road Haulage Executive they suggested that this would soon become all too obvious. The 1953 Transport Act gave the Minister the authority to abolish both, which he duly did, and for the first time the BTC had a free hand to run the railways.[28] Eighteen months later they published their plan for the future. The *Modernisation and Re-Equipment of British Railways*, more commonly known as the Modernisation Plan, set five major objectives to be achieved within ten years: improvement of track and signalling, replacement of steam as a form of motive power, replacement of much of the existing passenger rolling stock, drastic remodelling of freight services, and expenditure on sundry other items such as the packet ports, staff welfare and office mechanisms.[29]

Action was swift. The BTC proposed that no new express passenger or suburban steam locomotives would be built after the 1956 programme, and any steam locomotive would cease to be built 'within a few years'.[30] They saw the future of motive power to be a combination of electric and diesel traction, although they stressed that the plan was flexible enough to enable advantage to be taken of any technical developments, 'including gas turbine propulsion'.[31] History has viewed many of the BTC's proposals as being idealistic, and too reliant on change being achievable simply by the use of technology. But, as Tanya Jackson has noted, their proposals need to be seen in the context of the prevailing belief in the ability of technology to make things better.[32] Sensibly, the BTC dismissed the idea of atomic-powered locomotives, accepting that the use of nuclear power in relation to railways was likely to be indirect, through the use of electricity derived from nuclear power stations.[33]

The BTC was keen on the 'importance of incorporating good modern design in all construction and decoration'.[34] To this end they established a Design Panel whose first major project, the Blue Pullman, was hailed a critical triumph.[35] Hitherto Pullmans had been privately-owned and operated carriages which offered a premium service on other companies' trains. In 1954 the BTC indulged in an early example of brand building by purchasing a controlling stake in the Pullman Car Company. The Blue Pullmans, named after the Nanking Blue of their livery, were train-sets that embodied the BTC's vision – diesel-electric multiple units which offered fast, luxurious and air-conditioned travel between important business

Fig 112 Metropolitan Cammell eight car Blue Pullman DMU W60097 at Old Oak Common July 1967 (Hugh Llewelyn CC-SA-2.0)

centres.[36] The Western Region was allocated three sets. BTC guidelines stipulated that diesel multiple units (DMUs) were to be serviced in a separate section of a motive power depot from steam locomotives.[37] With Old Oak Common still primarily a steam locomotive depot, the pre-war carriage paint shop was selected for conversion (Gazetteer No. 20). Plans were issued in the autumn of 1959, and the building was converted during the course of the following year, in time for the trains to enter service in September 1960 (Fig 112).[38] The shed's first-floor offices and messrooms were retained, and the former WWII dormitories on the ground floor were converted into the carpet-cleaning shop. A dedicated 6,000 gallon fuel tank and fuel unloading point for the Pullmans were also provided.

Although the BTC regarded diesel traction as a half-way house to electrification it accepted that the 'dieselisation' of British Railways was a far quicker and cheaper option that avoided significant investment in civil engineering or signalling work.[39] Three years after the Modernisation Plan was published one of the BTC's first diesel locomotives, the North British Locomotive Company's largely unloved D600 'Warship' class of diesel-hydraulic locomotives (later Class 41), was delivered to Swindon. Later that year the Western Region's own Type 4 diesel-hydraulic locomotive, the D800 'Warships' (Class 42), arrived at Laira, their Plymouth depot.[40] Soon, the D800s were joined at Laira by the little Type 2 diesel-hydraulics, the D6300 'Baby Warships' (Class 22). The introduction of these locomotives marked the start ofa process which would in time render whole areas of Old Oak Common redundant.

Preliminary plans for full conversion of the depot to diesel traction were issued at the beginning of the 1960s.[41] A further batch of D3000 (Class 08) shunters arrived during Spring 1960, and later that year plans were issued for the upgrading of the depot's main refuelling point.[42] The 170,000 gallon tank was to be converted from heavy oil to light oil storage, although its smaller horizontal neighbour was to remain a heavy oil tank in order to cater for 'gas turbine locomotives'. The plural was used even though the BTC were by then down to a single example, and this was to be withdrawn from service a few months later. Additional fuelling columns were to be installed in place of the traverser outside the Factory repair shop, and the boiler house was to be removed.

In 1962 D1000 'Western' diesel-hydraulic locomotives (Class 52) started appearing at Old Oak Common, the first main-line diesel locomotives to be allocated to the depot.[43] These were followed in summer 1963 by D7000 diesel-hydraulic 'Hymeks' (Class 35), and in autumn by the first of what became many Class 47 diesel-electric locomotives (Fig 113). The lightweight D6300 began arriving in numbers during 1964, primarily to shuttle empty carriages between Paddington and the depot.

Fig 113 D1000 'Western' locomotives at Old Oak Common in April 1964, with two D7000 Hymeks behind. To the right, just in shot, is the front of a Class 47 diesel-electric locomotive. (R C Riley)

Old Oak Common was therefore expected to maintain four types of main-line diesel locomotive, several of them unique to the Western Region, as well as the Pullmans, the shunting fleet and the residue of their steam locomotive allocation. There were few economies of scale available, and with the collapse of the North British Locomotive Company in 1962 maintenance of NBLC locomotives soon became difficult. The 1967 National Traction Plan called for some order to be applied to the BTC's chaotically assembled locomotive fleet, and in so doing sounded the death knell for diesel-hydraulic traction.

By the time the report appeared Old Oak Common had been free of steam locomotives for several years (although a Ransomes & Rapier 45-ton steam crane, which had been delivered new to the depot in 1940, survived until the late 1970s). Once underway the withdrawal of steam locomotives had been swift, as illustrated by the fate of the GWR's durable 'Castle' class locomotive. In February 1960 there were still 162 examples in operation, of which 33 had lately been allocated to Old Oak Common.[44] Seven were withdrawn that year and three the year after, but 55 left service in 1962 (25 in September alone) and 49 in 1963. By January 1965 there were only a dozen left in service.[45] Old Oak Common became an assembly point for locomotives being prepared for their last journey (Fig 114). In 1964 British Railways had an annual turnover of £20m from scrap alone, and redundant rolling stock travelled far and wide.[46] For example, British Railways issued a Special Traffic Notice in November 1963 to describe the intended route from Old Oak Common to Norwich of three condemned Castles that were 'dead on their own wheels'.[47]

Old Oak Common closed to steam on 27 March 1965.[48] By that time there had been much demolition in order to prepare the depot for its new

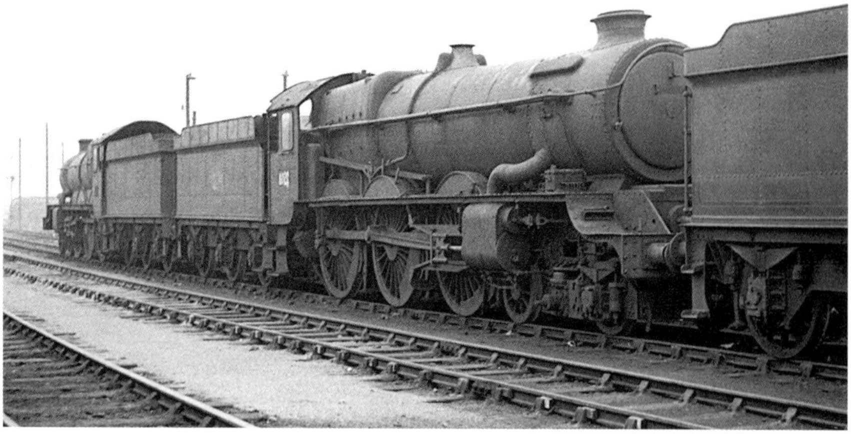

Fig 114 'King' class King George VI at Old Oak Common in December 1963, awaiting removal to Newport for scrapping (Peter Brumby)

Fig 115 By 1966 Old Oak Common had been transformed into one of British Rail's new diesel maintenance depots

role. The largest building to be removed, the Engine Shed, was demolished progressively whilst locomotives continued to shelter beneath it. Demolition had begun in March 1964 but it is clear from a photograph in Chris Leigh's volume on Old Oak Common that the work was still in progress in June 1965.[49]

The new train maintenance depot was officially opened on 20 October 1965 (Fig 115). It offered facilities for the full maintenance of 70 main

A - Carriage Lifting Shed	E - Amenity and Office Block	I - Water Tower	M - Underframe Cleaning Plant	
B - Pullman Shed	F - Stores	J - Water Softening Plant	N - Oil Refueling Facility	
C - Workshop	G - Oil Interceptor	K - Lifting Shop	O - Shunter's Cabin	Q - Signal Box
D - Turntable	H - Sub-station	L - Steam Raising Plant	P - Mess Hut	R - Grand Junction Canal

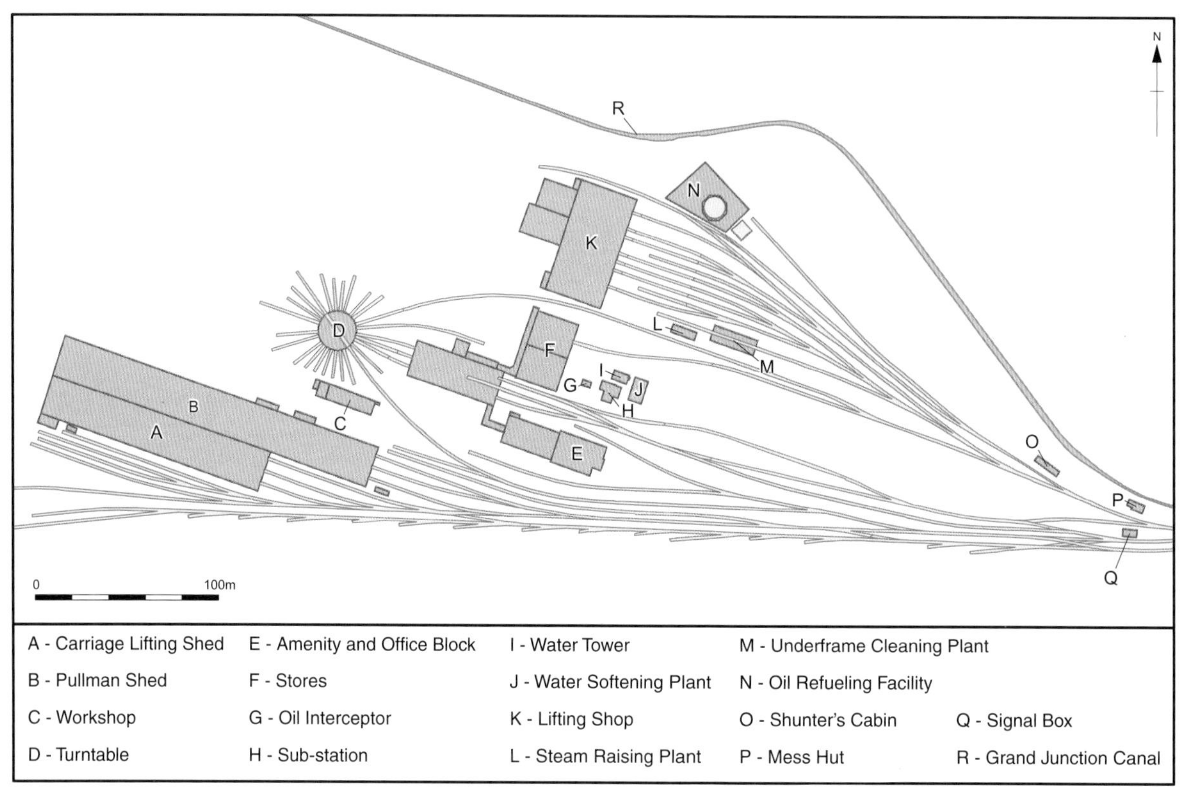

line and 25 shunting diesel locomotives, with daily servicing for 65 locomotives.[50] The transition from steam to diesel locomotion was complete, and with the demise of steam locomotives came the demise of many hitherto essential tasks, almost all of them dirty, dangerous and repetitive. The skills of building and maintaining a fire in a steam locomotive were no longer required. Gone too was the need to laboriously clean out a locomotive's tubes, drop and remove its ash and clinker and rake its firebox clean. Perhaps most importantly, it was no longer necessary for hundreds of tons of coal a week to be transferred by hand from wagons to tubs to tenders.[51]

A diesel locomotive required none of these procedures. At the beginning of each shift the engines could be started with the push of a button and the headlamps lit with the flick of a switch. With a cab at each end the need for turntables was dispensed with, and generally a locomotive needed simply to be refuelled between trips. This systemic change was embodied at Old Oak Common by the replacement in March 1965 of the 'bottom passenger' turntable with a bright and airy steel-framed Cleaning and Servicing Shed (Gazetteer No. 24, Figs 116 to 118). The building spanned three through roads over brightly-lit, half-length pits. Clerestory windows ran the length of the walls above RSJ wall plates. Eight large, projecting roof vents on each pitch kept the building ventilated should the roller doors at either end be closed. Here locomotives were refuelled, their axles and gearboxes topped up with oil and minor parts such as brake blocks replaced. Alongside, a new double-height sand house maintained the supply of dry sand that aided wheel adhesion.

Fig 116 The new versus the old: Old Oak Common on 19 December 1964. The new Cleaning and Servicing Shed had been built and the Engine Shed was in the process of being demolished (David Lennon)

Fig 117 (left) Old Oak Common's Cleaning and Servicing Shed opened in March 1965. This image shows it being readied for demolition in 2010

Fig 118 (right) Old Oak Common's Cleaning and Servicing Shed and semi-detached sand house in 1975 (Martin Addison CC-BY-SA-2.0)

Old Oak Common's turntables, although now surplus to requirements, were not old. In June 1951 Western Region had ordered two replacement 65ft models and a 70ft example from Cowans Sheldon & Co. Ltd of Carlisle, prolific suppliers of turntables to the industry. The larger unit (Gazetteer No. 21, Fig 119) survived the demolition of the engine shed and in 2010 was donated by Crossrail to Swanage Railway Museum (Fig 120).[52] It is assumed that the larger turntable was ordered so that Old Oak Common could accommodate British Railways's 'Britannia' class locomotives, construction of which had begun in January 1951 and which, at 68ft 9in in length, were too long for the depot's existing turntables.

Nothing at Old Oak Common embodied the BTC's Modernisation Plan quite like the New Amenity Building (Gazetteer No. 30, Fig 121). Clean, modern lines, bright colours and extensive use of glass ensured that when it opened in March 1963 it stood in complete contrast to neighbouring

Fig 119 Old Oak Common's 70ft turntable in 2010, immediately prior to its removal

Fig 120 Parts of Cowans Sheldon's 70ft turntable leaving Old Oak Common for Swanage in 2010. The Pullman Shed is in the background

buildings, especially Churchward's office building to which it was connected. Built from a concrete-rendered steel frame with infilling brickwork and first-floor glazed curtain walling, both floors consisted of large open plan rooms with a central row of 'Y'-shaped concrete pillars. The stair tower at the eastern end wrapped round a vertical services duct and climbed to a second-floor plant room. The building was a clear outcome of the BTC's observation in their Modernisation Plan that 'The standards of accommodation and working amenities have a powerful influence on staff recruitment.'[53]

Fig 121 Old Oak Common's new Amenity Building opened in 1963

Fig 122 An interesting feature of the New Amenity Building was an incinerator set into a recess in the wall of the main first-floor office. This had been fabricated by Heenan and Froude of Worcester, and was labelled a 'Horsfall No 5 Destructor'

The BTC's modernisation programme cut deeply into staff numbers and at Old Oak Common many of its semi-skilled and unskilled jobs quickly became obsolete. At the same time, skilled footplate work was transformed. A new redundancy system encouraged older employees to apply for release, and this suited many. As one driver remembered:

> *'A lot of the old steam drivers couldn't accept the change and those 60 and above were offered early retirement. They couldn't be bothered, and there was so much uncertainty regarding the job. Nobody knew what the job would entail, where depots would be sited.'*[54]

In 1953 the number of people employed on the railways had stood at 594,768; by the end of 1962 this number had shrunk to 474,538 and by 1973 the total workforce numbered little more than 250,000.[55] A near halving of the workforce in a decade could not be wholly attributed to the effects of the BTC's Modernisation Plan. At the height of the programme the politicians had taken fright. Modernisation was costing money, and British Railways was deeply in debt. The 1962 Transport Act abolished the BTC and established the British Railways Board (BRB), a new body charged with taking into consideration 'deficits on revenue account arising at any time after the vesting date'.[56] The BRB's first chairman was to be Dr Richard Beeching.

NOTES

1 Davies 1908
2 The paper, by William Coates and Alfred Robinson, was entitled 'The Transport Problem in Great Britain' (Gourvish 1986, 17)
3 The Transport Bill (HMSO) was published on 27 November 1946
4 GWR Minutes of the Board of Directors No. 58, 1945-1947, TNA RAIL 250/62, 46. In 1946 the Central Office Of Information produced a short film in the 'Britain Can Make It' series to emphasise the contribution the railways were making to saving coal.
5 GWR Minutes of the Board of Directors No. 58, 1945-1947, TNA RAIL 250/62, 82
6 GWR drawing 'Old Oak Common Locomotive Yard. Proposed Locomotive Oil Fuelling Plant', September 1946. Drawing No. 123770A, superseded by Drawing No. 123770/B, WSHC 2515/403/2185; GWR drawing 'Old Oak Common Locomotive Yard Proposed Locomotive Oil Fuelling Plant', Drawing No. 123770B, October 1946, WSHC 2525/410/1187; Hawkins and Reeve 1987, 98
7 Hansard HC Deb 24 July 1946 vol 426 cc45-162
8 Hansard HC Deb 17 October 1946 vol 427 c263W
9 The potential costs were estimated to total £300,000 per annum.
10 Hawkins and Reeve 1987, 106
11 GWR Minutes of the Board of Directors No. 58, 1945-1947, TNA RAIL 250/62, 72, 94
12 The Swiss locomotive was given the number 18000, the British example 18100
13 BR (WR) drawing 'Proposed Fuelling Facilities for Gas Turbine Locomotives, Locomotive Oil Fuelling Depot Old Oak Common', March 1949, BR (WR) 127624
14 BR (WR) drawing 'Arrangement of Fuelling Facilities for Diesel and Gas Turbine Locos, Old Oak Common Motive Power Depot', February 1952, WSHC 2515/406/1388
15 These William Dean-designed locomotives had been built in Swindon between 1883 and 1899
16 Four D3000 diesel shunters arrived in October 1953 (www.brdatabase.info, accessed 18 December 2015)
17 Hawkins and Reeve 1987, 106
18 BR (WR) drawing 'Old Oak Common – Motive Power Depot, Pro. Acc. for Gas Turbine and Diesel Elec. Locos', August 1952, BR (WR) 131763, WSHC 2515/403/2194
19 This used the standard 1500V DC overhead system until November 1960 when British Railways switched to a 25KV AC system.
20 Railway Executive drawing, 'Ilford Carriage Sheds and Sidings Proposed Electric Lighting', July 1948, ERO D-Z 346-5003-34
21 Railway Executive drawing, 'Ilford Carr. Depot', 1953, ERO D-Z 346-3003-53. See also 'Safety Line', a 10 minute film devoted to the activities undertaken at the depot. This was produced in 1956 by the Essex Education Committee County Film Service, East Anglian Film Archive Cat. No. 594.
22 Railway Executive drawing, 'Ilford Carriage Sheds', 1955, ERO D-Z 346-3003-74
23 British Railways Eastern Region, 'Proposed Inspection and Cleaning Shed and Alterations', January 1956, ERO D-Z 346-3003-57
24 Jackson and Croome 1962, 310
25 Loc. cit.
26 Ibid, 330
27 'Rehabilitating British Main Lines', The Railway Magazine, September 1953, 577
28 HMSO, Transport Act 1953, 23
29 British Transport Commission 1955, 6-7
30 Ibid, 11
31 Ibid, 13
32 Jackson 2013, 63

33 British Transport Commission 1955, 13
34 Haresnape 1979, 111
35 Jackson 2013, 72
36 Quoted from an introductory brochure, *Introduction of Pullman Diesel Express Services*, published by British Railways (Western Region) in 1960
37 British Transport Commission, *Modernisation and Re-equipment of British Railways: Design of Motive Power Depots. Part I: Planning a DMU Depot*, 31/03/1956, TNA AN 8/16, 1
38 BR (WR) drawing, 'Old Oak Common Proposed Conversion of Carriage Paint Shop for Diesel Pullman Maintenance', October 1959, WSHC 2525/410/0690
39 British Transport Commission 1955, 12, 16
40 These were scaled-down versions of the German Federal Railway's V200 which used Maybach engines. David Maidment, a WR Traffic Apprentice and former student of German, remembers whilst being based at Old Oak Common being asked by the Shedmaster to translate engine drawings that had arrived from Germany (Maidment 2014, 37)
41 BR (WR) drawing ' Old Oak Common Conversion to Diesel Depot' ('Preliminary Drawing not to be worked to'), undated, WSHC 2515/410/1781
42 BR (WR) drawing, 'Old Oak Common: Proposed Additional Facilities for Servicing Diesel Locos', September 1960, BR (WR) drawing 152798, WSHC 2515/403/2196
43 www.brdatabase.info, accessed 18 December 2015
44 The Old Oak Common figure is for 21 March 1959 (Leigh 1993, 80)
45 The last, *Clun Castle*, was withdrawn in December 1965 but survives (with *Barbury Castle*) in trust ownership at Tylseley Locomotive Works. *Caerphilly Castle* is preserved at Swindon Steam Railway Museum, and *Pendennis Castle* and *Drysllwyn Castle* (now *Earl Bathurst*) are preserved at Didcot Railway Centre. *Thornbury Castle* and *Nunney Castle* are in private hands, and *Ogmore Castle* (now *Defiant*) is held by Quainton Railway Society Ltd.
46 Turnover reference from the 1964 film *'Look at Life – Turn of the Wheel'*, Rank Organisation. Taking into account inflation, this figure was equivalent in 2014 to £362m.
47 Special Traffic Notice, 28th Nov 1963, British Rail, London Midland Region (Western Lines) Z 298/88 (Bedfordshire and Luton Archives and Record Service). Their destination was almost certainly R A King's well-known yard on Hall Road in Norwich where, incidentally, the fate of Castle class locomotive *G J Churchward* was sealed in early 1963.
48 Leigh 1993, 2
49 Ibid, 78
50 Opening ceremony of the new Western Region Diesel Depot Old Oak Common, 02/10/1965, TNA AN 91/12
51 For the sources of the information in this paragraph see McKenna 1980, Joby 1984, Spooner 1986 and Hawkins and Reeve 1987. A fantastic introduction is also provided by *'The Railwaymen: One of a Film Series About Jobs'* produced for the Ministry of Transport by the Central Office of Information, B/C7228, June 1946. The film is partly shot at Old Oak Common and Paddington.
52 Cowans Sheldon & Co Ltd drawings 'General Arrangement for 65' Articulated Engine Turntable', April 1952, WSHC 2515/406/0908; 'General Arrangement for 70' Articulated Engine Turntable', December 1952, WSHC 2515/406/1414
53 British Transport Commission 1955, 28
54 Interview with retired steam engine driver Denis Mansell, who at 16 began as a locomotive cleaner in Gloucestershire in 1947, www.theguardian.com/society/2002/feb/08/publicvoices, accessed 17 February 2014
55 British Railways Board 1963, 50; Gourvish 2002, 67
56 1962 Transport Act, Section 22

CHAPTER 8

DECLINE AND RENEWAL: LONDON'S RAILWAYS 1963 – 2010

Fig 123 Beeching launched the BRB's *The Re-shaping of British Railways* report at Paddington Station on 27 March 1963 (Moore/Hulton/Getty Image 3062681)

In 1963 the newly formed British Railways Board (BRB), under its first chairman, Dr Richard Beeching, published *The Re-shaping of British Railways* (Fig 123). This report, known forever afterwards as the Beeching Report, has been regarded as 'one of the most important single publications on transport on the post-war period'.[1] The report set out the BRB's plans, as enabled by the 1962 Transport Act, for remodelling the railway system 'to suit current needs' and for adapting the Modernisation Plan 'to this new shape'. Although now remembered principally for its public confession of what the BRB had planned for the country's branch lines the provisions it described also had a profound effect on the business of moving freight by rail.

Traditionally, this had been divided into coal-class traffic, mineral traffic and general merchandise, the last itself divided into two groups dependent on whether consignments were large enough to constitute wagonload movement.[2] Wagonload traffic was formed by individual wagons loaded at private sidings or small goods depots before being transferred to marshalling yards for sorting, transporting onwards to destination marshalling yards, and finally taken to other goods depots or private sidings. A sub-category, by the late 1970s all but eradicated by the repeal in 1962 of the railway's common carriers obligation, had been formed by the traffic in sundries (smaller or sometimes individual items hand-stowed and unloaded from 12-ton covered wagons or guard's vans). Whilst in 1961 coal-class traffic remained profitable large swathes of the complex, labour intensive and unprofitable wagonload operation were in inexorable decline.

Beeching analysed the profitability of wagonload movements and concluded that the only group of traffic making a contribution above direct costs was that where private sidings were involved at both ends.[3] Amongst the report's proposals was the closure of small goods depots in order to reduce the passage of uneconomic freight through them. In 1962 the nation's railways still had 5,175 freight stations and goods depots but by 1968 this number had fallen to 912, and by 1973 to 542.[4] Most goods yards were adjuncts of small Victorian stations that served local, often rural, communities. Almost always old and antiquated, these had borne the brunt of the closures. Paddington New Yard in Westbourne Park, London, however, was a city freight depot that had opened in 1908. The site's dominant three-storey transit shed and warehouse was even younger, having been erected in 1938 to store the heavy, seasonal produce of the GWR's rural hinterland (Gazetteer No. 45, Fig 124). It was, perhaps, the country's last classical railway warehouse, and closely resembled the company's warehouse in South Lambeth which had been built in 1929.[5] Both were promoted by the GWR as places where companies could '*Rent a space – the charges are very low – and maintain a stock for your customers. Leave the rest to us; we will execute your orders, performing any services such as sampling, labelling, stocktaking* etc'.[6] After the freight depot closed in December 1972 Alfred Road Warehouse (as it had been named) became a lost property store for British Rail. The yard's sidings outlived the depot, and at least one was later adopted by Tarmac to service the concrete batching plant they established on the site in 1975.[7] The warehouse was demolished in 2010 in preparation for the construction of approach lines to Crossrail's western tunnel portal.

Also affected by Crossrail, and more typical of the small station goods yard, was Plumstead Goods Depot in Kent, which had opened in July 1859 (Gazetteer No. 148, Figs 125 and 126). Like many, this had been both a station goods yard and an exchange point for a nearby works, in this case the sprawling Royal Woolwich Arsenal. It was the closure of this site which had hastened the yard's demise in December 1967.[8] Uncommonly, for Plumstead there was to be a temporary reprieve when

Fig 124 Alfred Road Warehouse, pictured in October 1963 (R C Riley)

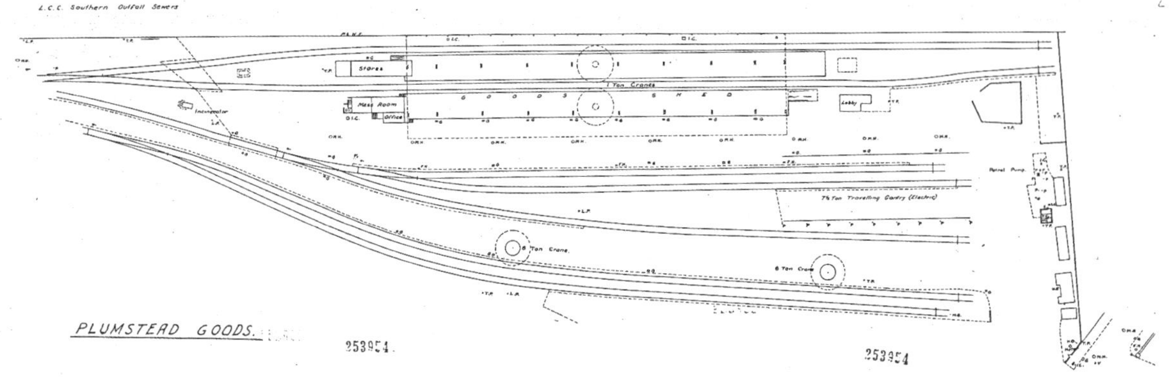

Fig 125 Plumstead Goods Depot in 1951 (Network Rail drawing 253954)

the yard re-opened in December 1971 to serve paper and coal traffic. There was to be no such stay of execution for many of the other goods yards which later became incorporated within Crossrail's works. Maidenhead Goods Yard, which had opened in 1871, closed in 1966 (Gazetteer No. 1); North Woolwich Goods Yard closed in December 1970 and most of Ilford Goods Depot closed in May 1968, although the United Dairies milk dock remained marked on maps until *c* 1980.[9] By then British Rail was carrying little more than half the freight it had in 1950 and its trainload operations (the operation of a complete train for a single end user) now far outstripped its wagonload business.[10]

Fig 126 A 1970s goods shed at Plumstead Goods Depot shortly before its demolition in 2012

Explicit in Beeching's report was the need for much greater efficiency on the railways. The adoption in the early 1970s of TOPS, the American computerised Total Operations Processing System, was a successful part of British Rail's response to this need, although it came too late to save the wagonload business.[11] Another 1970s success was the Inter-City 125 (the HST), a train widely regarded as one of the finest of its generation.[12] To facilitate its deployment on the Western Region a new depot was built at Old Oak Common, on the site of Churchward's 1905 carriage shed. This continues in use under the control of First Great Western.

A further development from the same period was the resurrection of ideas for a cross-London railway. In 1974 a steering group was set up by the Department of the Environment and the Greater London Council. Its remit was to look at future transport needs and strategic plans for London and the South East. The London Rail Study's 1974 report advocated a northern tunnel to join British Rail's Western Region to its Eastern Region (Fig 127). There would be new stations at Paddington, Marble Arch, Bond Street, Leicester Square, Holborn and Liverpool Street. A southern tunnel would connect the Southern Region's Central Division services via stations at Victoria, Piccadilly, Leicester Square, Blackfriars, Monument and London Bridge.

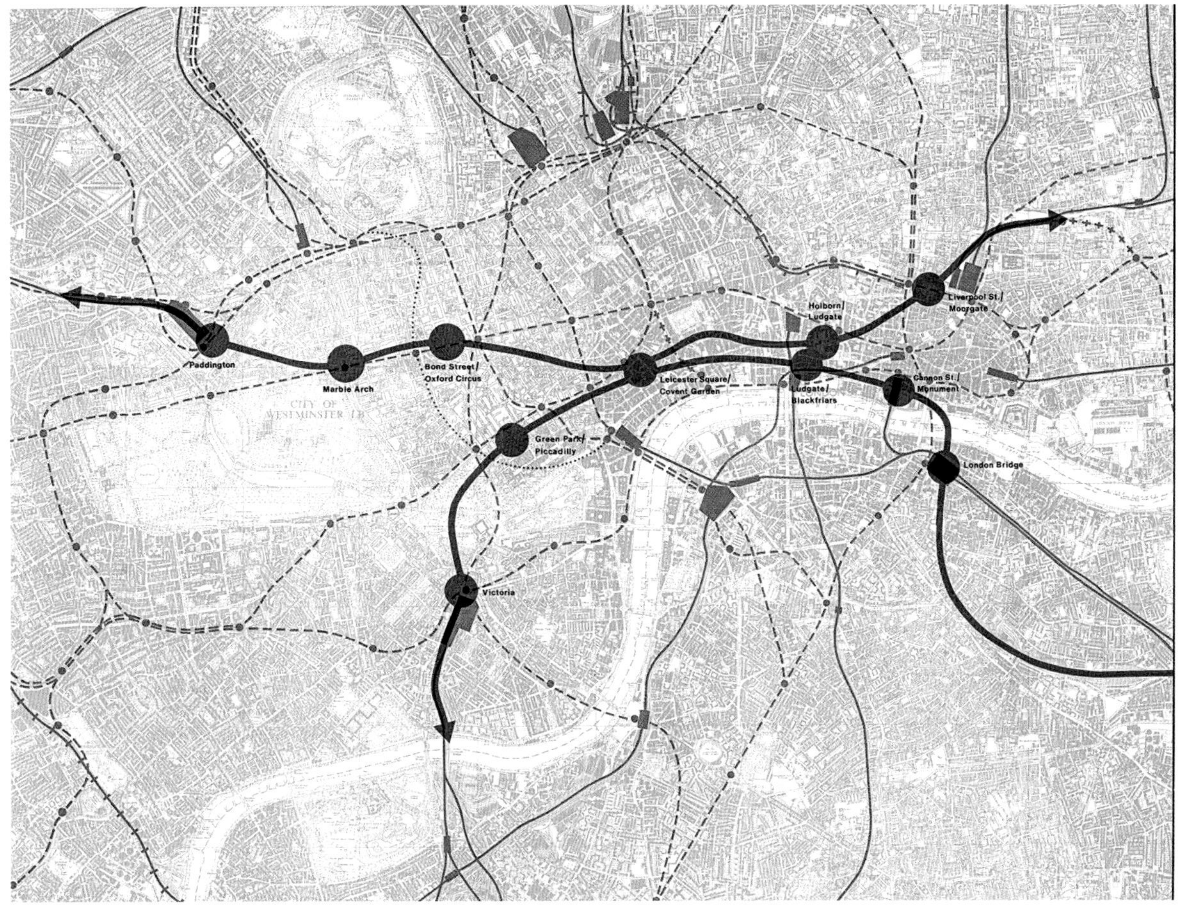

Fig 127 The 1974 London Rail Study advocated new tunnels to connect British Rail's Western Region with its Eastern Region, and Victoria station with London Bridge (Crossrail)

Crucially, the 1974 study acknowledged the conclusions of earlier reports that Crossrail needed to be a main-line railway that just happened to spend a good deal of time underground. It was, the steering group, noted 'an imaginative and exciting solution to the problems of overcrowded public transport in central London.'

An estimated cost of £300 million meant that the proposal remained just that. As Terry Gourvish has noted, 'In the 1970s and 1980s such schemes had little or no chance of attracting government support', and this was the predictable result of the next proposal as well.[13] In 1980 a BRB discussion paper proposed a cross-London rail link that featured three route options, all involving deep bored tunnels, and a cost of £330 million.[14] The favoured option linked existing infrastructure north and south of London, rather than focusing on east to west travel, with the major connection points being at Victoria and Euston. Benefits included a reduction in the overall journey time and the removal of a need for one or two interchanges. It also considered how such a route would relate to other major schemes, with the Channel Tunnel, the various schemes to improve rail access to London airports and the Electrification Review all being singled out for mention.[15] Further, indirect benefits were seen to include a transfer of traffic from London Transport Underground services, something that is still very much an objective of Crossrail today.

Although the 1980 paper, like its predecessor, did not lead to any immediate development of the concept, its prediction of looming transport congestion proved accurate. By the late 1980s, it was clear that existing Underground and rail capacity was approaching its limits. The Government therefore commissioned a joint study by the Department of Transport, Network South East, London Regional Transport and London Underground. Their Central London Rail Study, published in January 1989, further evaluated many of the 1974 options, including East-West Crossrail (Fig 128).[16] The total cost of the many schemes presented in the 1989 paper was in the region of £5 to £6 billion, sums deemed unacceptable by the Government. Therefore, only two schemes were chosen for further study; the Jubilee line extension and the £1.4 billion East-West Crossrail.

Fig 128 Crossrail route options given in the 1989 Central London Rail Study. Image from the Railways Archive website (Department of Transport)

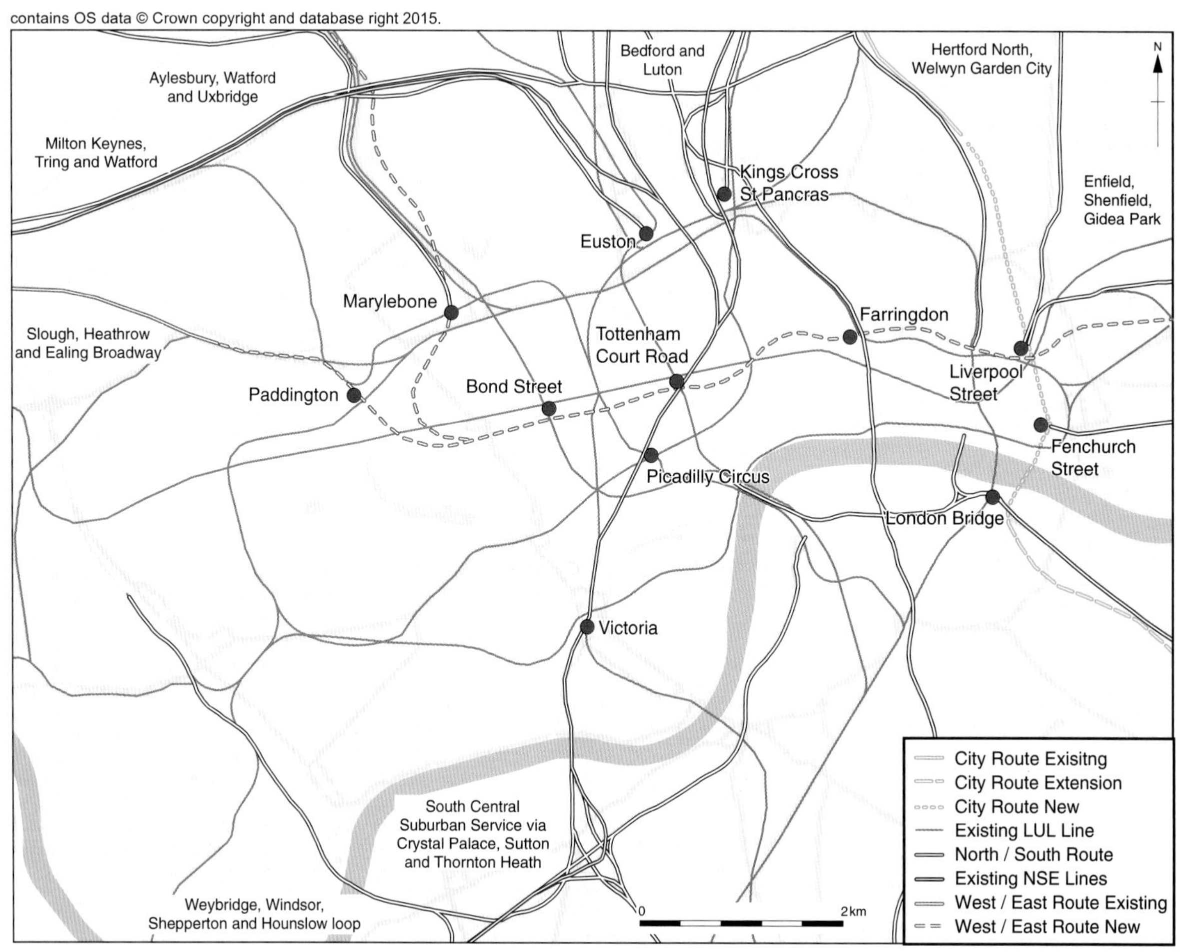

In October 1990 the Government endorsed the Crossrail scheme and gave a limited go-ahead to London Transport and the BRB to start developing it, with the intention of opening in 1999.[17] In January of the following year a Bill promoted by the two transport organisations was submitted to Parliament. It provided for the construction of a new underground railway commencing west of Paddington station and terminating east of Liverpool Street station, to connect on either side with existing BRB railways. It also provided for the construction of a new railway on what it termed the Thames Valley railway at Old Oak Common, which would have connected the new underground railway with the Metropolitan and Chiltern lines.[18]

Hopes that the scheme would proceed were high, but a significant hurdle was introduced when the Government announced that Crossrail should proceed only as a joint venture with the private sector.[19] The passengers who would benefit and the developers of nearby property who would gain were identified as major sources of such income. This financing model became increasingly less certain once both groups began to feel the effects of an economic recession in the early 1990s, and with the estimated costs of Crossrail rising to £2.38 billion in 1992, the project was 'effectively put on a care and maintenance basis'.[20] The bill was finally scuppered by a Private Bill Committee decision in May 1994 that a case had not been made.

This was not, however, the end of the matter. In July 1994 it was announced that the project would be pushed forward under the Transport and Works Act (TWA), and in November a major advance was achieved when the route was legally safeguarded.[21] Thereafter, any development proposal within the route corridor had to ensure that it did not conflict with the proposal. A small team was set up within London Underground to manage the safeguarding.

Work on the application for powers under the TWA continued into 1995. In May, the Secretary of State for Transport reported that this was being done in parallel with a study which the promoters were undertaking at his request.[22] The study was charged with examining Crossrail's proposed structure and ownership under the railway privatisation arrangements, as well as the advantages and disadvantages of possible small-scale alternatives to the scheme.

However, by April 1996 it had become apparent that the Government was in no hurry to proceed with the project. In a written answer to the House of Lords the Under Secretary of State for Transport reported that the Government had asked the chairs of London Transport, Railtrack and British Rail not to proceed for the time being with an application under the TWA.[23] Further, he reported that the chairman of Railtrack had been asked to consider the project further once Railtrack was in the private sector, 'in the light of the Government's continued firm policy that Crossrail should proceed only as a joint venture with a substantial private sector contribution'. The Crossrail project was once more to be cast in a different light, this time the dawn of a new era; rail privatisation.

Privatisation

In the early 1980s the Government began identifying BRB businesses that could be privatised. Those activities of an obviously non-core nature, such as Seaspeed (the hovercraft division), Superbreak (British Transport Hotel's provider of mini holidays) and British Transport Hotel's wines division were quickly sold. Larger assets like Sealink, the descendant of the railways' pre-nationalisation packet port operations, were disposed of from 1984 onwards. At the same time there had now begun a process known as 'sectorisation', whereby British Rail's regional structure gave way to business-led sectors such as Parcels and Inter-City. By the late 1980s some of these sectors were themselves fragmenting into new companies, usually wholly-owned by the BRB and established with the intention of being transferred into private hands. British Rail Maintenance Limited (BRML), for example, was a company formed in 1987 to operate some of British Rail's maintenance depots, of which Ilford was one. This was sold in June 1995 to ABB Customer Support Services, a division of the conglomerate which as Brown, Boveri had built the GWR's first gas turbine locomotive.

It was during this period that BR Telecommunications Limited (BRT) was formed to capitalise on the railway's valuable communication networks.[24] Telecommunications had been a core component of the railways almost from the start, the GWR laying its first electric telegraph cables as early as 1839. Designed by William Fothergill Cooke these had consisted of copper wires clothed in silk and threaded through 1in diameter underground gas pipes. The drawback with this system was that the wires were very difficult to get at and they were soon replaced with iron wires suspended from poles. Daniel Gooch, the GWR's first locomotive superintendent, described the system as one of the marvels of the world, although he noted that in early years '*no-one seemed to believe in it and we did not use it for railway purposes*'.[25] By the 1980s the BRB had amassed one of the largest telecommunication systems in Britain, one consisting of 17,000kms of fibre optic and copper cable that connected every major town and city in the country. It also operated its own national trunked radio network and held substantial wayleave rights. These were the long-term fruits of the BTC's recognition in 1955 that:

'Efficient telecommunications ... constitute a vital service for railways. The existing telegraph and telephone systems must be considerably modernised, and advantage taken of all available developments in telecommunications.' [26]

In the early 1990s the Parcels sector was rebranded as Rail Express Systems. In 1993 it renewed its contract with the Post Office which meant that when it was bought by the newly-established North and South Railways in 1995, the operation of the Royal Mail's travelling post offices (which Old Oak Common had continued to maintain) passed into the private sector.[27] The following year North and South Railways acquired all three of BR's recently established trainload companies (Loadhaul, Mainline Freight and Transrail Freight) and changed its name to English, Welsh and Scottish Railway (EWS).[28] In 1997 it acquired Railfreight Distribution, meaning that all bar one of BR's recently fragmented freight operation was once again in the hands of a single organisation.[29]

Sectorisation meant that by the second half of the 1980s the locomotives serviced and maintained at Old Oak Common were operated by Network South-East, Inter-City or freight operators rather than by British Rail. The first two of these were by then well advanced in their plans to switch from the use of locomotives to fleets of diesel or electric multiple units. As the demand for passenger locomotive maintenance fell, the older parts of Old Oak Common concentrated increasingly on the stabling, servicing and repair of rolling stock for the freight and heritage sectors, or were used by external contractors to dismantle locomotives for scrap (Figs 129-130). Charter traffic was also important, and its turntable, by the turn of the century one of only two left in London, proved popular.[30] On the privatisation of British Rail in 1994 the parts of the depot not used by

Fig 129 Railfreight's Class 37 locomotive 37373 pictured at Old Oak Common in January 1997. This locomotive was scrapped at the depot later that year. (Ron Halestrap)

Fig 131 Signs showing some of the activities undertaken by EWS at Old Oak Common in its last years

Great Western Trains to stable and service their Inter-City 125 trainsets, or by Heathrow Express for their airport shuttles, passed to EWS (Fig 131).[31]

Although privatisation removed it from the headlines, plans for Crossrail did not go away. In 1999 the Government asked the Shadow Strategic Rail Authority to carry out a review of the issues relating to rail travel on an east-west axis across London. Their 'London East-West Study', published in November 2000, echoed the support for Crossrail which had appeared in the Government's ten year transport plan, 'Transport 2010', earlier that year.[32] In 2002 Cross London Rail Links Ltd was formed to undertake project definition work on a Crossrail link, and in July of the following year the Crossrail Business Case was presented to the Secretary of State for Transport.

Fig 130 Under EWS control Old Oak Common added the refurbishment and stabling of historic rolling stock to its list of activities (Tulyarman)

The Crossrail Hybrid Bill was presented to Parliament in February 2005 and the principle of the scheme was established at the second reading debate in July. In 2008 the Bill received Royal Assent and the Crossrail Act 2008 passed into statute. The seemingly interminable questionmark over funding was also removed; the cost would be shared between the Government, Transport for London (TfL) and the business community.

In April 2009, a little over a century after it had opened, most of Churchward's Old Oak Common depot closed to allow work on Crossrail's tunnel segment factory to begin. The following month, thirty-five years after the idea of an east-west railway across London had first been seriously considered, Crossrail broke ground at Canary Wharf.

As this book goes to press, passenger services through Crossrail's tunnelled section are on course to begin in 2018, with full completion of the line the following year. Already, work is well advanced on planning the next generation of railways for the capital. Parliament has passed legislation allowing expenditure on the planning of a high speed railway network, with the design of the first phase of High Speed 2 (HS2) advancing swiftly. HS2 will provide an all-new high speed line between London Euston and Birmingham, with a major transport interchange at Old Oak Common. Further ahead, work continues on the development of Crossrail 2, a joint project by TfL and Network Rail to improve links between south-west and north-east London. The driver behind these projects is the desire to cater for, and promote growth. As Joe Brown puts it in his indispensable *London Railway Atlas* 'London ... owes its growth and continuing success to its intricate network of railways, which have been a part of the landscape for over 170 years and show no sign of losing their relevance or importance'.[33]

NOTES

1 British Railways Board 1963, 1; Gourvish 1986, 401
2 British Railways Board 1963, 25-26
3 Ibid, 80
4 Gourvish 2002, 80
5 Atkins 2007, 117-123, 165
6 Advert in *The Railway Gazette* 'GWR Special Centenary Number' supplement, August 30, 1935
7 This plant was demolished by Crossrail in summer 2014, and has been replaced by a new facility alongside.
8 Closure date given in Brown 2012, 42
9 Ibid, 29, 41
10 Serpell 1983, 7; In 1981 trainload freight (coal/coke, iron/steel, petroleum/chemicals and aggregates/building materials) accounted for 137 million tonnes whilst only 17 million tonnes were classified as wagonload (Serpell 1983, 21)
11 Gourvish 2002, 93
12 Jackson 2013, 133
13 Gourvish 2002, 313
14 British Railways Board 1980
15 Ibid, 27
16 'Central London Rail Study', January 1989, published jointly by the Department of Transport, London Regional Transport and British Rail
17 Gourvish 2002, 314
18 Crossrail Bill, 22 January 1991, HMSO
19 Hansard HC Deb 24 May 1993 vol 225 cc407-8W
20 Hansard HC Deb 03 March 1992 vol 205 c87W; Gourvish 2002, 314
21 Hansard HC Deb 08 July 1994 vol 246 c348W; HC Deb 16 January 1991 vol 183 c496W
22 Hansard HC Deb 22 May 1995 vol 260 cc400-1W
23 Hansard, HL Deb 02 April 1996 vol 571 c19WA
24 BRT was bought by Racal Electronics in December 1995 and became Racal-BRT. It is now part of Thales.
25 Burdett Wilson 1972, 45-46
26 British Transport Commission 1955, 11
27 North and South Railways was owned by a consortium lead by the American company Winconsin Central Tranportation Corporation.
28 Gourvish 2002, 512. EWS was sold in November 2007 to Deutsche Bahn and was rebranded in January 2009 as DB Schenker.
29 The sixth, Freightliner, remained as an independent company.

30 At the time of writing (October 2014) the only railway turntable left in the capital is at Hither Green TMD in Lewisham.
31 EWS Crossrail Petition Session 2005-06. Paddington New Yard and Plumstead Goods Depot also passed to EWS.
32 sSRA, *London East-West Study,* 2000, 11;
33 Brown 2012, Preface to the Third Edition

GAZETTEER

This section offers further details of the railway heritage structures discussed in this book. The entries are drawn from, and use the numbering system of, Crossrail's comprehensive gazetteer of the buildings and structures affected by the project. This master gazetteer may be accessed at www.crossrail.co.uk, as may many of the bibliographic sources cited in this volume.

The Monument Type classifications used are drawn from Historic England's Monument Type Thesaurus. The Site Code has been provided by the Museum of London Archaeological Archive.

1: Maidenhead Station – Goods Shed

Maidenhead Station's goods shed in 2012. West-facing elevation (left), interior (right)

Monument type	CL Transport, BT Railway Transport Site, NT Goods Shed
Address	Boyn Valley Road, Maidenhead, Berkshire, SL6 4EE
NGR	488170, 180642
Local Planning Authority	Royal Borough of Windsor and Maidenhead
Date built	1890–1893
Recording note	Recorded in advance of demolition to faciliate construction of Network Rail offices
Architect	Not known
Builder/Manufacturer	Not known
Original railway company	GWR
Field events	2012, EH Level 2 NLBH record, Wessex Archaeology
Bibliography and sources	Wessex Archaeology, 2012, *Maidenhead Railway Goods Shed; Archaeological Evaluation and Historic Building Record Report*, WOT1B-HEN-REP-MSA-000003 C02
Site code	N/A
Archive location	N/A
Volume references	CRL Series No.4, p102
Characterisation	Maidenhead goods yard was re-established in the 1890s after the main line was doubled in width. The goods shed was constructed from red bricks in English bond, roofed in slate, with a chimney located centrally. Single through road. All doorways had bullnose blue brick quoin and jamb details. An original office (heated) attached to east elevation, later extended eastwards in Fletton bricks.

18: Old Oak Common TMD – Sub-station

1906 sub-station (left) and 1960s extension

Monument type	CL Industrial, BT Electrical Production Site, RT Electricity Sub Station
Address	Old Oak Common, Acton, London NW10 6DU
NGR	521825, 182303
Local Planning Authority	Hammersmith and Fulham Council
Date built	1906
Recording note	Building demolished in 2012 to facilitate construction of Crossrail's temporary tunnel segment factory.
Architect	GWR
Builder/Manufacturer	Messrs Pattinson & Sons
Original railway company	GWR
Field events	2010, EH Level 3 NLBH record, Oxford Archaeology/Ramboll
Bibliography and sources	Crossrail, 2010, *Old Oak Common Worksites, Archaeological Detailed Desk Based Assessment: Non-Listed Built Heritage*, C150-CSY-T1-RGN-CR076_PT001-00011 Crossrail, 2015, *Old Oak Common Non-Listed Built Heritage Recording Report*, C254-OXF-T1-RGN-CRG05-50001
Site code	XSU10
Archive location	LAARC
Volume references	CRL Series No.4, p44
Characterisation	In 1906 termed the Electric Distributing Centre. Plans to extend the sub-station were issued in May 1939 but appear not to have been enacted, presumably because WWII intervened. Extension eventually constructed in mid 1960s. 1906 structure of red brick in stretcher bond, on a deep plinth of blue bricks and a stepped shoulder of two chamfered brick courses. Door stamped with maker's mark 'Ratner Safe Co Ltd'. Original roof structure of cast concrete, the underside shuttered into shallow barrel vaults.

19: Old Oak Common TMD – Carriage Lifting Shed

Eastern gable (left); internal view of the shed, looking west (right)

Monument type	CL Transport, BT Railway Transport Site, NT Railway Carriage Shed
Address	Old Oak Common, Acton, London NW10 6DU
NGR	521566, 182274
Local Planning Authority	Hammersmith and Fulham Council
Date built	1939
Recording note	Demolished by Crossrail in 2014 in advance of construction of Bombardier's TMD
Architect	GWR Swindon
Builder/Manufacturer	Not known
Original railway company	GWR
Field events	2010, EH Level 2 NLBH record, Oxford Archaeology/Ramboll
Bibliography and sources	Crossrail, 2010, *Old Oak Common Worksites*, Archaeological Detailed Desk Based Assessment: Non-listed Built Heritage, C150-CSY-T1-RGN-CR076_PT001-00011 Crossrail, 2015, *Old Oak Common Non-Listed Built Heritage Recording Report*, C254-OXF-T1-RGN-CRG05-50001 Hawkins, C and Reeve, G, 1987, *An Illustrated History of Great Western Railway Engine Sheds*, Wild Swan Publications
Site code	XSU10
Archive location	LAARC
Volume references	CRL Series No.4, p94
Characterisation	Constructed as part of a government-backed employment programme. It measured 412ft long by 70ft 5in wide, with three 350ft roads beyond which lay a machine shop. Constructed from brick panel walls between steel stanchions at 12ft centres. Roof clad in metal sheeting with four lengths of 9ft 3in deep glazing. Both roofs surmounted by continuous glazed lanterns. Provided with two 20 ton travelling cranes constructed by Wharton of Stockport and supported independently from the building on high-level rails carried on eleven stanchions by Dorman Long & Co. The floor largely of concrete, but at the western end of re-used teak wedges from dismantled wooden Mansell wheels.

20: Old Oak Common – Carriage Paint Shop / Pullman Shed

Offices/shelters at the western end of the shed (left); west gable (facing Old Oak Common) (right)

Monument type	CL Transport, BT Railway Transport Site, NT Railway Carriage Shed; CL Industrial, BT Engineering Industry Site, NT Paint Shop; CL Defence, BT Civil Defence Site, NT Air Raid Shelter
Address	Old Oak Common Lane, Acton, London NW10 6DW
NGR	521585, 182285
Local Planning Authority	Hammersmith and Fulham Council
Date built	1939-1940
Recording note	Demolished by Crossrail in 2014 in advance of construction of Bombardier's TMD.
Architect	GWR Swindon
Builder/Manufacturer	Not known
Original railway company	GWR
Field events	2010, EH Level 2 NLBH record, Oxford Archaeology/Ramboll
Bibliography and sources	Crossrail, 2010, *Old Oak Common Worksites*, Archaeological Detailed Desk Based Assessment: Non-listed Built Heritage, C150-CSY-T1-RGN-CR076_PT001-00011 Crossrail, 2015, *Old Oak Common Non-Listed Built Heritage Recording Report*, C254-OXF-T1-RGN-CRG05-50001 Hawkins, C and Reeve, G, 1987, *An Illustrated History of Great Western Railway Engine Sheds*, Wild Swan Publications
Site code	XSU10
Archive location	LAARC
Volume references	CRL Series No.4, p78
Characterisation	Constructed as a carriage paint shop of 592ft length by 69ft 6in width with three full length roads and steel-framed windows. Lightweight steel truss roof clad in Robertson's Protected Metal V-Beam Sheeting with 9ft 3in deep glazed panels glazed lanterns fitted with fixed louvres and running the length of the building. High-level bull's-eye windows in both end gables. At the Old Oak Common end an internal two-storey block of single depth rooms was built to accommodate stores, the trimming shop and the piecework checker's office on the ground floor and a messroom and offices for the shop clerks and foreman on the first. Seigwart floor. In 1940 this block converted to blast-protected ARS with 96 bunks. Building converted in 1960 to a maintenance shop for BR's new Blue Pullmans.

21: Old Oak Common TMD – 70' turntable

Old Oak Common's last working turntable in 2010, looking south-west

Monument type	CL Transport, BT Railway Transport Site, NT Railway Turntable
Address	Old Oak Common Lane, Acton, London NW10 6DW
NGR	521665, 182335
Local Planning Authority	Hammersmith and Fulham Council
Date built	1952/1953
Recording note	Turntable relocated to Swanage Railway Museum in 2010
Architect	Cowans & Sheldon Ltd
Builder/Manufacturer	Cowans & Sheldon Ltd
Original railway company	BR (WR)
Field events	2010, EH Level 2 NLBH record, PCA
Bibliography and sources	Crossrail, 2010, *Old Oak Common Worksites Non-Listed Built Heritage Recording of 70' Turntable*, C150-CSY-T1-RGN-CR076_PT001-00019
Site code	XSU10
Archive location	LAARC
Volume references	CRL Series No.4, p96
Characterisation	Originally one of four Ransome & Rapier 65' turntables dating from 1906. Adapted to house a 70' diameter table in 1952-3, probably so that Old Oak Common could accommodate British Railways's new 68ft 9in long 'Britannia' class locomotives. Retained when the other three turntables were removed in the mid 1960s. Powered manually or with a 12.5 hp x 945 rpm electric motor with a current supply of 400V supplied by Crompton Parkinson Ltd. Turntable guide track measured 33' 4" in diameter.

22: Old Oak Common TMD – Sand Furnace House

1906 sand furnace house, with mid to late 1940s extension in the foreground. Looking north-east

Monument type	CL Transport, BT Railway Transport Site; CL Industrial, BT Furnace; later: CL Unassigned, BT Building Component; NT Canteen
Address	Old Oak Common, Acton, London NW10 6DU
NGR	521661, 182297
Local Planning Authority	Hammersmith and Fulham Council
Date built	Sand furnace 1906, altered to a canteen 1937. Mid to late 1940s additions. Final use as a stores/workshop.
Recording note	Building demolished in 2012 to facilitate construction of Crossrail's temporary tunnel segment factory.
Architect	GWR Swindon
Builder/Manufacturer	William Walkerdine
Original railway company	GWR
Field events	2010/2011, EH Level 3 NLBH record, Oxford Archaeology/Ramboll
Bibliography and sources	Crossrail, 2010, *Old Oak Common Worksites, Archaeological Detailed Desk Based Assessment: Non-Listed Built Heritage*, C150-CSY-T1-RGN-CR076_PT001-00011 Crossrail, 2015, *Old Oak Common Non-Listed Built Heritage Recording Report*, C254-OXF-T1-RGN-CRG05-50001 Hawkins, C and Reeve, G, 1987, *An Illustrated History of Great Western Railway Engine Sheds*, Wild Swan Publications
Site code	XSU10
Archive location	LAARC
Volume references	CRL Series No.4, p41
Characterisation	Second of two sand furnace houses attached to the outside walls of the depot's engine shed. There is evidence this may have been added to the TMD as an afterthought, although it was present by the time it opened. In 1937 it was gutted, its chimney removed and extended by 24 feet to the west to allow conversion into a canteen. The canteen had a kitchen and seating and tables for 170 diners. New pedestrian doors allowed access from the shed. A low extension was added to the eastern elevation in the mid to late 1940s for use as an 'Ambulance Room'. Last used as a stores/workshop with full-height sliding doors in northern elevation.

23: Old Oak Common TMD –Engine Shed

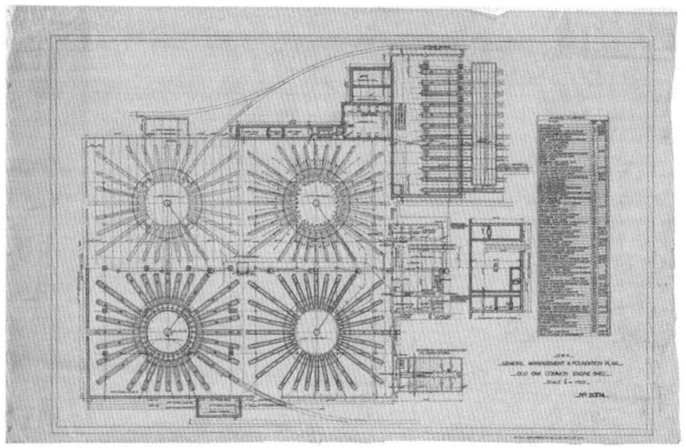

Layout of Old Oak Common's engine shed as it was built in 1906 (left); part of the north-west turntable was re-exposed in 2015. Here the junction of a road with the turntable pit is shown (right)

Monument type	CL Transport, BT Railway Transport Site, NT Engine Shed; NT Railway Turntable
Address	Old Oak Common Lane, Acton, London NW10 6DW
NGR	521697, 182343
Local Planning Authority	Hammersmith and Fulham Council
Date built	1906
Recording note	Engine shed progressively demolished during 1964 and 1965
Architect	GWR
Builder/Manufacturer	William Walkerdine
Original railway company	GWR
Field events	NW turntable partially archaeologically excavated in 2015
Bibliography and sources	Crossrail, 2010, *Old Oak Common Worksites, Archaeological Detailed Desk Based Assessment: Non-Listed Built Heritage*, C150-CSY-T1-RGN-CR076_PT001-00011 Crossrail, 2015, *Old Oak Common Non-Listed Built Heritage Recording Report*, C254-OXF-T1-RGN-CRG05-50001 Hawkins, C and Reeve, G, 1987, *An Illustrated History of Great Western Railway Engine Sheds*, Wild Swan Publications
Site code	XSU10
Archive location	LAARC
Volume references	CRL Series No.4, p32
Characterisation	Vast brick-built engine shed containing four 65ft Ransomes & Rapier turntables. Each turntable served 28 roads, providing total accommodation for 112 locomotives. Internal dimensions of 444ft by 360ft. Each turntable had a working load of 114 tons and two electrically-driven hinged tractors, placed diagonally at each end of the girders Together these turned the table at a speed of one revolution in 90 seconds.

24: Old Oak Common TMD – Diesel Cleaning and Servicing Shed

Old Oak Common's mid-1960s Cleaning and Servicing Shed, facing north-east (left); interior (right)

Monument type	CL Transport, BT Railway Transport Site, NT Engine Shed
Address	Old Oak Common, Acton, London NW10 6DU
NGR	521754, 182292
Local Planning Authority	Hammersmith and Fulham Council
Date built	1964
Recording note	Building demolished in 2012 to facilitate construction of Crossrail's temporary tunnel segment factory.
Architect	BR (WR)
Builder/Manufacturer	Not known
Original railway company	BR
Field events	2010/2011, EH NLBH Level 1 record, Oxford Archaeology/Ramboll
Bibliography and sources	Crossrail, 2010, *Old Oak Common Worksites, Archaeological Detailed Desk Based Assessment: Non-listed Built Heritage*, C150-CSY-T1-RGN-CR076_PT001-00011 Crossrail, 2015, *Old Oak Common Non-Listed Built Heritage Recording Report*, C254-OXF-T1-RGN-CRG05-50001
Site code	XSU10
Archive location	LAARC
Volume references	CRL Series No.4, p95
Characterisation	Steel-framed shed built over the south-eastern turntable of the depot's demolished 1906 engine shed. Officially opened for traffic in March 1965. Three internal roads with inspection pits whose western ends respected the arc of the underlying turntable ring wall. Four diesel refuelling pumps. Clerestory windows and projecting roof vents. Workshops and offices attached to the northern elevation.

25: Old Oak Common TMD – Stores

External view of the Stores looking north-west

Monument type	CL Transport, BT Railway Transport Site, NT Railway Storehouse
Address	Old Oak Common, Acton, London NW10 6DU
NGR	521787, 182329
Local Planning Authority	Hammersmith and Fulham Council
Date built	1906
Recording note	Building demolished in 2012 to facilitate construction of Crossrail's temporary tunnel segment factory
Architect	GWR Swindon
Builder/Manufacturer	William Walkerdine
Original railway company	GWR
Field events	2010, EH Level 3 NLBH record, Oxford Archaeology/Ramboll
Bibliography and sources	Crossrail, 2010, *Old Oak Common Worksites, Archaeological Detailed Desk Based Assessment: Non-Listed Built Heritage*, C150-CSY-T1-RGN-CR076_PT001-00011 Crossrail, 2015, *Old Oak Common Non-Listed Built Heritage Recording Report*, C254-OXF-T1-RGN-CRG05-50001 Hawkins, C and Reeve, G, 1987, *An Illustrated History of Great Western Railway Engine Sheds*, Wild Swan Publications
Site code	XSU10
Archive location	LAARC
Volume references	CRL Series No.4, p38
Characterisation	Formed from two identically-sized and conjoined blocks. Internally, a large central open-plan stores area (originally with an internal rail head) with various rooms along the north and south sides. A mezzanine level provided additional storage. English-bond red brick with a plinth of dark blue bricks and a slate-covered roof. Multi-light metal windows with segmental window arches. The roof had two identical east-to-west bays, each with sets of north-to-south Polonceau-type trusses. These of composite construction with softwood members in compression and steel rods acting in tension. Each truss included two large cast connector rings which linked the various members. A central east-to-west spine comprised a steel composite beam with underslung latticework bracing, supported at midpoint by a cast-iron column which also acted as a downpipe for the gutter in the central valley. Stamped 'GWR W'hampton Dec 1903'.

26: Old Oak Common TMD – Offices

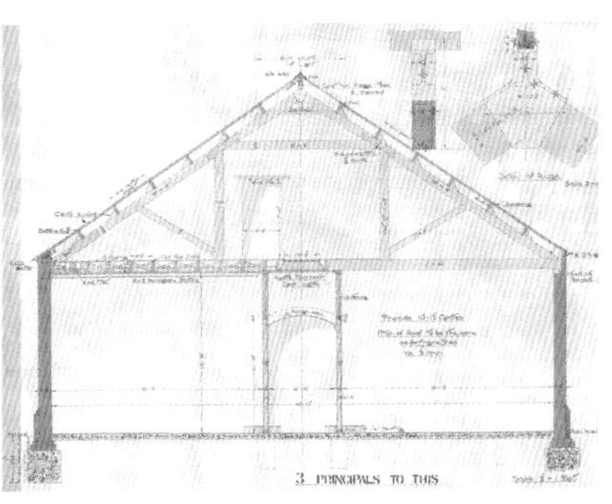

Old Oak Common's 1906 office block shed, looking east (left); 1903 cross-section through the building (right)

Monument type	CL Transport, BT Railway Transport Site, NT Office
Address	Old Oak Common, Acton, London NW10 6DU
NGR	521787, 182276
Local Planning Authority	Hammersmith and Fulham Council
Date built	1906
Recording note	Building demolished in 2012 to facilitate construction of Crossrail's temporary tunnel segment factory.
Architect	GWR Swindon
Builder/Manufacturer	William Walkerdine
Original railway company	GWR
Field events	2010, EH Level 3 NLBH record, Oxford Archaeology/Ramboll
Bibliography and sources	Crossrail, 2010, *Old Oak Common Worksites, Archaeological Detailed Desk Based Assessment: Non-Listed Built Heritage*, C150-CSY-T1-RGN-CR076_PT001-00011 Crossrail, 2015, *Old Oak Common Non-Listed Built Heritage Recording Report*, C254-OXF-T1-RGN-CRG05-50001 Hawkins, C and Reeve, G, 1987, *An Illustrated History of Great Western Railway Engine Sheds*, Wild Swan Publications
Site code	XSU10
Archive location	LAARC
Volume references	CRL Series No.4, p81
Characterisation	Free-standing red brick structure, part of the original depot layout. Offices at ground floor level arranged on either side of a central corridor, with WCs at the north-west corner and a spiral staircase in the north-eastern part of the building. Brick work essentially English bond with occasional inconsistencies; bullnose bricks softened the corners of the structure and a high plinth of blue bricks wrapped around the building. Twelve full-height windows on the south elevation, each with segmental arches and sloped blue brick sills. Converted into a canteen during WWII and substantially altered in the mid 1960s when the construction of the adjoining Amenity Block allowed a partial return to office accommodation. The first floor was originally given over to a one large room, later partitioned into smaller spaces.

27: Old Oak Common TMD – Lifting Bay, formerly Smith's Shop

Inside the engine lifting bay, looking north-west (left); west gable of the former smith's shop, with former carpenters and coppersmiths shops to the left (right)

Monument type	CL Transport, BT Railway Transport Site, NT Railway Engineering Workshop
Address	Old Oak Common, Acton, London NW10 6DU
NGR	521788, 182388
Local Planning Authority	Hammersmith and Fulham Council
Date built	1906
Recording note	Building demolished in 2012 to facilitate construction of Crossrail's temporary tunnel segment factory
Architect	GWR Swindon
Builder/Manufacturer	William Walkerdine
Original railway company	GWR
Field events	2010, EH Level 3 NLBH record, Oxford Archaeology/Ramboll
Bibliography and sources	Crossrail, 2010, *Old Oak Common Worksites, Archaeological Detailed Desk Based Assessment: Non-Listed Built Heritage*, C150-CSY-T1-RGN-CR076_PT001-00011 Crossrail, 2015, *Old Oak Common Non-Listed Built Heritage Recording Report*, C254-OXF-T1-RGN-CRG05-50001 Hawkins, C and Reeve, G, 1987, *An Illustrated History of Great Western Railway Engine Sheds*, Wild Swan Publications
Site code	XSU10
Archive location	LAARC
Volume references	CRL Series No.4, p38
Characterisation	Formerly Smith's Shop, 74ft by 47ft, equipped with seven hearths, a fan and a power hammer. Floor of 3in of fine ashes on top of 6in of dry ash. Converted into a lifting bay in mid 1960s. Changes at that time included insertion of a large opening with roller shutter doors to allow through movement of rolling stock, and removal of much of the east wall to unite this space with the adjacent lifting shop. The track through the room featured an inspection pit with four sets of lifting jacks on simple tracks set 0.75m apart. Jacks had a SWL of 25 tons and were made by Matterson Ltd of Rochdale.

28: Old Oak Common TMD – Boiler and Compressor House, formerly Carpenter's and Coppersmith's Shops

North elevation of former Carpenter's Shop (left); iInternal view of the boiler house, facing west

Monument type	CL Industrial, BT Railway Engineering Site, NT Railway Worksop; CL Industrial, BT Boiler House
Address	Old Oak Common, Acton, London NW10 6DU
NGR	521790, 182397
Local Planning Authority	Hammersmith and Fulham Council
Date built	1906, altered *c* 1965
Recording note	Building demolished in 2012 to facilitate construction of Crossrail's temporary tunnel segment factory
Architect	GWR Swindon
Builder/Manufacturer	William Walkerdine
Original railway company	GWR
Field events	2010, EH Level 3 NLBH record, Oxford Archaeology/Ramboll
Bibliography and sources	Crossrail, 2010, *Old Oak Common Worksites, Archaeological Detailed Desk Based Assessment: Non-Listed Built Heritage*, C150-CSY-T1-RGN-CR076_PT001-00011 Crossrail, 2015, *Old Oak Common Non-Listed Built Heritage Recording Report*, C254-OXF-T1-RGN-CRG05-50001 Hawkins, C and Reeve, G, 1987, *An Illustrated History of Great Western Railway Engine Sheds*, Wild Swan Publications
Site code	XSU10
Archive location	LAARC
Volume references	CRL Series No.4, p33
Characterisation	Originally two equally-sized rooms of 48ft by 23ft created for use by coppersmiths and carpenters. Converted in mid 1960s to accommodate a compressor room in the west part of the former carpenter's shop and a boiler house and lube oil room in the former coppersmith's shop. Built from red brick laid in English bond with same general constructional form and architectural detailing as elsewhere in the depot. The larger room in the former Carpenter's Shop housed three large horizontal, cylindrical boilers; at the east end of this room were pumps.

29: Old Oak Common TMD – Lifting and Repair Shop

Old Oak Common Lifting and Repair Shop, facing north-west (left); Internal view (right)

Monument type	CL Transport, BT Railway Transport Site, NT Railway Engineering Workshop
Address	Old Oak Common, Acton, London NW10 6DU
NGR	521816, 182378
Local Planning Authority	Hammersmith and Fulham Council
Date built	1906
Recording note	Building demolished in 2012 to facilitate construction of Crossrail's temporary tunnel segment factory
Architect	GWR Swindon
Builder/Manufacturer	William Walkerdine
Original railway company	GWR
Field events	2010, EH Level 3 NLBH record, Oxford Archaeology/Ramboll
Bibliography and sources	Crossrail, 2010, *Old Oak Common Worksites, Archaeological Detailed Desk Based Assessment: Non-Listed Built Heritage*, C150-CSY-T1-RGN-CR076_PT001-00011 Crossrail, 2015, *Old Oak Common Non-Listed Built Heritage Recording Report*, C254-OXF-T1-RGN-CRG05-50001 Hawkins, C and Reeve, G, 1987, *An Illustrated History of Great Western Railway Engine Sheds*, Wild Swan Publications
Site code	XSU10
Archive location	LAARC
Volume references	CRL Series No.4, p37
Characterisation	Rectangular structure comprising two large north-to-south bays of different sizes. The roof had pairs of gables at each end and long continuous sets of roof lights with walkways adjacent. Internal measurements of 195ft by 101ft with twelve 52ft inspection pits. Each road had a separate entrance in the eastern gable with double timber doors (later, roller shutter doors). A thirteenth door at the northern end did not have a corresponding road. Beyond the end of the pits lay the fitters and machine area, originally laid out with rows of workbenches. When opened this contained four lathes, two wheel lathes, two buffing machines, two shapers, two

drilling machines, a automatic cold sawing machine, a slotting machine, a punching and shearing machine, a screwing machine, a drill slotter and a grindstone. A travelling crane with a span of 49ft was supplied by Vaughan & Son Ltd, Manchester, replaced in the late 1920s with a 50 ton overhead beam crane from S H Heywood & Co Ltd. Each bay of the roof had 12 composite trusses dividing the 13 bays, with each truss of Polonceau form. Each truss comprised pine members in compression and steel tie-rods acting in tension. The rods were formed of three sections with the central section raised and further steel rods formed a triangle at the centre of each truss. Each truss included two large cast connecting members, one to each side of the truss, to link the various members.

30: Old Oak Common TMD – Amenity Block

The northern and southern elevations of Old Oak Common's purpose-built amenity building. This abutted and was connected to the depot's original 1906 office building, which is pictured on the right-hand side of the left-hand image

Monument type	CL Unassigned, BT Building, NT Office; CL Water Supply and Drainage, BT Water Disposal Site, NT Toilet
Address	Old Oak Common Lane, Acton, London NW10 6DW
NGR	521832, 182270
Local Planning Authority	Hammersmith and Fulham London Borough Council
Date built	March 1963
Recording note	Building demolished in 2012 to facilitate construction of Crossrail's temporary tunnel segment factory.
Architect	Not known
Builder/Manufacturer	Not known
Original railway company	BR
Field events	2010, EH NLBH Level 1 record, Oxford Archaeology/Ramboll
Bibliography and sources	Crossrail, 2010, *Old Oak Common Worksites, Archaeological Detailed Desk Based Assessment: Non-Listed Built Heritage*, C150-CSY-T1-RGN-CR076_PT001-00011 Crossrail, 2015, *Old Oak Common Non-Listed Built Heritage Recording Report*, C254-OXF-T1-RGN-CRG05-50001
Site code	XSU10
Archive location	LAARC
Volume references	CRL Series No.4, p96
Characterisation	Two-storey building with flat roof and staircase tower at the eastern end. Constructed using a concrete rendered steel frame with brick infilling to gables. The first floor jettied outwards by 1.4m on both long elevations and was glazed with metal-framed windows above original lime green panelling. The ground floor housed a small female WC and a larger male WC. First floor divided into large open-plan space and five small offices. One of these contained a Horsfall No 5 Destructor incinerator by Heenan and Froude of Worcester.

31: Old Oak Common TMD – oil refuelling facility

The 170,000 gallon storage tank, fuel pump house and tanker off-loading siding pictured in 2010 all dated from 1946. Looking north-west

Monument type	CL Transport, BT Fuelling Station
Address	Old Oak Common Lane, Acton, London NW10 6DW
NGR	521876, 182388
Local Planning Authority	Hammersmith and Fulham London Borough Council
Date built	Locomotive heavy oil fuelling plant established in 1946; altered in 1949 to allow fuelling of gas turbine and diesel locomotives. Converted to fully diesel refuelling in the early 1960s.
Recording note	Facility dismantled and removed by Crossrail to facilitate construction of tunnel segment factory.
Architect	GWR Swindon
Builder/Manufacturer	Not known
Original railway company	GWR
Field events	2010, EH Level 3 NLBH record, Oxford Archaeology/Ramboll
Bibliography and sources	Crossrail, 2010, *Old Oak Common Worksites, Archaeological Detailed Desk Based Assessment: Non-listed Built Heritage*, C150-CSY-T1-RGN-CR076_PT001-00011 Crossrail, 2015, *Old Oak Common Non-Listed Built Heritage Recording Report*, C254-OXF-T1-RGN-CRG05-50001
Site code	XSU10
Archive location	LAARC
Volume references	CRL Series No.4, p85
Characterisation	The coal shortage of 1946 prompted the installation of a heavy oil fuelling depot to allow the fuelling of converted steam locomotives. In 1949 the depot was adapted to allow refuelling of experimental gas turbine locomotives. By the mid 1960s the facility was being used to unload and store diesel oil, with refuelling taking place elsewhere on the site.

32: Old Oak Common TMD – Coal Stage

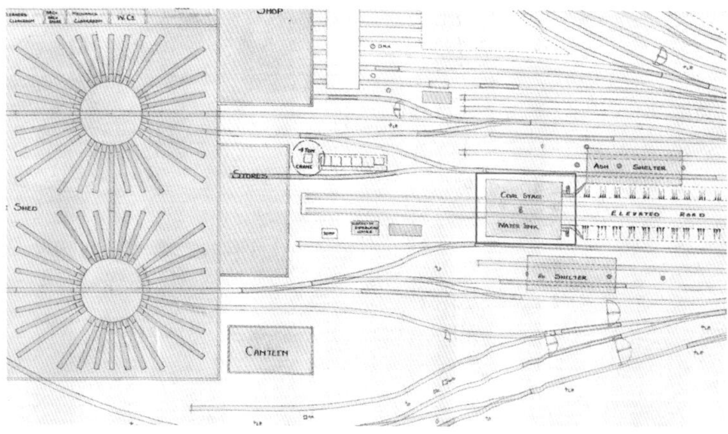

Old Oak Common's coal stage (highlighted on the plan by a red box) lay to the east of the engine shed. An incline carried on a series of brick arch allowed two sets of coal wagons to be fed through the elevated coal stage by gravity throughout the day

Monument type	Cl Transport, BT Fuelling Station
Address	Old Oak Common, Acton, London NW10 6DU
NGR	521920, 182253
Local Planning Authority	Hammersmith and Fulham Council
Date built	1906
Recording note	Demolished 1965
Architect	GWR Swindon
Builder/Manufacturer	William Walkerdine
Original railway company	GWR
Field events	2010, archaeological trial trenching, PCA
Bibliography and sources	Crossrail, 2010, *Old Oak Common Worksites, Archaeological Detailed Desk Based Assessment: Non-Listed Built Heritage*, C150-CSY-T1-RGN-CR076_PT001-00011 Hawkins, C and Reeve, G, 1987, *An Illustrated History of Great Western Railway Engine Sheds*, Wild Swan Publications
Site code	XSU10
Archive location	LAARC
Volume references	CRL Series No.4, p41
Characterisation	Elevated and inclined two-road siding allowed loaded coal wagons to be slowly gravity-fed through the coal stage throughout the day. The gradient was at 1:80. The coal was hand transferred from the wagons into iron tubs which were wheeled onto sprung flaps that projected outwards when pushed flat. The tubs were tipped from the flaps into waiting locomotive tenders below. Four double and two single tips were available. A 290,000 gallon water tank on top of the building, divided into four sections, supplied the whole depot. The tank in turn was supplied with water from the Grand Junction Canal via 10in. and 12in. pipes and a pump house.

33: Old Oak Common TMD – ash shelters

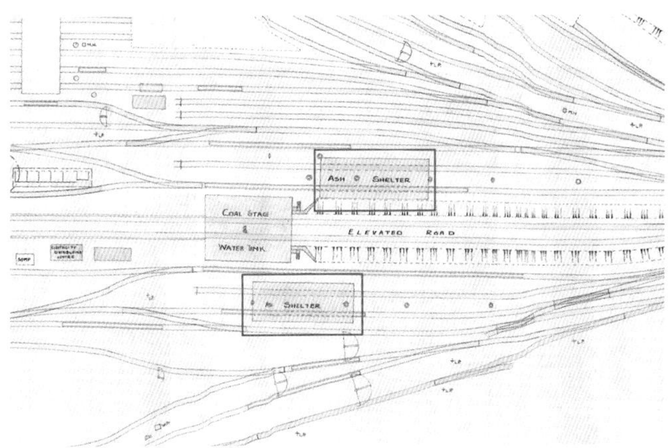

WWII ash shelters pictured on a 1943 plan of Old Oak Common

Monument type CL Defence, BT Passive Air Defence Site

Address Old Oak Common, Acton, London NW10 6DU

NGR 521920, 182253

Local Planning Authority Hammersmith and Fulham Council

Date built 1941

Recording note Dismantled and removed in the mid 1950s

Architect Not known

Builder/Manufacturer Smith Walker Ltd

Original railway company GWR

Field events Research for Old Oak Common DDBA

Bibliography and sources Crossrail, 2010, *Old Oak Common Worksites, Archaeological Detailed Desk Based Assessment: Non-listed Built Heritage*, C150-CSY-T1-RGN-CR076_PT001-00011

Hawkins, C and Reeve, G, 1987, *An Illustrated History of Great Western Railway Engine Sheds*, Wild Swan Publications

Site code N/A

Archive location LAARC

Volume references CRL Series No.4, p76

Characterisation Two steel-framed and asbestos sheet-clad shelters were erected at Old Oak Common during 1941. Built for a cost of over £2,000 these were intended to prevent the glowing embers raked from steam locomotives help enemy aircraft locate the site. In the 1950s the shelters were dismantled and removed, possibly for re-use at Llanelli Docks.

34: Old Oak Common TMD – 1906 mess hut

The mess hut at the eastern throat of Old Oak Common TMD dated to 1906

Monument type	CL Transport, BT Railway Transport Site, NT Railway Building
Address	Old Oak Common, Acton, London NW10 6DU
NGR	522099, 182236
Local Planning Authority	Hammersmith and Fulham Council
Date built	1906
Recording note	Building demolished to facilitate construction of Crossrail's temporary tunnel segment factory
Architect	Not known
Builder/Manufacturer	Not known
Original railway company	GWR
Field events	2010, EH Level 3 NLBH record, Oxford Archaeology/Ramboll
Bibliography and sources	Crossrail, 2010, *Old Oak Common Worksites, Archaeological Detailed Desk Based Assessment: Non-Listed Built Heritage*, C150-CSY-T1-RGN-CR076_PT001-00011 Crossrail, 2015, *Old Oak Common Non-Listed Built Heritage Recording Report*, C254-OXF-T1-RGN-CRG05-50001
Site code	XSU10
Archive location	LAARC
Volume references	CRL Series No.4, p32
Characterisation	Single-storey structure with double-pitched slate roof located at the eastern edge of the site. Interior divided into a lobby and two rooms by a timber tongue and groove partition fitted with original coat hooks. Main room heated with corner fireplace with stepped chimney breast. Bricks laid to Flemish bond with burnt headers particularly noticeable in the west gable end. Inconsistent use of blue headers and red stretchers (mirrored by adjacent retaining wall to canal), except on the eastern and western elevations where the effect was of a chequerboard. Some bricks stamped 'HAMBLET'S LTD'.

35: Westbourne Park Depot – standard gauge engine shed

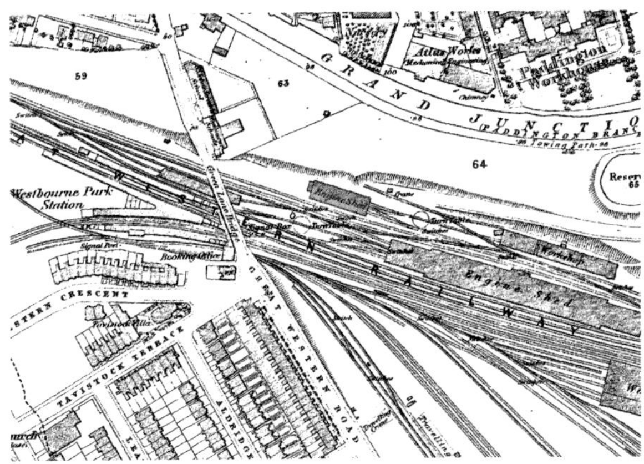

Extract from 1872 OS map showing the position of the standard-gauge engine shed at Westbourne Park Depot (left); its remains as excavated in 2014 (right)

Monument type	CL Transport, BT Railway Transport Site, NT Engine Shed
Address	Great Western Road, Westbourne Park, London W2
NGR	525015, 181785
Local Planning Authority	Westminster City Council
Date built	1862
Recording note	Demolished in 1906
Architect	Not known
Builder/Manufacturer	Not known
Original railway company	GWR
Field events	Archaeological excavation 2014
Bibliography and sources	Oxford Archaeology/Ramboll 2015, *Paddington New Yard, Westbourne Park, London W9: Archaeological Fieldwork Report*, C254-OXF-T1-RGN-CRG03-50251 Hawkins, C and Reeve, G, 1987, *An Illustrated History of Great Western Railway Engine Sheds*, Wild Swan Publications
Site code	XSI10
Archive location	LAARC
Volume references	CRL Series No.4, p9
Characterisation	Built to accommodate the GWR's standard-gauge locomotives that began arriving in Paddington in 1861. Initially contianed 3 roads but doubled to 6 in 1873. Known within the GWR as the Narrow Gauge or NG Shed. Brick walls, slate roof and iron roof principals. Each line was 147ft long and included an inspection pit of 140ft. Demolished as part of the re-development of the depot into a goods depot during 1906/7.

36: 56 Great Western Road, London W9

Former GWR Coffee Tavern on Great Western Road, Westbourne Park. Looking west

Monument type	CL Commercial, BT Eating and Drinking Establishment
Address	56 Great Western Road, London W9 3BT
NGR	524937, 181733
Local Planning Authority	Westminster City Council
Date built	1901
Recording note	Originally considered for inclusion within an adjacent Crossrail worksite but later removed from the scheme
Architect	Not known
Builder/Manufacturer	Not known
Original railway company	GWR
Field events	N/A
Bibliography and sources	None
Site code	N/A
Archive location	N/A
Volume references	CRL Series No.4, p17
Characterisation	Built in 1901, probably to replace an earlier coffee tavern beside Green Lane Bridge. Run by the Great Western Coffee Tavern Company Ltd as a temperance bar for employees until 1921 when it was converted into a GWR Deeds Office. Two-storey structure (first floor at road level), later with with living accommodation. Since the early 1980s it has been occupied by 'Big Table', a furniture manufacturer.

37: Westbourne Park Depot – 45' turntable

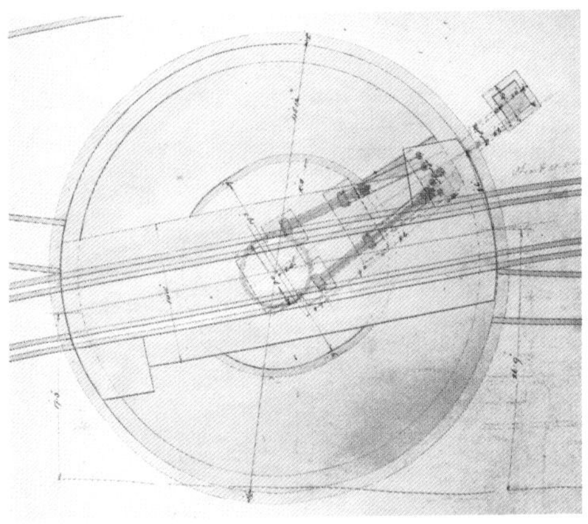

Westbourne Park Depot's 45' turntable, looking west towards Westbourne Park station (left);

Monument type	CL Transport, BT Railway Transport Site, NT Railway Turntable
Address	Great Western Road, Westbourne Park, London W2
NGR	524977, 181791
Local Planning Authority	Westminster City Council
Date built	1881
Recording note	Dismantled and removed in 1906
Architect	GWR Swindon
Builder/Manufacturer	GWR Swindon
Original railway company	GWR
Field events	Archaeological excavation 2014
Bibliography and sources	Oxford Archaeology/Ramboll 2015, *Paddington New Yard, Westbourne Park, London W9: Archaeological Fieldwork Report*, C254-OXF-T1-RGN-CRG03-50251 Hawkins, C and Reeve, G, 1987, *An Illustrated History of Great Western Railway Engine Sheds*, Wild Swan Publications, 65
Site code	XSI10
Archive location	LAARC
Volume references	CRL Series No.4, p14
Characterisation	Replacement for an earlier 40ft turntable to the south. The turntable deck was equipped with a hydraulic slewing mechanism, presumably because space was so limited at the west end of the depot. Hinged extension rails. The floor of the turn table pit was of brick, the full circle girders were of wrought iron and the deck (on which a small hut with windows, a vertical engine and a boiler sat) was of timber. Once operational, the nearby 42ft turntable was decommissioned and removed.

38: Westbourne Park Depot – Sand House

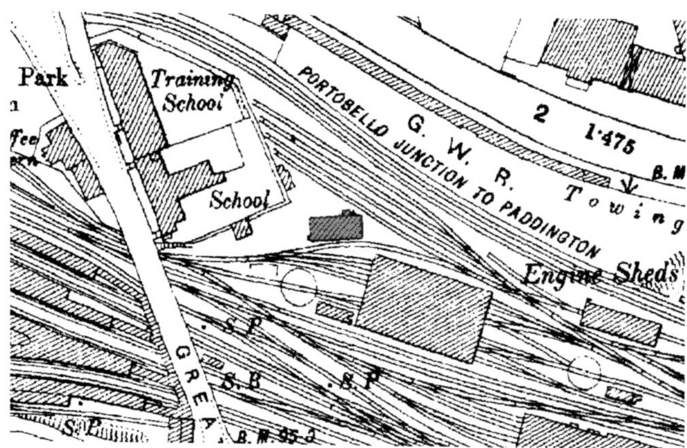

Westbourne Park Depot's Sand House, marked in red on the 1896 1:2500 OS map

Monument type	CL Transport, BT Railway Transport Site; CL Industrial, BT Furnace
Address	Great Western Road, Westbourne Park, London W2
NGR	524996, 181807
Local Planning Authority	Westminster City Council
Date built	1880
Recording note	Demolished mid 1970s
Architect	GWR Swindon
Builder/Manufacturer	Not known
Original railway company	Swindon
Field events	None
Bibliography and sources	Crossrail 2014, *Paddington New Yard, Archaeological Site Specific Written Scheme of Investigation*, C254-OXF-T1-GMS-CRG03-50006 Hawkins, C and Reeve, G, 1987, *An Illustrated History of Great Western Railway Engine Sheds*, Wild Swan Publications
Site code	N/A
Archive location	LAARC
Volume references	CRL Series No.4, p12
Characterisation	Small brick building, 27ft 10in width by 63ft length. Slate roof, iron roof principals. Two rooms, larger room of 15ft by 30ft contained sand furnace constructed from rail iron and plates, lined with firebricks. Four 'standard doors'. Three full length arched flues shown on GWR plans (although only two noted in an inventory from 1901 [Hawkins and Reeve, 65]). Also present in this room bunkers for coal and the resulting dry sand. Smaller room (13ft 10in by 24ft) held wet sand. Seven high-level windows behind the furnace, one chimney stack. Late, a small Engine men's Cabin added to external northern wall.

39: Westbourne Park Depot – 40' turntable

Westbourne Park Depot's 40' turntable inside its 55' 6" replacement

Monument type	CL Transport, BT Railway Transport Site, NT Railway Turntable
Address	Great Western Road, Westbourne Park, London W2
NGR	525134, 181721
Local Planning Authority	Westminster City Council
Date built	*c* 1861
Recording note	Enlarged in 1896 to 55' 6". Removed in *c* 1907
Architect	GWR Swindon
Builder/Manufacturer	GWR Swindon
Original railway company	GWR
Field events	Archaeological excavation 2014
Bibliography and sources	Oxford Archaeology/Ramboll 2015, *Paddington New Yard, Westbourne Park, London W9: Archaeological Fieldwork Report*, C254-OXF-T1-RGN-CRG03-50251 Hawkins, C and Reeve, G, 1987, *An Illustrated History of Great Western Railway Engine Sheds*, Wild Swan Publications, 65
Site code	XSI10
Archive location	LAARC
Volume references	CRL Series No.4, p11
Characterisataion	Originally turned by a pair of hand winches. The 40' table was replaced in 1896 by a 55' 6" diameter Swindon surface table, possibly with an eye to accommodating the new 4-6-0 locomotives being investigated by Swindon.

41: Westbourne Park Depot – 42' turntable

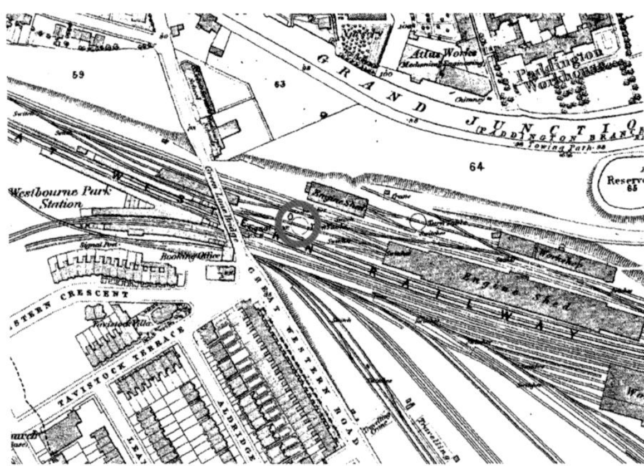

Extract from 1872 OS map showing the turntable and its control hut highlighted in red

Monument type	CL Transport, BT Railway Transport Site, NT Railway Turntable
Address	Great Western Road, Westbourne Park, London W2
NGR	525000, 181775
Local Planning Authority	Westminster City Council
Date built	Before 1872 (probably *c* 1853)
Recording note	Removed in *c* 1881
Architect	GWR Swindon
Builder/Manufacturer	Not known
Original railway company	GWR
Field events	Research for SSWSI prior to Crossrail works
Bibliography and sources	Crossrail 2014, *Paddington New Yard, Archaeological Site Specific Written Scheme of Investigation*, C254-OXF-T1-GMS-CRG03-50006 Hawkins, C and Reeve, G, 1987, *An Illustrated History of Great Western Railway Engine Sheds*, Wild Swan Publications, 61
Site code	N/A
Archive location	LAARC
Volume references	CRL Series No.4, p11
Characterisation	This 42' diameter turntable was located to the west of Westbourne Park's 1853 Engine Shed. A small hexagonal structure immediately to the north-west of the turntable housed an engine and boiler, the power it generated being transmitted to the table by means of a chain and a horizontal sprocket wheel in the engine shed. Believed to have been the only turntable on the line powered by steam.

42: Westbourne Park Depot – Lifting Shop

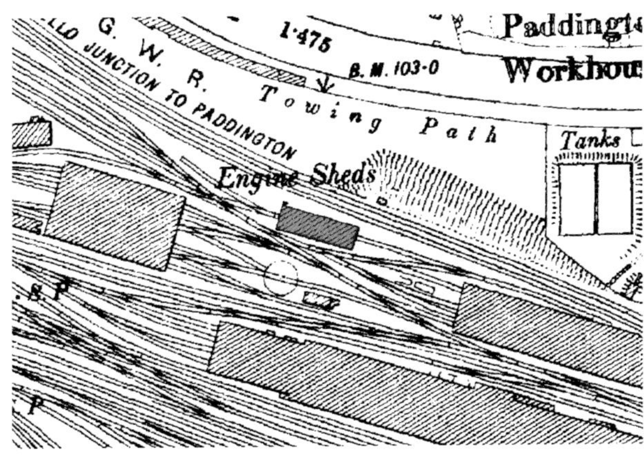

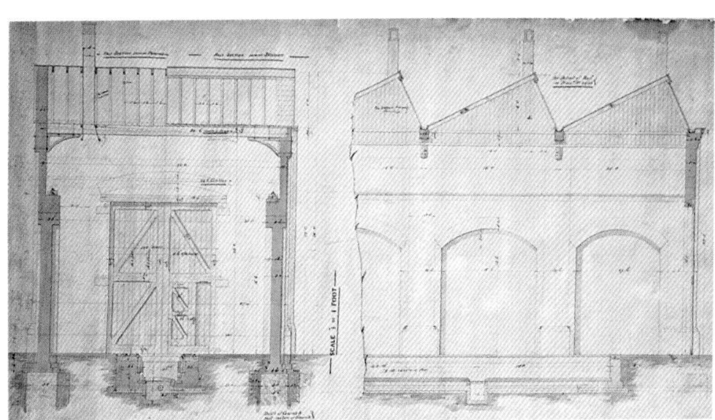

1896 1:2500 OS map showing the location of the lifting shop (left); details from a plan issued by the GWR in 1879 (right)

Monument type CL Industrial, BT Railway Engineering Site, NT Railway Workshop

Address Great Western Road, Westbourne Park, London W2

NGR 525112, 181769

Local Planning Authority Westminster City Council

Date built 1879

Recording note Demolished in 1938 to make way for Alfred Road Warehouse

Architect GWR Swindon

Builder/Manufacturer Not known

Original railway company GWR

Field events Archaeological excavation 2014

Bibliography and sources Oxford Archaeology/Ramboll 2015, *Paddington New Yard, Westbourne Park, London W9: Archaeological Fieldwork Report*, C254-OXF-T1-RGN-CRG03-50251

Hawkins, C and Reeve, G, 1987, *An Illustrated History of Great Western Railway Engine Sheds*, Wild Swan Publications

Site code XSI10

Archive location LAARC

Volume references CRL Series No.4, p12

Characterisation Westbourne Park Depots' lifting shop was erected in 1879 or 1880 to the north-west of the locomotive department workshops. Referred to in a 1901 schedule as the "Shear Legs" Shed, presumably in reference to two cranes. One of these was fixed, the other a hydraulic travelling unit. The slate-covered roof was of part-glazed, saw-tooth construction and the roof principals were of timber. One through road, with associated inspection pit. Measured 91ft x 23ft 6in. When the locomotive depot moved to Old Oak Common the road was removed and the structure converted into a goods shed.

43: Westbourne Park Depot – broad gauge engine shed

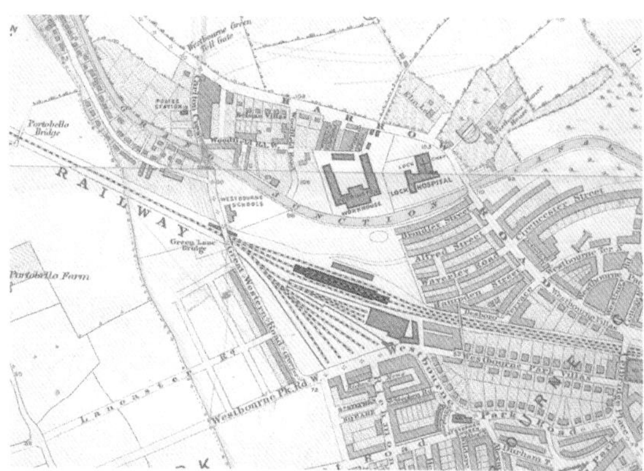

Extract from Stanford's 1862 map of London (1st edition) with the engine shed highlighted in red (left); inspection pit for the northernmost road of the shed (right)

Monument type	CL Transport, BT Railway Transport Site, NT Engine Shed
Address	Great Western Road, Westbourne Park, London W2
NGR	525134, 181721
Local Planning Authority	Westminster City Council
Date built	*c* 1853
Recording note	Demolished in May 1906
Architect	Not known
Builder/Manufacturer	Locke and Nesham
Original railway company	GWR
Field events	Archaeological excavation 2014
Bibliography and sources	Oxford Archaeology/Ramboll 2015, *Paddington New Yard, Westbourne Park, London W9: Archaeological Fieldwork Report*, C254-OXF-T1-RGN-CRG03-50251 Hawkins, C and Reeve, G, 1987, *An Illustrated History of Great Western Railway Engine Sheds*, Wild Swan Publications
Site code	XSI10
Archive location	LAARC
Volume references	CRL Series No.4, p6
Characterisation	Engine shed built to accommodate the company's 7ft broad gauge locomotives. Dubbed the BG Shed by GWR staff to differentiate it from the NG Shed where standard gauge locomotives were serviced. Dimensions: 663ft x 68ft 6in (middle section) 56ft 6in (end sections). Roof single span with tied wrought iron trusses. Four full-length roads, each with engine pits. Demolished in 1906 in advance of site conversion to a goods depot.

44: Westbourne Park Depot – engine department workshops and offices

The foundations of Westbourne Park's workshops and offices were exposed in 2014. A forge base and quenching pit in the smiths' shop (later termed the smithy) lie in the foreground, with the inspection pits of the c 1873 Repair & Paint Shop in the background

Monument type	CL Industrial, BT Railway Engineering Site, NT Railway Workshop
Address	Great Western Road, Westbourne Park, London W2
NGR	525145, 181744
Local Planning Authority	Westminster City Council
Date built	*c* 1853; substantial re-configurations in *c* 1873 and *c* 1906
Recording note	Demolished in 1938
Architect	Not known
Builder/Manufacturer	Possibly Locke and Nesham
Original railway company	GWR
Field events	Archaeological excavation 2014
Bibliography and sources	Oxford Archaeology/Ramboll 2015, *Paddington New Yard, Westbourne Park, London W9: Archaeological Fieldwork Report*, C254-OXF-T1-RGN-CRG03-50251 Hawkins, C and Reeve, G, 1987, *An Illustrated History of Great Western Railway Engine Sheds*, Wild Swan Publications
Site code	XSI10
Archive location	LAARC
Volume references	CRL Series No.4, p5
Characterisation	Complicated history of partial demolitions and rebuilds. Originally, a pair of two-storey blocks, each with a double-height bay, book-ending single storey workshops for smiths, carpenters, coppersmiths and fitters. The western block contained stores, enginemen's sleeping and waiting quarters and a night foreman's office. The eastern block housed a general office, and individual offices for 'Mr Andrews', Daniel Gooch and his clerks. Major reconfiguration in *c* 1873. Western block demolished, replaced by Repair & Paint Shop with 3 roads, each 89ft long with inspection pits. Fourth road and additional workshop space added against northern elevation in the 1880s. Eastern block demolished in *c* 1906 and remainder converted to a goods shed with two through roads. Finally all demolished in 1938.

45: Paddington New Yard – Alfred Road Warehouse

Alfred Road Warehouse, looking north-east (left) and west (right).

Monument type	CL Commercial, BT Warehouse; CL Transport, BT Railway Transport Site, NT Goods Station; CL Recreational, BT Artists Studio
Address	Great Western Road, Westbourne Park, London W2
NGR	525150, 181750
Local Planning Authority	Westminster City Council
Date built	1938
Recording note	Demolished in 2010 in advance of construction by Crossrail of a replacement concrete batching plant at Westbourne Park
Architect	Chief Engineer's Office, Paddington
Builder/Manufacturer	Not known
Original railway company	GWR
Field events	2010, EH Level 2 NLBH record, MOLA
Bibliography and sources	Crossrail, 2010, C150, *Westbourne Park, Non-listed Built Heritage Recording Report*, C150-CSY-T1-RGN-CR076_PT001-00015 Atkins, T, 2007, *GWR Goods Services Part 2A: goods depots and their operation*, Wild Swan Publications
Site code	XSA10
Archive location	LAARC
Volume references	CRL Series No.4, p101
Characterisation	Three-storey transit shed and warehouse built by GWR to handle perishable goods. Comprised a concrete-encased steel frame with brick infilling at first and second floors. At ground floor, two internal roads (only one through) separated from two external roads by a central platform. Access to upper floors via two sets of dog-leg stairs, two spiral staircases and two goods lifts. Canopy over inner external road. Used as a goods shed until December 1972, then by BR as a lost property store. From 1994 until 2009 named Great Western Studios.

47: Westbourne Park Depot – Alfred Villa

Basement of Alfred Villa, looking south east

Monument type	CL Domestic, BT Transport Workers House
Address	Great Western Road, Westbourne Park, London W2
NGR	525285, 181736
Local Planning Authority	Westminster City Council
Date built	*c* 1853
Recording note	Probably demolished to ground level in 1950s. Basement archaeologically excavated in 2011. Removed during Crossrail works.
Architect	Not known, possibly GWR
Builder/Manufacturer	Not known
Original railway company	GWR
Field events	Archaeological excavation 2011
Bibliography and sources	Oxford Archaeology/Ramboll, 2015, *Paddington New Yard, Westbourne Park, London: Archaeological Fieldwork Report*, C254-OXF-T1-RGN-CRG03-50251
Site code	XSI10
Archive location	LAARC
Volume references	CRL Series No.4, p57-8
Characterisation	Double-fronted GWR house, possibly constructed for Daniel Gooch, the company's first Locomotive Superintendent, or his deputy. The 2011 excavation exposed seven basement level rooms including a coal cellar and recorded surviving features including steps, doorways and timber door jambs.

48: Paddington Station – Platform 12 milk ramp

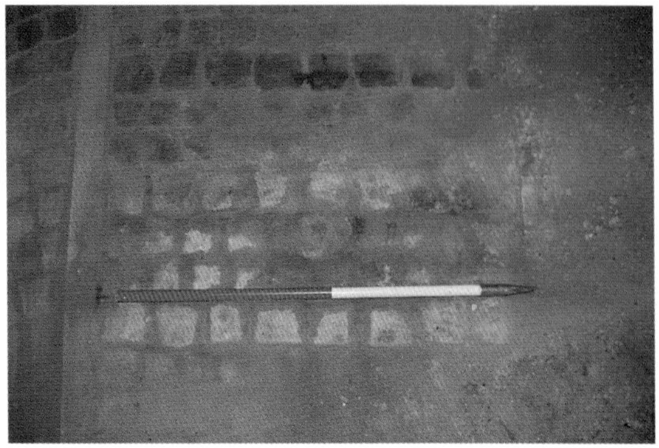

(left) Eastern elevation of the ramp between Stanchion S5 and S6, (right) detail of stone sett surface

Monument type	CL Transport, BT Ramp, NT Carriage Ramp
Address	Paddington Station, London St, London W2
NGR	526486, 181513
Local Planning Authority	Westminster City Council
Date built	1911-1916
Recording note	Demolished in advance of Crossrail works
Architect	Great Western Railway
Builder/Manufacturer	Not known
Original railway company	GWR
Field events	2009, EH Level 3 historic buildings record, Mott MacDonald Ltd
Bibliography and sources	Crossrail, 2011, C131 *Paddington Integrated Project, Building Recording, Paddington Station Milk Ramp*, C131-MMD-T1-RAN-B071-00001 Oxford Archaeology/Ramboll, 2015, *Building Recording: Paddington Station Milk Ramp*, C254-OXF-T1-RGN-CRG03-50215
Site code	N/A
Archive location	LAARC
Volume references	CRL Series No.4, p 65-6
Characterisation	As part of the modifications to Paddington Station between 1909 to 1916 a series of new platforms were provided on the arrivals side of the station and new rail access for parcels and milk was provided alongside the new fourth span. At platform level a special sunken roadway was provided, to ease the loading of wagons with milk churns. Surface access from Platform 12 was provided by a steel frame ramp, the milk ramp, which emerged along the north side of London Street. The ramp was supported by a grid of steel girder stanchions and laid with a stone sett surface and channel irons to guide wagons. During the 1930s the milk ramp became redundant and was truncated and sealed with concrete.

49: Paddington Station – shunt tunnel

Entrance to shunt tunnel from the west. Crossrail works underway.

Monument type	CL Transport, BT Railway Tunnel, RT Underground Railway Tunnel
Address	London Street, Paddington Station, London W2
NGR	526518, 181524
Local Planning Authority	Westminster City Council
Date built	1930s
Recording note	Recorded during Crossrail's alterations to the northern side of Paddington station
Architect	Not known
Builder/Manufacturer	Not known
Original railway company	GWR
Field events	2010, EH Level 2 NLBH record, Scott Wilson
Bibliography and sources	Crossrail, 2010, C131 *Paddington Integrated Project, Historic Building Recording PIP Triangle Site*, C131-MMD-T1-RAN-B071-00002
Site code	N/A
Archive location	LAARC
Volume references	CRL Series No.4, p 66
Characterisation	During the 1930s Bishop's Bridge Road Station was incorporated into Paddington Station and a shunt tunnel was built. The spur housed electric locomotives which took over from steam locomotives on their approach to the underground network to the east. The structure was formed of engineering bricks on its external envelope and red bricks internally to its ceiling. A large proportion of its historic fabric had been obscured by concrete render to the south and a modern day retaining wall to the north.

50: Paddington Station – Departures Road

Departures Road canopy looking north-west (left), railings on Eastbourne Terrace (right)

Monument type	CL Transport, BT Railway Transport Site, NT Railway Station; CL Monument, BT Barrier, NT Railings; CL Unassigned, BT Covered Way
Address	Departures Road, Paddington Station, London W2
NGR	526534, 181308
Local Planning Authority	Westminster City Council
Date built	1851-54
Recording note	Dismantling and removal of canopy, retaining wall and railings to facilitate construction of Crossrail station box. Railings retained for re-use.
Architect	Not known
Builder/Manufacturer	Fox, Henderson & Co
Original railway company	GWR
Field events	2009 and 2012, EH Level 3 historic buildings record, Scott Wilson Ltd and Oxford Archaeology/Ramboll
Bibliography and sources	Crossrail, 2009, *Paddington Station Building Recording at Departures Road*, CR-DV-PAA-X-RT-00047 Crossrail, 2015, *Building Recording, Departures Road, Paddington Station*, C254-OXF-T1-RGN-CRG03-50214
Site code	XSD10
Archive location	LAARC
Volume references	CRL Series No.4, p 63
Characterisation	Departures Road and the adjacent Eastbourne Terrace lay to the south of Grade I Listed Paddington station. The former gave access to the main station office and booking office at the base of inclines to east and west. At its lower level Departures Road was covered by a canopy and seperated from Eastbourne Terrace (which was at a higher level) by a retaining wall surmounted by cast iron railings. Roof structure an unusual variant on the Paxton-style ridge and furrow glazed roofing employed elsewhere in the station. Distinctive curved trusses rising above the line of the glazing and supporting the guttering from above. The Deaprtures Road area, and the canopy in particular, suffered significant damage during WWII. Railings restored in the late 1950s.

51: Paddington Station – Departures Road

Departures Road ramp retaining wall, looking west (left); one of two flights of steps between Departures Road and Eastbourne Terrace, looking south-east (right)

Monument type	CL Transport, BT Ramp, NT Carriage Ramp
Address	Departures Road, Paddington Station, London W2
NGR	526534, 181308
Local Planning Authority	Westminster City Council
Date built	1851-54
Recording note	Construction of Crossrail's Paddington station box requires extension of Departure Road's lowest levels into the area of Eastbourne Terrace.
Architect	Not known
Builder/Manufacturer	Fox, Henderson & Co
Original railway company	GWR
Field events	2009, EH Level 3 historic buildings record, Scott Wilson
Bibliography and sources	Crossrail, 2009, *Paddington Station Building Recording at Departures Road*, CR-DV-PAA-X-RT-00047
Site code	N/A
Archive location	LAARC
Volume references	CRL Series No.4, p 63
Characterisation	Departures Road and the adjacent Eastbourne Terrace lay to the south of Grade I Listed Paddington station. The former gave access to the main station office and booking office at the base of inclines to east and west. To retain the higher level a buttressed brick wall was constructed and two flights of stairs provided to allow pedestrian access between the two roads.

53: Paddington Station – Mint Stables

The Mint Wing of St Mary's Hospital, formerly the GWR's Mint Stables

Monument type	CL Transport, BT Stable, NT Railway Stable
Address	London Street, Paddington Station, London W2
NGR	526669, 181370
Local Planning Authority	Westminster City Council
Date built	1878
Recording note	Unaffected by Crossrail's work
Architect	Lancaster Owen
Builder/Manufacturer	Fox, Henderson & Co
Original railway company	GWR
Field events	None
Bibliography and sources	Brindle, S, 2004, *Paddington Station: Its History and Architecture*, English Heritage
Site code	N/A
Archive location	N/A
Volume references	CRL Series No.4, p 59, fn 2
Characterisation	Grade II Listed structure, formerly the Mint Stables beside Paddington station goods yard. Named after the Mint public house which had formerly stood on the site. Built to stable company horses, hundreds of which shunted railway wagons and delivered goods by road. Three-storey yellow brick building arranged around an irregular courtyard. The yard area had two levels connected by ramps leading to openings in stables. Building acquired by St Mary's Hospital in 1965.

83: Oxford House, 9-15 Oxford Street, London W1

9-15 Oxford Street, facing south

Monument type	CL Transport, NT Underground Railway Station, CL Commercial, NT Shopping Parade; CL Commercial, BT Commercial Office
Address	Oxford House, 9-15 Oxford Street, W1D 2DG
NGR	529789,181361
Local Planning Authority	Westminster City Council
Date built	Late 1890s
Recording note	Recorded in 2008 in advance of part demolition to faciliate construction of Crossrail's Tottenham Court Road eastern ticket hall
Architect	Station (ground floor and basement): Harry Bell Measures; Upper storeys: Delissa Joseph
Builder/Manufacturer	Not known
Original railway company	Central London Railway
Field events	2008- 2009, EH Level 1 NLBH record, MOLA
Bibliography and sources	MOLA, 2009, *Tottenham Court Road Station Upgrade. 1–15 Oxford Street, 157–167 and 138148 Charing Cross Road*, 1-6 Falconberg Court, London WC2
Site code	GCI08
Archive location	LAARC
Volume references	CRL Series No.3, p71; CRL Series No.4, p28
Characterisation	CLR's architect Measures designed a string of stations. These were specifically intended to carry upper storeys that had been designed and constructed by others. The parts of the building demolished by Crossrail largely corresponded to Joseph's development.

103: Smithfield Market: GWR Depot Shunters Rooms

One of the shunter's rooms (Room 3) in the GWR depot beneath Smithfield Market (looking west) (left). View of the eastern door to the mess room (Room 9) and five storage cabins (Rooms 8, 7, 6, 5 and 4), looking east (right)

Monument type	CL Transport, BT Railway Transport Site, NT Railway Storehouse
Address	Smithfield Market, London EC1A 9LH
NGR	531900, 181830
Local Planning Authority	City of London Corporation
Date built	1869
Recording note	Recorded in 2011 before demolition to facilitate construction of Crossrail's Farringdon Station eastern ticket hall
Architect	Not known
Builder/Manufacturer	Not known
Original railway company	GWR/MR
Field events	2011, EH Level 2 NLBH record, MOLA
Bibliography and sources	Crossrail, 2013, *Built Heritage Recording Report, Farringdon Station, Shunters Rooms*, C257-MLA-X-RGN-CRG03-50038
Site code	XTE12
Archive location	LAARC
Volume references	CRL Series No.4, p70
Characterisation	Series of small rooms (called the Shunters' Rooms) below Lindsey Street and to the south of the former northernmost wall of the depot sidings beneath Smith field Market. The series comprised a succession of smaller rectangular rooms, with barrel vaulted ceilings, ending with a larger room to the west. The height of the smaller rooms was *c* 6.80m and their length varied between 1.68m and 1.88m. The series ended to the west with a bigger rectangular room with a fireplace. This room had its own access to the sidings and tracks.

106: 3 Lindsey Street, London EC1 – GWR Goods Depot

View of the rooms under 3 Lindsey Street (left), view looking west showing blocked up arches at platform level (right)

Monument type	CL Transport, BT Railway Transport Site, NT Goods Station
Address	3 Lindsey Street, London EC1A 9HP
NGR	531921, 181801
Local Planning Authority	City of London Corporation
Date built	1869
Recording note	Altered and stabilised in advance of construction of Crossrail's Farringdon Station eastern ticket hall
Architect	Not known
Builder/Manufacturer	Not known
Original railway company	GWR/MR
Field events	2011, EH Level 2 NLBH record, Scott Wilson Ltd
Bibliography and sources	Crossrail 2008, *Archaeology Detailed Desk Based Assessment Farringdon Station*, CR-SD-FAR-EN-SR-00001 Crossrail, 2011, *Farringdon Station: Level II Historic Building Record*, C136-SWN-T1-RGN-M123-50002 London Metropolitan Archives, Smithfields Goods Station, Armour and Company Limited (1916-1959) GLC/AR/BR/22/BA/043620
Site code	XRU10
Archive location	LAARC
Volume references	CRL Series No.4, p70
Characterisation	Smithfield GWR goods depot built by the Corporation of London, with contributory funds from GWR and MR. Two levels were located beneath 3 Lindsey Street but were not directly accessed from it. The upper level was a basement used by GWR at 4 Lindsey Street and the lower level led to Smithfild goods depot railway platforms and sidings. Platform level was accessed from a courtyard to the rear of 3 Lindsey Street, from the adjoining 4 Lindsey Street and from a lift to 8-9 Hayne Street. Platform level rooms were initially used to house an engine and boiler, and from *c* 1931 as stores for meat before it was transferred to 8-9 Hayne Street.

108: 3 Lindsey Street, London EC1

3 Lindsey Street, western facade, looking east

Monument type	CL Commercial, NT Butchers Shop; CL Commercial, NT Meat Cellar
Address	3 Lindsey Street, London EC1A 9HP
NGR	531940, 181799
Local Planning Authority	City of London Corporation
Date built	Late 19th century
Recording note	Recorded in 2011 before demolition to facilitate construction of Crossrail's Farringdon Station eastern ticket hall
Architect	Not known
Builder/Manufacturer	Not known
Original railway company	By 1916 basement level linked to GWR office at 4 Lindsey Street and to the railway below
Field events	2011, EH Level 2 NLBH record, Scott Wilson Ltd
Bibliography and sources	Crossrail, 2011, *Farringdon Station: Level II Historic Building Record*, C136-SWN-T1-RGN-M123-50002 London Metropolitan Archives, Smithfields Goods Station, Armour and Company Limited (1916-1959) GLC/AR/BR/22/BA/043620
Site code	XRU10
Archive location	LAARC
Volume references	CRL Series No.3, p51; CRL Series No.4, p70
Characterisation	Single-storey structure situated over the eastern throat of Smithfield Market's sidings. It was likely to have been used as a meat store throughout its history. Four levels to the building; a platform at rail level, a basement, a ground floor and a mezzanine. Blocked doorways suggest the building could have been linked to the GWR railway offices at 4 Lindsey Street. From 1916 the basement was used as a meat storage area for 8-9 Hayne Street.

118: Liverpool Street Station – Queen Victoria Tunnel

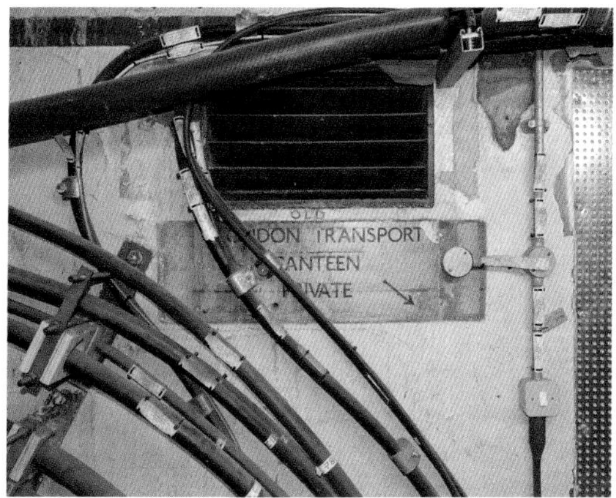

Demolition of a section of Queen Victoria Tunnel in 2014 shows that it was located not far below ground level (left). Sign on south wall of subway to Broad Street station's Underground ticket hall (right)

Monument type CL Transport, BT Railway Transport Site, NT Underground Railway Tunnel; CL Unassigned, BT Building Component, NT Canteen; CL Transport, BT Pedestrian Transport Site, NT Subway; CL Communications, BT Transmitter Site

Address Liverpool Street Station, London EC2M 2RH

NGR 533070, 181602

Local Planning Authority City of London Corporation

Date built Opened February 1875, altered to canteen mid 20th century, partly altered to a subway mid 1980s and used in 21st century as a London Regional Transport canteen and Communications Equipment Room

Recording note Partly demolished to facilitate construction of a Crossrail concourse from Broadgate ticket hall to other services

Architect Not known

Builder/Manufacturer Not known

Original railway company MR

Field events 2013, EH Level 2 NLBH record, MoLA

Bibliography and sources Crossrail, 2014, *Former Broad Street Ticket Hall and Queen Victoria Tunnel, Built Heritage Recording Report*, C257-MLA-T1-RGN-C101-50001

Site code XSM10

Archive location LAARC

Volume references CRL Series No.4, p27

Characterisation Great Eastern Railway Connection Tunnel (later Queen Victoria Tunnel) was built to provide a temporary link between the MR and Liverpool Street Station (LST) because of delays in opening their station at Bishopsgate. Terminated on Platforms 1 and 2 of LST. Regular services ended July 1875, used thereafter only very occasionally. The curved section above Broad Street ticket hall was also called the Queen Victoria Curve. During the mid 20th century the curve was converted into canteens.

119: Broad Street station – Broadgate ticket hall

Sub-station cabinets in Broad Street station's underground ticket hall, looking east (left). One of the original lengthened columns that supported the roof where the area was double-height, with blocked arched entrances to the hall's 1912 'A'-type escalators behind (right)

Monument type	CL Transport, BT Railway Transport Site, NT Railway Office; CL Industrial, BT Electricity Production Site, NT Electricity Sub Station
Address	100 Liverpool Street, London EC2M 2RH
NGR	533073, 181625
Local Planning Authority	City of London Corporation
Date built	*c* 1912
Recording note	Structure removed in 2014 to facilitate construction of Crossrail's Liverpool Street station Broadgate ticket hall
Architect	Not known
Builder/Manufacturer	Not known
Original railway company	CLR
Field events	2013, EH Level 2 NLBH record, MoLA
Bibliography and sources	Crossrail, 2014, *Former Broad Street Ticket Hall and Queen Victoria Tunnel, Built Heritage Recording Report*, C257-MLA-T1-RGN-C101-50001
Site code	XSM10
Archive location	LAARC
Volume references	CRL Series No.4, p27
Characterisation	A large subterreanean area built in *c* 1912 when the Central Line was extended from Bank to Liverpool Street. It was the last surviving part of Broad Street station, all else being demolished in the 1980s. The concrete roof was supported by iron columns and beams. The booking hall originally had ticket windows in the south partition wall (accessed via a staff doorway in the west wall), a Passimeter and turnstiles and two early escalators down to the Central Line platform. The ticket hall also had a cylindrical shaft through which two lifts connecting the underground platform with Broad Street station passed. After the station closed in 1985 the ticket hall was converted into a sub-station.

121: Whitechapel station – subways

Subway stairs connecting Platform 1/2 to Platform 5 (left); detail of glazed tiles in subway from Platform 1/2 (former Platform 1) (right)

Monument type	CL Transport, BT Railway Transport Site
Address	Whitechapel station, 277 Whitechapel Rd, E1 1BY
NGR	534650, 181850
Local Planning Authority	Tower Hamlets Council
Date built	1935
Recording note	Removal of subways as part of Crossrail's redevelopment of Whitechapel station
Architect	Not known
Builder/Manufacturer	Not known
Original railway company	LPTB
Field events	2012, EH Level 1 NLBH record, MoLA
Bibliography and sources	Crossrail, 2013, C261 *Archaeology Early East. Built Heritage Recording Report Whitechapel Station*, C261-MLA-X-RGN-CR140-50165 Crossrail 2008, *Conservation Area Consent- Heritage and Planning Statement: Whitechapel Bridges and Walls*, C140-HYD-Z-QAP-D061-00032
Site code	XSH10
Archive location	LAARC
Volume references	CRL Series No.4, p23
Characterisation	Two low level subways linking Platforms 1/2 and 3/4 on the Hammersmith and City Line to Platform 5 on the former ELR. Although of different shapes in plan, the tunnels have the same orientation, similar size and run partly parallel. Finishes include extensive use of Poole large profile ceramic tiles, in oatmeal/yellow, with decorative bands in blue, green and orange (cream tiles measure 302 x 423mm, blue tiles 74 x 302mm, green and orange tiles 350 x 423mm). Above the staircases two 'Way Out' bronze-framed signs in 1938 Standard Signs Manual pattern.

124: Whitechapel station – 1902 footbridge

1902 footbridge, southern side of staircase to former Platform 2 (left); western elevation of footbridge (right)

Monument type	CL Transport, BT Bridge, NT Footbridge; CL Transport, BT Pedestrian Transport Site, NT Steps
Address	Whitechapel station, 277 Whitechapel Road, E1 1BY
NGR	534680, 181860
Local Planning Authority	Tower Hamlets Council
Date built	1902
Recording note	Partial demolition to facilitate Crossrail's redevelopment of Whitechapel station
Architect	Not known
Builder/Manufacturer	Not known
Original railway company	WBR, a joint venture between MDR and LTSR
Field events	2012, EH Level 2 NLBH record, MoLA
Bibliography and sources	Crossrail, 2013, *C261 Archaeology Early East. Built Heritage Recording Report Whitechapel Station*, C261-MLA-X-RGN-CR140-50165
	Crossrail 2008, *Conservation Area Consent- Heritage and Planning Statement: Whitechapel Bridges and Walls*, C140-HYD-Z-QAP-D061-00032
Site code	XSH10
Archive location	LAARC
Volume references	CRL Series No.4, p23
Characterisation	Timber and cast-iron footbridge linking former MDR Booking Hall with Platforms 1 and 2 (now 1/2 and 3/4). Double-pitch timber roof covered in sheet corrugated iron and supported on cast iron ribs. In *c* 1914 the the northern end of the bridge and the staircase were replaced with a raised structure built in the same materials.

125: Whitechapel Station – Metropolitan District Railway Booking Hall

Whitechapel station's Metropolitan District Railway Booking Hall, looking south (left) and from above (right)

Monument type CL Transport, BT Railway Transport Site, NT Railway Office

Address Whitechapel station, 277 Whitechapel Road, E1 1BY

NGR 534701, 181849

Local Planning Authority Tower Hamlets Council

Date built 1884

Recording note Partial demolition to facilitate Crossrail's redevelopment of Whitechapel station

Architect MDR

Builder/Manufacturer Not known

Original railway company MDR

Field events 2012, EH Level 2 NLBH record, MoLA

Bibliography and sources Crossrail, 2013, *C261 Archaeology Early East. Built Heritage Recording Report Whitechapel Station*, C261-MLA-X-RGN-CR140-50165

Crossrail, 2008, *Conservation Area Consent- Heritage and Planning Statement: Whitechapel Bridges and Walls*, C140-HYD-Z-QAP-D061-00032

Site code XSH10

Archive location LAARC

Volume references CRL Series No.4, p24

Characterisation Former MDR booking hall which served as its terminus and was known as Whitechapel (Mile End) to differentiate it from the adjoining ELR station. In 1902, to allow the new Whitechapel and Bow Railway extension to use the station, the booking hall was shortened and used as a link between a new ticket hall and footbridge.

126: Whitechapel station – 1902 ticket hall

1902 ticket hall, looking north (left). The roof is supported by cast-iron ribs, formed by the bolting together of an upper pointed rib and a lower elliptical rib (right)

Monument type	CL Transport, BT Railway Transport Site, NT Railway Office
Address	Whitechapel station, 277 Whitechapel Rd, E1 1BY
NGR	534710, 181845
Local Planning Authority	Tower Hamlets Council
Date built	1902
Recording note	Partial demolition to facilitate Crossrail's redevelopment of Whitechapel station
Architect	Not known
Builder/Manufacturer	Not known
Original railway company	WBR, a joint venture between MDR and LTSR
Field events	2012, EH Level 2 NLBH record, MOLA
Bibliography and sources	Crossrail, 2013, *C261 Archaeology Early East. Built Heritage Recording Report Whitechapel Station*, C261-MLA-X-RGN-CR140-50165 Crossrail 2008, *Conservation Area Consent- Heritage and Planning Statement: Whitechapel Bridges and Walls*, C140-HYD-Z-QAP-D061-00032
Site code	XSH10
Archive location	LAARC
Volume references	CRL Series No.4, p25
Characterisation	Built in 1902 as part of a redevelopment of the station to accommodate the addition of a new line (the WBR) to Bromley-by-Bow. Comprising five bays with decorative cast iron ribs supporting its roof. Rooms flanking the hall were originally used as lavatories, offices, a waiting room and a booking office. Linked to the shortened remains of the former MDL booking hall, which it replaced.

135: Pudding Mill Lane station, London E15

The entrance to the DLR's 1996 Pudding Mill Lane station, looking north-west

Monument type	CL Transport, BT Railway Transport site; NT Railway Station
Address	Pudding Mill Lane, Stratford, London E15 2NQ
NGR	537823, 183533
Local Planning Authority	Newham Council
Date built	1996
Recording note	Demolished to allow construction of Crossrail ramp down to tunnel portal. Station rebuilt to the south
Architect	Fletcher Priest Architects
Builder/Manufacturer	Not known
Original railway company	DLR
Field events	None
Bibliography and sources	Crossrail, 2008, *Pudding Mill Lane Portal (including HAM and Wick Sewer Diversion), Archaeological Detailed Desk Based Assessment*, CR-SD-CT1-EN-SR-00001
Site code	XPM09 and XSK10
Archive location	LAARC
Volume references	CRL Series No.4, p19
Characterisation	Station closed on 11 April 2014; demolished shortly afterwards. Comprised two platfoms with a 'Y'-shaped central canopy. A dinstinctive feature was a tall post beside the entrance which carried a circular structure with the station name on it. Platforms accessed via a narrow central stair with one stage which lead upwards from a lobby under the tracks (entered at approximately at ground level). This housed the station's ticket machines.

138: Connaught Tunnel, Silvertown, London E16

The twin-bore section of Connaught Tunnel (left), view south from the southern portal (right)

Monument type	CL Transport, BT Railway Transport site; NT Railway Tunnel
Address	Connaught Tunnel, Silvertown, London E16
NGR	541441, 180859 to 541847, 180273
Local Planning Authority	Newham Council
Date built	1879
Recording note	Recorded before the tunnel was reinforced, cleaned and widened by Crossrail, with the twin-bore section altered to one tunnel by July 2014.
Architect	Not known
Builder/Manufacturer	1879 London & St Katherine Docks Company; 1935 steel lining to the twin-bore section by Charles Brand & Sons Ltd, Merton, Surrey
Original railway company	GER
Field events	2011, EH Level 3 NLBH record, MOLA
Bibliography and sources	Crossrail, 2011, *Connaught Tunnel, Pumphouse and Air Vents: Non-listed Built Heritage Recording*, C263-MLA-X-RGN-CRG07-50039
Site code	XSY11
Archive location	LAARC
Volume references	CRL Series No.4, p80
Characterisation	Built to carry the North Woolwich Line under Connaught Passage, a short canal which links the Royal Victoria and Royal Albert docks. The brick-lined tunnel is 600m long with a set of 15 concrete buttresses at either end of the tunnel. When Connaught Passage was deepened in 1935 the central twin-bore section of the tunnel was strengthened with steel linings to mitigate the reduction in thickness of each tunnel's apex. It is only in recent times that it has come to be known as Connaught Tunnel, its previous name being Silvertown Tunnel.

139: Connaught Tunnel – Pump House and Air Vents

The southern facade of the pump house (left); the southern air vent, looking north (right)

Monument type	CL Water Supply and Drainage, BT Water Disposal Site, Pumping Station; CL Unassigned, BT Shaft, NT Ventilation Shaft
Address	Connaught Tunnel, Silvertown, London E16
NGR	Pump house 541691, 180657 (vents 30m NW and 88m SSE from this)
Local Planning Authority	Newham Council
Date built	1879
Recording note	Recorded before Crossrail's redevelopment of the area. Pump house dismantled for re-use elsewhere.
Architect	Not known
Builder/Manufacturer	London & St Katherine Docks Company
Original railway company	GER
Field events	2011, EH Level 3 NLBH record, MOLA
Bibliography and sources	Crossrail, 2011, *Connaught Tunnel, Pumphouse and Air Vents: Non-listed Built Heritage Recording*, C263-MLA-X-RGN-CRG07-50039
Site code	XSY11
Archive location	LAARC
Volume references	CRL Series No.4, p22
Characterisation	Two identical surface air vents and an octagonal Gault brick pump house serviced Connaught Tunnel. Pump house covered a shaft containing original pumping apparatus, operational until 2012. Roofed in grey slate with lead flashing along the edge of each roof segment. Surmounted with louvred timber vent, also roofed in slate. Five windows, formerly six, original decorative metal frames. Air vents constructed from yellow London stock brick coursed entirely in snapped headers. Each vent plinth is 3.03m wide x 0.85m high and culminates in two courses of chamfered bricks.

141: North Woolwich: miscellaneous items of railway infrastructure

Former siding tracks on Factory Road (left); granite sett road surface opening into Factory Road from railway line to the north (right)

Monument type	CL Transport, BT Railway Transport site, NT Railway, NT Goods Yard, NT Signal Box
Address	Factory Road, North Woolwich, London
NGR	Sidings centred at 542772, 179984; signal box at 543241, 179802; road junction to railway at 542866, 179968; level-crossing gates at 542776, 180000
Local Planning Authority	Newham Council
Date built	Later 19th to mid 20th century
Recording note	Recorded in 2013 before removal to allow construction of Crossrail's North Woolwich Portal
Architect	Not known
Builder/Manufacturer	Not known
Original railway company	ECR
Field events	2012, EH Level 2 NLBH Record
Bibliography and sources	Crossrail, 2012, *North Woolwich Portal Archaeological Written Scheme of Investigation*, C122-OVE-T1-GMS-CR146-50003
Site code	XSV11
Archive location	LAARC
Volume references	N/A. Example of recorded railway street heritage
Characterisation	A number of items relating to railways in the area were recorded in 2012. These included the tracks of three former sidings where they crossed Factory Road to connect the North Woolwich line with dock-side industries (such as Tate & Lyle) to the south. Other items included level-crossing posts (comprising two bullhead rails bolted together and closed at the top) and the remainder of their gates, a granite sett road surface on a junction from Factory Road into the railway corridor, the former goods yard to North Woolwich station and a former timber-framed and iron-reinforced signal box south of the railway tracks near Woolwich Pier.

142: North Woolwich – Henley's Footbridge

Henley's Footbridge, looking west (left) and north (right). Note replacement steel column

Monument type	CL Transport, BT Railway Transport site, NT Footbridge
Address	Albert Road and Factory Road, North Woolwich, London
NGR	542876, 179966
Local Planning Authority	Newham Council
Date built	1892
Recording note	Dismantled by Crossrail and relocated to Whitwell & Reepham Railway, Norfolk
Architect	Not known
Builder/Manufacturer	Eastwood, Swingler and Co. Ltd, Derby
Original railway company	GER
Field events	2011, EH Level 3 NLBH record, MOLA
Bibliography and sources	Crossrail, 2011, *Non-Listed Built Heritage Recording Report North Woolwich Railway Footbridge*, C263-MLA-X-RGN-CRG07-50024
Site code	XSV11
Archive location	LAARC
Volume references	CRL Series No.4, p2
Characterisation	Wrought iron footbridge supported on twelve ornate Tuscan cast-iron columns. Panels of lattice ironwork, rivetted to lengths of iron in 'T' or 'L' profiles. Provided workers' access to Henley's Electric Cable works.

145: Ilford Depot EMU – Workshop B

Ilford Depot's Workshop B, facing east

Monument type	CL Transport, BT Railway Transport Site, NT Railway Engineering Workshop
Address	Ley Street, Ilford, IG1 4BP
NGR	544465, 186849
Local Planning Authority	Redbridge Council
Date built	1948
Recording note	Alterations in connection with establishment of a Crossrail stabling yard
Architect	Not known
Builder/Manufacturer	Not known
Original railway company	BR (ER)
Field events	2016, EH Level 1 NLBH record, Oxford Archaeology/Ramboll
Bibliography and sources	Crossrail 2013, *Ilford Depot Site Specific Written Scheme of Investigation*, C254-OXF-T1-GMS-CRG03-50007
Site code	N/A
Archive location	LAARC
Volume references	CRL Series No.4, p88
Characterisation	Large rectangular building with three through roads, established as a Carriage Cleaning Shed. An integral extension attached to the north elevation housed Plant, Stores and Messrooms.

146: Plumstead Goods Depot – air raid shelters

Shelter 1's escape shaft (left); interior of Shelter 2, looking west (right)

Monument type	CL Defence, BT Civil Defence Site, NT Blast Shelter
Address	White Hart Road, Plumstead, London SE18 1DE
NGR	Shelter 1: 545708, 178933 Shelter 2: 545278, 178904
Local Planning Authority	London Borough of Greenwich
Date built	Between 1939-45
Recording note	Recorded before removal to facilitate construction of Crossrail's tunnel portal at Plumstead
Architect	Not known
Builder/Manufacturer	Not known
Original railway company	SR
Field events	2011, EH Level 2 NLBH record, MOLA
Bibliography and sources	Crossrail, 2011, *Non-listed Built Heritage Recording Report, Plumstead Portal, Worksites West and East*, C263-MLA-X-RGN-CRG07-50025
Site code	XSW11
Archive location	LAARC
Volume references	CRL Series No.4, p77
Characterisation	Two WWII air raid shelters (not bomb proof) formed from pre-cast reinforced concrete posts, double-pitched trusses and panels. Shelters erected in trenches and covered with trench risings. Shelter 1 offered protection for those working in the yard's carriage sidings; Shelter 2 for those at eastern end of the goods yard. Each had two entrances in order that a means of escape remained should one became blocked. Shelter 1's entrance was at 90° to its axis, a short escape tunnel and hatch was situated midway down the shelter and a circular air vent was provided at the opposite end to the entrance. The design of Shelter 2 was difficult to identify due partial collapse of its structure.

148: Plumstead Station: East and West Goods Yards

Post-1951 concrete-framed shed in Plumstead station goods yards

Monument type	CL Transport, BT Railway Transport Site, NT Rail Depot, NT Railway, NT Railway Building
Address	Plumstead station, London, SE18 7EA
NGR	Centred on 545483, 178899
Local Planning Authority	London Borough of Greenwich
Date built	Mid 19th to late 20th centuries
Recording note	Recorded before removal to facilitate construction of Crossrail's tunnel portal at Plumstead
Architect	Not known
Builder/Manufacturer	Not known
Original railway company	SER
Field events	2011, EH Level 1 NLBH record, MOLA
Bibliography and sources	Crossrail 2011, *Non-listed Built Heritage Recording Report, Plumstead Portal, Worksites West and East*, C263-MLA-X-RGN-CRG07-50025
Site code	XSW11
Archive location	LAARC
Volume references	CRL Series No.4, p101
Characterisation	Post-1951 buildings, track and associated rail infrastructure relating to the goods yards at Plumstead station. This included concrete buffer blocks and iron railings. The structure pictured was formed from tall concrete uprights that divided the structure into seven bays and carried concrete roof trusses. Clad in corrugated asbestos and PVC materials. Waist-height brick infill to walls. One through road beside internal concrete apron.

152: Old Oak Common TMD – refuse incinerator

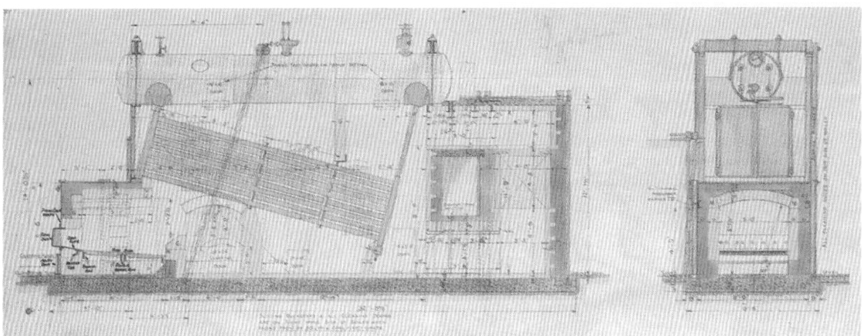

Sections through the Old Oak Common's refuse incinerator plant

Monument type	CL Industrial, BT Waste Disposal Site RT Refuse Destructor Station
Address	Old Oak Common, Acton, London NW10 6DU
NGR	521696, 182441
Local Planning Authority	Hammersmith and Fulham Council
Date built	1927
Recording note	Demolished when Old Oak Common converted to a diesel locomotive depot in the mid 1960s
Architect	GWR Swindon
Builder/Manufacturer	New Destructor Co. Ltd, Pershore, Worcs
Original railway company	GWR
Field events	None
Bibliography and sources	Crossrail, 2010, *Old Oak Common Worksites, Archaeological Detailed Desk Based Assessment: Non-Listed Built Heritage*, C150-CSY-T1-RGN-CR076_PT001-00011
Site code	N/A
Archive location	N/A
Volume references	CRL Series No.4, pp45-6
Characterisation	Refuse destructor (an incinerator) built a short distance to the north-east of the engine shed. Designed to burn waste in a coal-fired furnace which heated a boiler, the steam from which drove two new compound duplex pumps installed in the adjoining boiler house. The refuse was brought by wagons via the existing siding; smoke was expelled through an 80ft high brick chimney situated remotely beside the south-west corner.

153: Old Oak Common TMD – air raid shelter

The former WWII air raid shelter at the eastern throat of Old Oak Common TMD. Facing north

Monument type	CL Defence, BT Air Raid Shelter, NT Blast Shelter
Address	Old Oak Common, Acton, London NW10 6DU
NGR	522067, 182238
Local Planning Authority	Hammersmith and Fulham Council
Date built	1939-1943
Recording note	Building demolished to facilitate construction of Crossrail's tunnel segment factory
Architect	Not known
Builder/Manufacturer	Not known
Original railway company	GWR
Field events	2010, EH Level 2 NLBH record, Oxford Archaeology/Ramboll
Bibliography and sources	Crossrail, 2010, *Old Oak Common Worksites, Archaeological Detailed Desk Based Assessment: Non-Listed Built Heritage*, C150-CSY-T1-RGN-CR076_PT001-00011 Crossrail, 2015, *Old Oak Common Non-Listed Built Heritage Recording Report*, C254-OXF-T1-RGN-CRG05-50001
Site code	XSU10
Archive location	LAARC
Volume references	CRL Series No.4, p76
Characterisation	Surface air raid shelter, probably built during the earlier stages of WWII to offer blast protection to staff working in the remote eastern end of Old Oak Common TMD. Present on a drawing of the yard prepared in Sept 1943. Thin, single-storey rectangular building constructed from red engineering brick in English Bond except for the northern wall, which was of concrete block construction. Shallow double-pitched concrete roof with transverse shutter marks. A thick, 'L'-shaped rendered brick blast wall protected the original doorm which had been in the eastern elevation. This was later bricked-up. After the war it was converted to a Shunter's Cabin and all of the extant window and door openings dated from this post-war period.

154: Westbourne Park Depot – Marcon Sewer

The Marcon Sewer was exposed in 2010 (left) and 2014 (right).

Monument type	CL Transport, BT Railway Transport Site
Address	Great Western Road, Westbourne Park, London W2
NGR	523124, 181738 (centre)
Local Planning Authority	Westminster City Council
Date built	Probably 1853
Recording note	Exposed during excavations at Paddington New Yard and when it was locally diverted to allow construction of Crossrail's Royal Oak tunnel portal
Architect	GWR Swindon
Builder/Manufacturer	GWR Swindon
Original railway company	GWR
Field events	Archaeological excavation 2010-4
Bibliography and sources	Oxford Archaeology/Ramboll 2013, *Archaeological Watching Brief in the Vicinity of Westbourne Park and Royal Oak Stations, Paddington, London: Targeted and General Watching Brief Fieldwork Report*, C254-OXF-T1-RGN-CRG03-50047 Oxford Archaeology/Ramboll 2015, *Paddington New Yard, Westbourne Park, London W9: Archaeological Fieldwork Report*, C254-OXF-T1-RGN-CRG03-50251
Site code	XSI10
Archive location	LAARC
Volume references	CRL Series No.4, pp8-9
Characterisation	Westbourne Park Depot was drained by a east-to-west aligned brick conduit which later became known as the Marcon Sewer (after the name of a concrete manufacturer who occupied the site). This may have been constructed in the 1850s specifically to drain the depot, but it is also possible that it was laid when the GWR main line was constructed during the 1830s. The drain could be accessed in a number of locations in the depot via manholes attached to, or within buildings. Built from red unfrogged bricks bonded with pale grey mortar. It remains a live drain.

157: Ilford Depot EMU – Workshop A

Ilford Depot's Workshop A, facing north-east (left). The offices attached to the north elevation, facing east (right)

Monument type	CL Transport, BT Railway Transport Site, NT Railway Engineering Workshop
Address	Ley Street, Ilford, IG1 4BP
NGR	544487, 186884
Local Planning Authority	Redbridge Council
Date built	1948
Recording note	Internal alterations in connection with establishment of a Crossrail stabling yard
Architect	Not known
Builder/Manufacturer	Not known
Original railway company	BR (ER)
Field events	2014, EH Level 1 NLBH record, Oxford Archaeology/Ramboll
Bibliography and sources	Crossrail 2013, *Ilford Depot Site Specific Written Scheme of Investigation*, C254-OXF-T1-GMS-CRG03-50007
Site code	N/A
Archive location	LAARC
Volume references	CRL Series No.4, p88
Characterisation	Built as two large conjoining rectangular sheds with three through roads in each. In essence, two steel structures clad in lightweight materials, the northernmost of which was equipped with Babcock and Wilcox overhead travelling cranes with main load limits of 25 tons. The northern block housed a repair area; in the smaller building to the south trains were inspected on a four-day cycle. Smaller buildings attached to the northern elevation provided accommodation for a large machine shop, stores, offices and lavatories etc. In 1956 the inspection area had two of its three roads removed and its pits infilled. The stores were then re-located to the western part of the building.

BIBLIOGRAPHY

Manuscript sources

Wiltshire and Swindon History Centre

GWR DRAWINGS

WSHC 2515/403/0351 - 'Alteration to Turning Bar and Stop Lever, Ransomes & Rapier 65' Turntable Old Oak Common. Swindon', March 1906

WSHC 2515/403/0363 - 'Old Oak Common Extension of Electricity Sub-Station', May 1939

WSHC 2515/403/0361(A) - Old Oak Common New Carriage Lifting & Painting Shops, Drawing No. 4, Details of Offices, Stores &c' (drawing no. 112175, dated 26 Sept 1938). Includes overlay (drawing no. Q.3027: 'Proposed Sleeping Accommodation for Company's Staff (96 Bunks)', dated 21/11/1940

WSHC 2515/403/0774 - 'GWR Coffee Tavern at Westbourne Park Station: Proposed Conversion into Deeds Office', 1921

WSHC 2515/403/2185 - 'Old Oak Common Locomotive Yard. Proposed Locomotive Oil Fuelling Plant', September 1946. Drawing No. 123770A, superseded by Drawing No. 123770/B

WSHC 2515/403/2194 - 'Old Oak Common Loco Yard Survey, September 1943'

WSHC 2515/406/0852 - Westbourne Park's workshop engine, boiler and pump room, as proposed in 1886

WSHC 2515/406/0852/3– 'Westbourne Park - Arrangement of Boilers & Pumps', November 1886

WSHC 2515/406/0881/1 - 'Arrangement of pumps for 11'0" dia well, Westbourne Park', May 1898

WSHC 2515/406/1370 - 'Proposed new Messrooms in Old Sand Furnace House and new Cloakrooms in old Messrooms, Engine Shed Old Oak Common', August 1937

WSHC 2515/406/1551 - 'Arrangement of Electric Lighting Carriage Shed Old Oak Common', April 1906

WSHC 2515/406/1806 - 'Detail of Roof & Partition to General Offices Engine Shed', April 1903

WSHC 2515/406/2621 - Arrangement of LT Gear for 50-Tons 4 Motor Crane, S.H. Heywood & Co. Ltd Reddish. Order no. 1872, date 26/09/1928

WSHC 2515/406/3201 - 'Block Plan of Hydraulic Slewing Gears 45' Turntable Westbourne Park', March 1881

WSHC 2515/406/3348 - 'Detail of Offices, Lifting Shop, ES Old Oak Common', March 1903

WSHC 2515/406/3394 - Arrangement of LT Gear for 50-Tons 4 Motor Crane, S.H. Heywood & Co. Ltd Reddish. Order no. 1872, date 26/09/1928

WSHC 2515/406/3394 - Wiring diagram for 50 Tons 4 Motor E.O .T Crane, received 23/10/1929

WSHC 2515/409/0040 - Plan of the boiler and pump rooms at Westbourne Park

WSHC 2515/409/0051 - 'Sandhouse for Westbourne Park'

WSHC 2515/409/0056 - 'Lifting Shop for Westbourne Park', issued 1879

WSHC 2515/409/0075 - 'Boiler House Economical Boiler Washing Plant Old Oak Common', December 1910

WSHC 2515/409/0119/1 - 'Tank and Engine House: Centrifugal Pumps', December 1886

WSHC 2515/409/0135 - 'Arrangement of House Economical Boiler Washing Plant Old Oak Common', December 1910

WSHC 2515/409/0138 - 1911 proposal for altering the mess rooms and stores in the carriage shed at Old Oak Common

WSHC 2515/409/338 - 'New Carriage Shed at Old Oak Common', n/d. *c* 1905

WSHC 2515/409/0772 - 'Building for Refuse Destructor, Old Oak Common', May 1927

WSHC 2515/409/0774/1 - WR drawing 'Old Oak Common General Sections of Plant', July 1927

WSHC 2515/409/0803 - 'Old Oak Common Elevations of Furnace & Boiler', July 1927

WSHC 2515/409/0804 - 'Old Oak Common Refuse Destructor Building', May 1927

WSHC 2515/409/0862 - 'Old Oak Common General Plan of Plant, New Destructor Co. Ltd', June 1927

WSHC 2515/409/0863 - 'Old Oak Common Boiler Setting & Flues, New Destructor Co. Ltd', July 1927

WSHC 2515/409/0866 - 'Old Oak Common 400' & 500' Outside Pits Coal Stage Old Oak Common', December 1907

WSHC 2515/409/0869 - Old Oak Common's southern sand house, 1903 plan

WSHC 2515/409/1172 - '88' Outside Pit (Chair Road) Engine Shed Old Oak Common', December 1906

WSHC 2515/409/1180 - '226'6" Outside Pit (Chair Road) Engine Shed Old Oak Common', May 1907

WSHC 2515/409/0866 - 'Old Oak Common 400' & 500' Outside Pits Coal Stage Old Oak Common', December 1907

WSHC 2525/410/0062 - 'Old Oak Common Locomotive Yard Proposed Engine Pits', October 1906

WSHC 2515/410/0672 - Oak Common Locomotive Yard, Survey September 1943

WSHC 2515/410/0720 - 'Proposed New Engine Shed, Coaling Plant etc', December 1943

WSHC 2525/410/1187 - 'Old Oak Common Locomotive Yard Proposed Locomotive Oil Fuelling Plant', Drawing No. 123770B, October 1946

WSHC 2515/410/1773 - 'New Goods Depot at Westbourne Park', December 1907

BR (WR) DRAWINGS

WSHC (reference No. unknown) - 'Proposed Fuelling Facilities for Gas Turbine Locomotives, Locomotive Oil Fuelling Depot Old Oak Common', March 1949, BR (WR) 127624

WSHC 2515/403/2194 - 'Old Oak Common – Motive Power Depot, Proposed Accommodation for Gas Turbine and Diesel Elec. Locos', August 1952, BR (WR) 131763

WSHC 2515/403/2196 - 'Old Oak Common: Proposed Additional Facilities for Servicing Diesel Locos', September 1960, BR (WR) drawing 152798

WSHC 2515/406/0908 - Cowans Sheldon & Co Ltd drawings 'General Arrangement for 65' Articulated Engine Turntable', April 1952

WSHC 2515/406/1388 - 'Arrangement of Fuelling Facilities for Diesel and Gas Turbine Locos, Old Oak Common Motive Power Depot', February 1952

WSHC 2515/406/1414 - General Arrangement for 70' Articulated Engine Turntable', December 1952

WSHC 2515/410/0690 - 'Old Oak Common Proposed Conversion of Carriage Paint Shop for Diesel Pullman Maintenance', October 1959

WSHC 2515/410/1781 - ' Old Oak Common Conversion to Diesel Depot' ('Preliminary Drawing not to be worked to'), undated

TNA

TNA AN 91/12 - Opening ceremony of the new Western Region Diesel Depot Old Oak Common, 02/10/1965

TNA AN 8/16, 1 - British Transport Commission, *Modernisation and Re-equipment of British Railways: Design of Motive Power Depots. Part I: Planning a DMU Depot*, 31/03/1956

TNA RAIL 250/47 - GWR Minutes of the Board of Directors No. 44, 1903-05

TNA RAIL 250/48 - GWR Minutes of the Board of Directors No. 45, 1905-07

TNA RAIL 250/58 - GWR Minutes of the Board of Directors No. 55, 1938-1941

TNA RAIL 250/59 - GWR Minutes of the Board of Directors No. 56, 1941-1943

TNA RAIL 250/60 - GWR Minutes of the Board of Directors No. 57, 1943-1945

TNA RAIL 250/62 - GWR Minutes of the Board of Directors No. 58, 1945-1947

TNA RAIL 250/339 - GWR Traffic Committee Minutes No. 6, 1897-99

TNA RAIL 250/340 - GWR Traffic Committee Minutes No. 7, 1899-1900

TNA RAIL 250/270 - GWR Locomotive, Carriage & Stores Committee Minutes No. 3, 1898-1902

TNA RAIL 250/271 - GWR Locomotive, Carriage & Stores Committee Minutes No. 4, 1902-1904

TNA RAIL 252/1340 - General Conditions & Specification of Works

TNA RAIL 252/1340 - 'New Engine Shed & other works at Old Oak Common Acton', Specification, Schedule of Quantities & Contract, dated 04/01/1904

TNA RAIL 252/1462 - 'New Carriage Shed & other works at Old Oak Common, Acton. Thomas Rowbotham & the GWR Award', 19/03/1907

TNA RAIL 253/309 - Old Oak Common Division, Damage Caused by Enemy Action, 1940

ESSEX RECORD OFFICE

ERO D-Z 346-3003-53 - Railway Executive Eastern Region drawing 'Ilford Carr Depot', dated 1953

ERO D-Z 346-3003-57 - British Railways Eastern Region, 'Proposed Inspection and Cleaning Shed and Alterations', January 1956

ERO D-Z 346-3003-74 - Railway Executive drawing, 'Ilford Carriage Sheds', 1955

ERO D-Z 346-5003-34 - Railway Executive drawing, 'Ilford Carriage Sheds and Sidings Proposed Electric Lighting', July 1948

EAST ANGLIAN FILM ARCHIVE

Cat. No. 594 - 'Safety Line', a 10 minute film devoted to the activities undertaken at the depot. This was produced in 1956 by the Essex Education Committee County Film Service

LONDON METROPOLITAN ARCHIVES

LMA, GLC/AR/BR/22/BA/043620 – 1916, 1939, Smithfield Goods Station, Armour and Company Limited, 52-64 Charterhouse Street, 8-9 Hayne Street, 4 Lindsey Street, Long Lane, City of London: Building Act case file (Goods Stations and Shops)

MUSEUM OF LONDON DOCKLANDS, THE SAINSBURY STUDY CENTRE

MLDSSC 5/15/219 - London & St Katharine Docks Company General Meetings Minutes (1874-90)

Printed and secondary works

Atkins, P J, 1977 'London's Intra-Urban Milk Supply, circa 1790-1914', *Transactions of the Institute of British Geographers*, New Series, **2**, No. 3, 383-399

Atkins, T, 2007 *GWR Goods Services: Part 2A Goods Depots and their Operation*, Wild Swan Publications

Baker, J H, 1906 'Composite Roofs', *Transactions of the Swindon Engineering Society* 1906-7, 145-168

Bolton, D K, Croot, P E C, and Hicks, M A, 1982 'Willesden: Settlement and growth', in *A History of the County of Middlesex: Volume 7, Acton, Chiswick, Ealing and Brentford, West Twyford, Willesden*, ed. T F T Baker and C R Elrington (London), pp. 182-204 http://www.british-history.ac.uk/vch/middx/vol7/pp182-204 [accessed 15 March 2016]

Bell, R, 1946 *History of the British Railways During the War, 1939-45*, The Railway Gazette

Brindle, S, 2013 *Paddington Station: its history and architecture*, 2nd edition, English Heritage

British Railways Board, 1963 *The Re-shaping of British Railways: Part 1:Report*, HMSO

British Railways Board, 1980 *A Cross-London Rail Link: A British Railways Board discussion paper*, British Rail Publications

British Transport Commission, 1948 *British Railways: The New Organisation*

British Transport Commission, 1955 *Modernisation and Re-Equipment of British Railways.*

Brodribb, J, 2009 *The Main Lines of East Anglia*, Ian Allan

Brown, J, 2012 *London Railway Atlas,* 3rd Edition, Ian Allan

Brown, R, Munby, J, Shelley, A, and Smith, K, 2016 *The Changing Face of London. Historic Buildings and the Crossrail Route*, Crossrail Archaeology Publication, Oxford Archaeology

Burdett Wilson, R, 1972 *Sir Daniel Gooch: Memoirs and Diary*, David & Charles

Davies, E, 1908 *The Nationalisation of Railways*, Adam and Charles Black, London

Day, J R, and Reed, J, 2008 *The Story of London's Underground*, Capital Transport

Dobinson, C, 2001 *AA Command. Britain's Anti-Aircraft Defences of the Second World War*, Methuen

Dodd, George, 1856 *The Food of London: A Sketch of the Chief Varieties, Sources of Supply, Probable Quantities, Modes of Arrival, Processes of Manufacture, Suspected Adulteration, and Machinery of Distribution, of the Food for a Community of Two Millions and a Half*, London: Longman, Brown, Green and Longmans

Drummond, D, 2010 *Tracing Your Railway Ancestors*, Pen and Sword Family History

Faultless, A T, undated *True stories of the GWR footplate during the 1939-45 war,* unpublished

Forsythe, H G, 1981 *Steam Shed Portrait*, Atlantic Books

Fussell, G E, 1966 *The English Dairy Farmer*, London, Cass

Gourvish, T, 1986 *British Railways 1948-73*, Cambridge University Press

Gourvish, T, 2002 *British Rail 1974-97: From Integration to Privatisation*, Oxford University Press

Greeves, I S, 1980 *London Docks 1800-1900: a civil engineering history*, Thomas Telford Ltd

GWR, 1942 'Women Locomotive Builders at The Swindon works', *Great Western Railway Magazine* **54**, 123-4

Hall, S A, 1965 'The Cattle Plague of 1865', *Proceedings of the Royal Society of Medicine* **58**, 799-801

Hansard HC Deb = Hansard, *House of Common Reports*, 5th series, 1909-1981; 6th series, 1981 to date

Haresnape, B, 1979 *British Rail 1948-78: A Journey by Design*, Ian Allan

Hawkins, C and Reeve, G, 1987 *An Illustrated History of Great Western Railway Engine Sheds*, Wild Swan Publications

Hosegood, J, 1991 'Wartime' in *Great Western Echo* 116, 22-23

Jackson, A A, 1991 *Semi-detached London: Suburban Development, Life and Transport, 1900-39*, Wild Swan Publications

Jackson, A and Croome, D, 1962 *Rails through the Clay*, Allen and Unwin

Jackson, T, 2013 *British Rail: The Nation's Railway*, The History Press

Joby, R S, 1984 *The Railwaymen*, David & Charles

Klapper, C, 1976 *London's Lost Railways*, Routledge & Kegan Paul

Lardner, Dionysius, 1850 *Railway Economy. A Treatise on the New Art of Transport. Its management, prospects and relations*, London, Taylor, Walton and Maberley

Leigh, C, 1993 *The Heyday of Old Oak Common and its Locomotives*, Ian Allan

London Topographical Society 2005 *The London County Council Bomb Damage Maps 1939-1945*, LTS Publication No. 164

Lyons, E, 1972 *Great Western Railway Engine Sheds 1947*, Oxford Publishing Co. Ltd

Lyons, E and Mountford, E, 1979 *An Historical Survey of Great Western Engine Sheds 1837-1947*, Oxford Publishing Co. Ltd

Maidment, D, 2014 *The Toss of a Coin: An autobiography of a railway career*, PublishNation

Marden, D, 2013 *London's Dock Railways Part 2: The Royal Docks, North Woolwich and Silvertown*, Kestrel Railway Books

Matheson, R, 2007 *The Fair Sex: Women and the Great Western Railway*, Tempus

McKenna, F, 1980 *The Railway Workers 1840-1970*, Faber and Faber

Metcalfe, R S, 2012 *Meat, Commerce and the City: The London Food Market, 1800-1855*, London: Pickering and Chatto

Milburn, M M, 1952 *The Cow: Dairy husbandry and cattle breeding*, new edition, London: Wm. Orr & Co

Morton, J C, 1865 'On London Milk', *Journal of the Society of Arts* **14**, No. 682, 65-78

Norris, J, Lewis, J and Beale, G, 1987 *Edwardian Enterprise: GWR 1900-1910*, Wild Swan

PCA, 2010 *Archaeological Detailed Desk-Based Assessment: Non-Listed Built Heritage – Old Oak Common Worksites* Crossrail report C150-CSY-T1-RGN-CR076_PT001-00011

Porter, John Fletcher *London Pictorially Described*, 1890

Pratt, E A, 1921 *British Railways and the Great War: Organisation, Effects, Difficulties and Achievements*, London: Selwyn & Blount Limited

Serpell, D 1983 *Railway Finances: Report of a Committee Chaired by Sir David Serpell*, Department of Transport

Siviour, G, 2006 'The North Woolwich Branch', *Steam Days* 207, 660-670

sSRA, 2000 *London East-West Study*

Street, A J, 1952 *I Drove the 'Cheltenham Flyer'*, Nicholson and Watson

Spooner, A, 1986 *Old Oak Engineman*, Ian Allan

Taylor, D, 1971 'London's Milk Supply, 1850-1900: A Reinterpretation', *Agricultural History* **45**, No.1, 33-38

Tucker, M, 2010 *The 'Factory' Building (former locomotive lifting shop) at Old Oak Common Railway Depot – Its Significance*, (unpublished report)

Walters, L, 1993 *London: the Great Western Railway Lines*, Ian Allan Publishing

White, A J L, 1906 'New Locomotive Depot at Old Oak Common', *Great Western Magazine* March 1906, 85-86

Whitehead, P and Thomas, D, 1984 *The Great Western Railway: 150 Glorious Years*, David & Charles

Wilson, A, 2006 'Old Oak Common Locomotive Depot: A Cathedral of Steam' in *Steam Days* 200, 230-248

Wojtczak, H, 2005 *Railwaywomen: exploitation, betrayal, and triumph in the workplace*, Hastings Press

Internet sources

www.bbc.co.uk/history/ww2peopleswar/stories/02/a3936602.shtml, accessed 26 Mar 2014

www.britain-at-war.org.uk/WW2/Bristolian_Train_Driver, accessed 14 March 2014

www.brdatabase.info, accessed 18 December 2015

www.historywebsite.co.uk/Museum/Transport/Trains/Children.htm, accessed 8 March 2014

www.littlehamptonfort.co.uk/ accessed 1 Jul 2014

www.neighbourhood.statistics.gov.uk/HTMLDocs/dvc12/railway.html accessed 7 March 2014

www.parliament.uk/about/living-heritage/transformingsociety/towncountry/towns/tyne-and-wear-case-study/about-the-group/public-administration/the-1848-public-health-act/ Accessed 8 February 2016

www.people1st.co.uk/getattachment/Research-policy/Research-reports/State-of-the-Nation-Passenger-Transport-Travel, accessed 27 March 2015, 29

http://readingroom.skillsfundingagency.bis.gov.uk/sfa/nextstep/lmib/Next%20Step%20LMI%20Bitesize%20-%20Goskills%20-%20rail%20-%20Jun%202010.pdf

www.theguardian.com/society/2002/feb/08/publicvoices, accessed 17 February 2014

www.ww1hull.org.uk/index.php/ww1/women-in-the-first-world-war, accessed 27 March 2015